Music of the Night

Music of the Night

*Religious Influences and Spiritual
Resonances in Operetta and Musical Theatre*

IAN BRADLEY

OXFORD
UNIVERSITY PRESS

Oxford University Press is a department of the University of Oxford.
It furthers the University's objective of excellence in research, scholarship,
and education by publishing worldwide. Oxford is a registered trade mark of
Oxford University Press in the UK and in certain other countries.

Published in the United States of America by Oxford University Press
198 Madison Avenue, New York, NY 10016, United States of America.

© Ian Bradley 2025

All rights reserved. No part of this publication may be reproduced, stored in a retrieval system, transmitted, used for text and data mining, or used for training artificial intelligence, in any form or by any means, without the prior permission in writing of Oxford University Press, or as expressly permitted by law, by license or under terms agreed with the appropriate reprographics rights organization. Inquiries concerning reproduction outside the scope of the above should be sent to the Rights Department, Oxford University Press, at the address above.

You must not circulate this work in any other form
and you must impose this same condition on any acquirer.

Library of Congress Cataloging-in-Publication Data
Names: Bradley, Ian, author.
Title: Music of the night : religious influences and spiritual resonances in
operetta and musical theatre / Ian Bradley.
Description: [1.] | New York : Oxford University Press, 2025. |
Includes bibliographical references and index. |
Identifiers: LCCN 2024062171 (print) | LCCN 2024062172 (ebook) |
ISBN 9780197699744 (paperback) | ISBN 9780197699737 (hardback) |
ISBN 9780197699775 | ISBN 9780197699751 (epub)
Subjects: LCSH: Musicals—Religious aspects. | Operetta—Religious aspects. |
Musicals—History and criticism. | Operetta.
Classification: LCC ML3921 .B73 2025 (print) | LCC ML3921 (ebook) |
DDC 782.1—dc23/eng/20241231
LC record available at https://lccn.loc.gov/2024062171
LC ebook record available at https://lccn.loc.gov/2024062172

DOI: 10.1093/9780197699775.001.0001

Paperback printed by Marquis Book Printing, Canada
Hardback printed by Bridgeport National Bindery, Inc., United States of America

Contents

Acknowledgements	vii
Introduction	1
1. Jewish and Catholic influences in operetta	7
2. A matter of life and death: Darkness and light in Gilbert and Sullivan	28
3. The fatherhood of God and the brotherhood of man: Oscar Hammerstein II	50
4. Nuns and menorahs: *The Sound of Music* and *Fiddler on the Roof*	75
5. God don't answer prayers a lot: The secularism of Stephen Sondheim	93
6. The Reluctant Pilgrim: Stephen Schwartz	110
7. Spiritual yearning and High Church aesthetics: Andrew Lloyd Webber	130
8. The two Jesuses: *Godspell* and *Jesus Christ Superstar*	157
9. The road to Calvary and the circle of life: *Les Misérables* and *The Lion King*	178
10. The spiritual show goes on: *Mamma Mia!* and *The Book of Mormon*	195
Recommended further reading	205
Index	207

Acknowledgements

Many people have helped me in my research for this book. I have benefited from email exchanges on Offenbach with Donald Fox, editor of the *Jacques Offenbach Society Newsletter*, and Jacqueline and Hervé Roten from the Institut Européen des Musiques Juives. Thomas Gnedt, director of the Carl Zeller Museum in St Peter in der Au, Austria, kindly answered my queries on Zeller. I had an enjoyable and productive conversation about Viennese operetta over coffee and cakes in Zauner's café, Bad Ischl, with Dr Stefan Frey. Ulf Schirmer, former music director of Oper Leipzig, shared with me his interesting thoughts about the religious resonances in Lehár's operettas, many of which he has conducted and recorded. Maria Sams, director of the Bad Ischl Stadtmuseum, and her colleague, Franz Fuchs, made me welcome at the Lehár archives there. Dr Paul Seeley kindly shared with me his doctoral thesis on the works of Lehár, and I benefited from a conversation with him in the Gladstone Library in Hawarden, North Wales, which has, as always, been a congenial home from home while I have been working on the book.

My continuing work on Arthur Sullivan's religious beliefs and sacred music, something of a life-long obsession, has been encouraged by fellow enthusiasts, and I have given draft versions of my chapter 'A Matter of Life and Death' as papers to a conference of the Arthur Sullivan Society and to a fringe session of the International Gilbert and Sullivan Festival in Buxton, Derbyshire. I am grateful to the organisers of these events, Stephen Turnbull and Neil Smith, respectively, for their enduring support and friendship.

I have leant heavily on the superb doctoral thesis done by Dr Kathryn Bradley under my supervision on the influence of liberal Protestantism on Oscar Hammerstein. Mark Horowitz, senior music specialist in the music division of the Library of Congress, Washington, very kindly sent me transcripts of letters which do not appear in the collected edition of Hammerstein's correspondence, which he has edited for Oxford University Press. I am grateful to the representatives of the estate of Oscar Hammerstein II and their lawyer, Graham Coleman of Davis Wright Tremaine, for permission to quote extracts from Hammerstein's letters and papers of which they retain the copyright. Lauren Ziarko, archivist and Special Collections

viii ACKNOWLEDGEMENTS

librarian at Manhattanville College, Purchase, New York, assisted me greatly over Richard Rodgers' research there for the liturgical music in *The Sound of Music*.

Stephen Schwartz read through and commented on my chapter about his work and on my analysis of *Godspell*, and answered questions that I put to him by email. John Caird did the same in relation to his involvement in *Children of Eden* and *Les Misérables*. I am very grateful to these two leading practitioners in the musical theatre world for their generosity in sharing hitherto undisclosed insights into their creative processes and for their enthusiasm for my project.

Urs Mattmann has shared his encyclopaedic knowledge of musicals and directed me towards some lesser-known ones with religious resonances. Hester Greatrix and other students taking the Sacred Music MLitt degree at the University of St Andrews have sought valiantly, if not wholly successfully, to convince me of the religious dimension and spiritual side to Stephen Sondheim's musicals. I am grateful to them and to the many students who took my 'Theology of the Musical' module between 2000 and 2017 for indulging and even encouraging my obsession with this subject and contributing their own thoughts and ideas, some of which have found their way into this book. For any howlers, or serious lapses of judgement and critical detachment, I alone am responsible.

Introduction

The closely related genres of operetta and musical theatre are often dismissed as escapist, trivial, and shallow. They are also generally seen as essentially secular and superficial, neither plumbing the spiritual depths nor soaring to the sacred heights of opera and serious drama.

This book challenges these judgments and seeks to show that there have been both clear religious influences and strong spiritual resonances in operetta and musical theatre. It does this by examining the religious background and motivation of a number of prominent practitioners in the two genres and by identifying and exploring spiritual themes in some of their best-known works.

Among the topics covered are the formative religious influences, both Jewish and Christian, on Jacques Offenbach and some of his French contemporaries, the impact of Franz Lehár's Catholicism on his operettas, and the way in which Arthur Sullivan's liberal Christian faith and approach to life softened and lifted the rather gloomy tone of the lyrics of W.S. Gilbert, his collaborator in the Savoy Operas. There are chapters on the lives and work of Oscar Hammerstein, Stephen Sondheim, Stephen Schwartz, and Andrew Lloyd Webber. I also explore the religious influences and spiritual resonances in six musicals where both features are especially prominent: *The Sound of Music, Fiddler on the Roof, Godspell, Jesus Christ Superstar, Les Misérables*, and *The Lion King*.

In many ways, this book serves as a sequel to my 2004 study, *You've Got to Have a Dream: The Message of the Musical*, which broke new ground by looking at musicals from a religious perspective and arguing that many people derive their spirituality, theology, and view of life from musical theatre. I proposed the thesis there that the English-language musical as a distinct art form derives from Jewish and Protestant roots, being word-led and having the strong narrative structure and concern with story found especially prominently in these two religious traditions. I suggested that Continental European operetta, by contrast, owes more to Roman Catholicism with its

---

Music of the Night. Ian Bradley, Oxford University Press. © Ian Bradley 2025.
DOI: 10.1093/9780197699775.003.0001

2   MUSIC OF THE NIGHT

greater emphasis on movement, colour, and emotion. Both these themes are developed in this book.

The pages that follow also pick up and expand points that I made in *Arthur Sullivan: A Life of Divine Emollient*, published by Oxford University Press in its 'Spiritual Lives' series in 2021. The first study of the religious influences on Sullivan and of his own beliefs, which I locate firmly in the nineteenth-century Anglican Broad Church liberal tradition, it pointed out how many of his Continental contemporaries, who can be seen as the founding fathers of European operetta in its golden age, shared his upbringing in church music and his dual career as a composer of both sacred and stage works. Further research that I have done on this topic forms the basis for Chapter 1 of this book, while Chapter 2 develops my view that Sullivan's essentially spiritual love of life stood in opposition to, and eventually trumped, Gilbert's death obsession.

As with my earlier studies in this area, this book owes much to the nearly twenty years that I spent teaching what, as far as I am aware, was the only university course in the world focussed on the theology and spirituality of musical theatre. Now in retirement, I still teach a class on musical theatre as part of a master's degree in sacred music at the University of St Andrews.

This remains a largely neglected topic, at least in the academic world. *The Oxford Handbook of the American Musical*, published in 2011, has a section on 'Identities' which covers race, ethnicity, gender and sexuality, politics of nation, region, class, and culture but has nothing on religion. There have been serious studies of the Jewish impact on American musicals, notably Andrea Most's *Making Americans: Jews and the Broadway Musical* and Michael Kantnor's 2013 film, *Broadway Musicals: A Jewish Legacy*, shown in the US on the PBS network and in the UK by the BBC, but they have tended to look more at sociological and cultural factors rather than religious ones. There has been little, if any, academic study of Christian influences on operetta and musical theatre. I hope that this book begins a serious exploration of this subject that will continue.

Some of those writing about musical theatre are alive to its religious echoes and spiritual resonances. In his *The American Musical and the Performance of Personal Identity*, Raymond Knapp, Distinguished Professor of Musicology and Humanities at the University of California, Los Angeles, provides a fascinating analysis of the religious resonances of the song 'Feed the birds' in *Mary Poppins*, with its setting on the steps of St Paul's Cathedral, its echoes of familiar carols, with their 'hints of Christmas and thus of Christianity', its prayer-like character, references to saints and angels, and 'evocations of the eternal'.[1] But this is a relatively rare example of academic appreciation of the religious dimension of musical theatre.

Those who are involved in production and performance are less reticent about recognizing and acknowledging the spiritual side of the works with which they have an intimate relationship. Julie Taymor, director and costume designer of *The Lion King* since its inception as a stage show, has talked about musical theatre's ability 'to exorcise demons, to take people through the dark moment, through pain, acting in its original capacity as a shamanistic experience'. She describes *The Lion King*'s impact on a boy whose older sister had died and who related especially to Mufasa telling Simba how the spirits of the ancestors survive and go on living: 'He was able to absorb that spiritual song, that sense that beyond the physical body a human being can still live in you'.[2] Interviewed on 'The Big Night of Musicals', a live Saturday evening show broadcast on BBC television in January 2024, Beverley Knight, the English singer who had a strict Pentecostal upbringing and began her career by singing Gospel numbers in church, said, 'We have hospitals to heal our bodies, and we have musicals to heal our souls'. She then led a youth choir in the anthem 'Seasons of Love' from *Rent*, a musical which undoubtedly has a profound spiritual dimension.

I was delighted to see that the 2019/20 operetta and musicals season in the Stadttheater at Baden bei Wien, Austria, where I have regularly gone to indulge my passion for operetta, was focused around the theme of '*Religion und Glaube*' (religion and belief). It featured Leo Fall's *Die Rose von Stambul* about the conflict between Islam and the West; Rodgers and Hammerstein's *The King and I*, presented as an expression of Buddhism; and *Drei Engel Auf Erden*, a new musical by Beppo Binder and Pavel Singer very much in the Austrian operetta tradition about three archangels having too much fun in heaven and being banished to earth.

Faith communities have also recognized the religious and spiritual dimension of operettas and musicals. The performances of the Gilbert and Sullivan Yiddish Light Opera Company of Long Island, founded in 1983, in retirement homes and synagogues have been a major marker of Jewish identity and have played an important role in preserving the Yiddish language. I went to New York in 2005 to make a programme for the BBC about this fascinating and moving phenomenon and to explore the particular Jewish love affair with the Savoy Operas—I called it 'Pinafores, Buttercups and Bagels'. Several churches have themed worship services around musicals—I

4 MUSIC OF THE NIGHT

have done so myself, singing 'Love changes everything' from the pulpit and leading congregations in 'Do you hear the people sing?'. Between 2008 and 2015, the Metropolitan Community Church in Austin, Texas, ran a series of over thirty services under the title 'Bible on Broadway', in which the worship and the sermons drew on different musicals, including *Camelot, Carousel, Chicago, The Color Purple, Guys and Dolls, Fiddler on the Roof, Footloose, Into the Woods, Nashville, Oklahoma!, South Pacific, Camelot, The Lion King, Pippin, Sunset Boulevard, The Wiz*, and *Les Misérables*. An academic study found that those who had participated in the services and heard the sermons overwhelmingly felt that they had encouraged pro-social behaviour and raised their moral consciousness.[3]

I should clarify the terms that I use in this book. When I write about religious influences, I am thinking primarily of the effects of distinct and recognized faith traditions in which composers and librettists have been raised or to which they have adhered. In the case of those discussed here, these have overwhelmingly been either Jewish or Christian (or, in the case of Offenbach, both). Spirituality is an altogether wider and more nebulous term than religion. I use it in the sense that it is often defined, generally in contrast to a secular outlook, as involving and embracing the recognition of a feeling or belief that there is something greater than ourselves, something more to being human than sensory experience, and that the greater whole of which we are part is in some sense cosmic or divine in nature.

I should also say a word about the title. 'Music of the Night' hints at an important subsidiary purpose of this book, which is to point to the darker, more serious side of operetta and musical theatre, another aspect which is often neglected and ignored. This darker side can clash and jar with the religious and spiritual elements, but it can also take them to a deeper level. It prevents operettas and musicals from being the banal, sugar-coated, frivolous fripperies that they are so often taken for. This darker side has been identified by several of those writing about both genres. Stefan Frey, the leading scholar of Viennese operetta, entitles his biography of Emmerich Kálmán, *Laughter under Tears*, and James Agate famously described Ivor Novello's shows as 'tears in waltz time'. Several of the many studies of Stephen Sondheim's musicals have identified and probed their bitter-sweet quality and darker side. A good example of this, which also expresses the stereotypical view of the triviality of musicals, is the review of the first London performance of *Company* in 1972 by the distinguished British theatre critic, Harold Hobson. He wrote, 'It is extraordinary that a musical, the most trivial

INTRODUCTION 5

of theatrical forms, should be able to plunge as *Company* does with perfect congruity into the profound depths of human perplexity and misery'.[4]

There is plenty of this darker 'music of the night' in the later works of Lehár. In the case of his 1927 operetta, *Der Zarewitsch*, it is combined with undoubted religious influences and spiritual echoes. In Andrew Lloyd Webber's *The Phantom of the Opera*, the 'music of the night' seems more diabolical and subversive of religious and spiritual values. This is another neglected and overlooked aspect of operetta and musical theatre and another reason for taking both genres seriously.

I am not seeking to suggest that every operetta and every musical has religious roots or deep spiritual significance. Many do not. The composers and lyricists and the works that come under the microscope in this book are not necessarily a representative and certainly not a comprehensive selection, although they do include some of the most successful practitioners and some of the most enduringly popular shows of the last century and a half. I have chosen them because I think that they do display interesting and significant religious influences and spiritual resonances and because I think these aspects have been overlooked. There are other practitioners of musical theatre who are much more secular in their approach and message. Indeed, I would put Stephen Sondheim in this category and do so in the chapter that I devote to him. He is included for reasons that I explain and because there are many who clearly find his work deeply spiritual.

What I hope that I have done in this book is to shine a light on a neglected but important element in these two much loved and sadly still rather despised art forms. I explore several topics that have not really been looked at before: the impact of Franz Lehár's Catholicism; the importance of liberal Protestant idealism in the lives and work of both Arthur Sullivan and Oscar Hammerstein; the particular contribution that the Universalist faith to which he was exposed as a boy made to Hammerstein's later thinking; the extraordinary care which both he and Richard Rodgers took over the representation of Catholicism in *The Sound of Music*; the significance of Andrew Lloyd Webber's High Anglican aestheticism; and the progressive Christianization of *Les Misérables* through its various incarnations.

I believe that both operetta and musical theatre deserve to be taken more seriously as art forms and not dismissed as frivolous, commercially driven pariahs, as they are by many critics and dramatists, like the British playwright David Hare, who complains of their dominance in Broadway and the West End, writing that 'musicals have become the leylandii of theatre, strangling

6 MUSIC OF THE NIGHT

everything in their path'.[5] But I do not want to take them too seriously and diminish the sheer enjoyment and pleasure that they provide through over-analysis and conceptualization. Operettas and musicals exist primarily to be performed, sung, and enjoyed rather than to be subjected to detailed academic study, whether on the basis of their religious influences and spiritual resonances or anything else. For me, the life-enhancing joy that they exude is itself a spiritual quality, and it is what I want to celebrate and affirm above all.

Notes

1. Raymond Knapp, *The American Musical and the Performance of Personal Identity* (Princeton, NJ: Princeton University Press, 2006), 149.
2. Mike Wade, 'Theatre can still be shamanistic experience', *The Times*, 19 October 2019.
3. W. Bernard Lukenbill and William D. Young, 'Broadway Musicals and the Christian Sermon: Communicating Moral, Reasoning, Church Values, and Prosocial Behaviors', *Journal of Religious & Theological Information*, 16, no. 2 (March 2017), 52–67.
4. Quoted in Scott McMillan, *The Musical as Drama* (Princeton, NJ: Princeton University Press, 2006), 197.
5. 'Musicals are killing theatre', *The Spectator*, 25 March 2023.

1

Jewish and Catholic influences in operetta

European operetta, with its golden age between 1871 and 1901, and its silver age from 1901 to *c*.1930, is widely seen as the precursor of twentieth-century musical theatre. It is not generally regarded as having any serious or spiritual dimension but is rather dismissed as shallow and ephemeral, not least by critics from its Continental European heartland. Typical is the disparaging description of it by the German musicologist, Carl Dahlhaus, as 'trivial music'.[1] In the German-speaking world it has been relegated to the category of U-music (signifying *Unterhaltung*, or entertainment) as distinct from E-music (*Ernste*, or serious).

Operetta has, indeed, suffered from being seen primarily as an inferior kind of opera and defined in terms of what it is not rather than what it is. I prefer this definition by John Kenrick, which makes clear how it stands on its own as a perfectly respectable art form, not a poor relation to something else:

> Operetta is a versatile form of musical that integrates songs and musical sequences with dialogue to dramatize a story, retaining the vocal pyrotechnics and forms of grand opera (arias, choruses, act finales, etc.) but relying on more accessible melodies. The songs develop character and/or advance the plot.[2]

One might add that for singers, operetta can be just as demanding as opera. Many leading soloists have happily straddled both genres without feeling one is inferior to the other.

For me, operetta has a spiritual quality and value, if only for its feel-good factor and the uplifting, life-enhancing effect of its music, alternately stirring, ravishing and soulful. Richard Traubner acknowledges this when he opens his classic study of the genre with the observation that operetta is 'basically designed to promote good feeling and even joy ... sentiment and romance have traditionally played important roles in operetta, but rarely despair'.[3] Micaela Baranello begins her book *The Operetta Empire* by saying

Music of the Night. Ian Bradley, Oxford University Press. © Ian Bradley 2025.
DOI: 10.1093/9780197699775.003.0002

8 MUSIC OF THE NIGHT

that she was first attracted to the genre by its optimism: 'Amid the thickets of Schoenberg and Mahler, the works of Lehár and Kálmán seemed to suggest a world in which men and, most crucially, women could find happiness'. She ends it with the observation that 'operetta promised nothing less than a more harmonious, more beautiful, and happier life'.[4]

These are not insignificant qualities. Franz Lehár was right to suggest that while not everyone can appreciate the complexities of opera, for the great majority of people operetta can provide 'recuperation after the day's trouble and toil'.[5] In this respect, operatta offers more than mere escapism, providing both an emollient balm and a reviving tonic with therapeutic benefits. There is a directness and clarity in operetta—more so than in most operas—which to me also have a spiritual dimension. This has been well recognized by the English conductor, John Andrews, whose own self-proclaimed tastes are 'serious and Germanic—Beethoven, Wagner and Richard Strauss'. After recent exposure to Offenbach, Johann Strauss and Sullivan, he describes being 'captivated by the ability of comic opera and operetta to speak much more directly to audiences about their day-to-day lives and find the comedy and pathos'.[6] In other words, there is realism here as much as, if not more than, escapism.

There is, of course, a clear line of descent from later Viennese operetta to musical theatre via those Broadway composers who shared the Central European Jewish origins of the masters of operetta's silver age. Rudolf Friml's *Rose Marie* and Sigmund Romberg's *The Desert Song* are as much operettas as musicals. So is Rodgers and Hammerstein's *The Sound of Music*. Andrew Lloyd Webber also follows in this tradition, even though he claims not to be conscious of doing so. In his irreverent and unfailingly perceptive book on musicals, *Broadway Babies Say Goodnight*, Mark Steyn somewhat cheekily proposes an operetta lineage 'from the Golden Age (Strauss) to the Silver Age (Lehár) to the Rhinestone Cowboy (Lloyd Webber)'. He quotes Michael Kunze, who writes the German libretti for Lloyd Webber's hits and sees him standing firmly in the Viennese operetta tradition, and the distinguished German conductor Caspar Richter, who says: 'I have conducted many operettas at the Vienna Volksoper and in 1988 I began conducting musicals—mainly Andrew Lloyd Webber. I believe he is the Lehár of today . .. His orchestration, heavily based on strings, isn't far from the Viennese tradition'. Steyn goes on to comment that *The Phantom of the Opera* 'has made operetta hip, after half a century of being outflanked by musical comedy and the musical play'.[7]

If the soaring, soulful, bitter-sweet melodies and sense of yearning so evident in the works of Lehár and Kálmán provide operetta's clearest legacy to later twentieth-century musical theatre and also its most obvious spiritual dimension, we should not ignore the contribution made in both these areas by the earlier practitioners in the genre's golden age. Among them are several who experienced strong religious influences in their upbringing and musical training. These may not have been overtly expressed in their work, but they undoubtedly contributed to forming some of the earliest distinguishing marks of operetta as a distinct art form, notably its clarity and accessibility, melodic strength and directness, and perhaps, too, its hint of wistfulness amidst the overall joyful, life-affirming positivity.

Jacques Offenbach

In initiating the distinctive French traditions of *opéra bouffe* and developing *opéra comique*, Jacques Offenbach is generally seen as the founding father of operetta and, indeed, in John Kenrick's words, as 'the grandfather of musical theatre as we know it. *Oklahoma!*, *A Chorus Line*, *Hamilton*—all are direct descendants of his operettas'.[8] While Offenbach has often been portrayed as an essentially lightweight and frivolous figure, recent studies have sought to cast him in a more substantial and serious light, few more so than Laurence Selenick's *Jacques Offenbach and the Making of Modern Culture*, written, in the author's words, to dispel the prevailing impression 'that Offenbach is all champagne and petits fours' and to go beyond 'the easy stereotypes of high kicks and popping corks'.[9] For Selenick, Offenbach is anarchic and absurdist, an underminer of establishment values and deflator of unexamined certainities, exemplifying the untranslatable French word '*blague*', a mixture of topsy-turvydom, burlesque, satire, and subtle wit. In another recent study, Carolyn Abbate sees Offenbach as engaging in what she calls 'ethical frivolity', encouraging his audiences to make peace with impermanence and insouciance.[10] Although these re-appraisals present Offenbach as having a serious purpose, they do not suggest any specifically religious influences or spiritual resonances in his life and work.

In fact, I think that it is possible to discern both religious and musical influences on Jacques Offenbach coming from his father, Isaac Eberst, who later adopted the name of his home town, Offenbach-am-Main. Isaac combined his duties as *chazan*, or cantor, in the synagogue in Cologne with

10 MUSIC OF THE NIGHT

being an itinerant musician, playing the violin in dance halls and cafés. He had a strong commitment to Jewish liturgy, producing a German translation of the *Hagadah*, a compilation of chants and prayers for the Passover Seder, and a book of prayers for the young. He also wrote chants for synagogue use and songs for Jewish festivals. We can gain a very good idea of their quality and variety thanks to a CD recorded in 2020 by the Paris-based *Institut Européen des Musiques Juives* (IEMJ). It includes seven of his compositions, ranging from settings of Hebrew psalms and prayers to songs used after the Passover meal and at Purim. What is striking is both their lyrical, operatic quality—Isaac was well known for incorporating extracts from operas into synagogue worship—and the crossover between sacred and secular in their style. Much of the synagogue chant feels no more 'holy' or sacred in tone than the Purim drinking song. *Halelouyo*, a setting of Psalm 150 for tenor soloist, chorus and organ, is full of short, staccato, heavily accented notes and trills, much like many of his son's later operetta songs.[11]

The Belgian musicologist Robert Pourvoyeur has rightly observed that 'The spirit of Isaac Offenbach is one of the keys to understanding the work of his son'. Reflecting that the cantor acts as the liturgical centre of Jewish worship, maintaining and developing its tradition, he notes that 'cantors are often a curious mixture of seriousness and mischief' and that, in the case of Isaac, 'this spirit oscillating between irreverence and seriousness is a major key to understanding the music which his son later composes'. Pourvoyeur points out that before the reform of Jewish religious music from 1840, melodies from dance and opera were regularly used in religious services and that cantors often took pleasure in imitating different musical instruments, a technique which was to be frequently employed by Jacques Offenbach. He goes on to suggest that the tendency to have a somewhat disrespectful and iconoclastic attitude to 'great music' is characteristic of religious musicians and is the key to understanding Offenbach's approach and his personality.[12]

There is certainly no doubt that young Jacob, as he then was, was well schooled in Jewish liturgical music. He sang in the choir of one of the Paris synagogues while attending the Conservatoire there from the age of 14 and some of his earliest compositions were settings of Hebrew texts. Two of them are included in the IEMJ CD: soulful, modal, a capella choral versions of *Ochamnon* and *Tovo lefoné'ho* from the Yom Kippur prayer of confession that he wrote at the age of 22 when visiting his father in Cologne. A note in Hebrew by Isaac on the manuscript records: 'Widdui, by my son, Jacob, long may he live. He and his brother sing with me in the synagogue and assist me in the prayer of Mussaf in honour of the Eternal One and to honour me'.[13] One of Jacob's first secular pieces, the Rebecca waltz, written in 1837 when he was 16, incorporated melodies from medieval Jewish liturgical music. There were mutterings in the musical press that he had burlesqued 'melodies sanctified by religious observance' and turned them into 'a wanton waltz' but, as the German cultural critic Siegfried Kracauer noted, this was in keeping with his father's approach:

> Offenbach did not leave religious melodies as religious melodies but turned them into dance music; so that it was true that music that was sacred to the devout was converted to purposes of profane delight. But this lack of scruple was entirely consistent with the traditions in which the young Offenbach had been reared. Had his father ever had any hesitation in singing tunes from *Der Freischütz* in the synagogue?[14]

Several of Offenbach's biographers have made much of the feelings of loneliness and exile that assailed him when he was sent off to the Paris Conservatoire at the age of 14 and have suggested that they may account for a wistful and soulful strain in his music. Richard Fischer has argued that he retained something of the strong Jewish faith in which he was raised and that his loneliness heightened an identification with the Biblical theme of expulsion from Paradise and loss of childhood innocence to which he returned several times in his works.[15] Selenick makes a similar observation, suggesting that beneath his superficiality and cynicism Offenbach had a Utopian vision of paradise lost. The composer himself recalled in later life how he was consoled during his teenage years in Paris by a slow, gentle waltz tune, which his mother and sisters had sung to him as an infant to rock him to sleep. It came to haunt him in his loneliness, taking on 'quite extraordinary dimensions' and bringing back the voices he so much missed.

> It ceased to be an ordinary waltz and became almost a prayer, which I hummed to myself from morning to night, not as a prayer addressed to heaven, but because when I played it, it seemed to me that my dear ones heard me, and then, when it returned to my mind later, I could have sworn that they were answering me.[16]

Although that remark seems to suggest filial piety and strong family affection rather than deep faith, there are occasional expressions of religious belief

12 MUSIC OF THE NIGHT

in Offenbach's writings which can perhaps be taken to support Krakauer's assertion that he 'possessed a very genuine native piety'.[17] When his mother died in 1840, he wrote a poem about how she had suffered on earth and would be happy in heaven, and praising God that she would be reunited with her son Michael, the youngest of the ten Offenbach children, who had died of a cerebral fever at the age of fourteen. In his later years he wrote: 'I do not know what I have done to cause God to bestow so much happiness and so much melody upon me'.[18]

Biographers have differed in their assessment of Offenbach's conversion to Roman Catholicism, when he married his Spanish wife, Herminie, in 1844, and what it tells us about his religious beliefs. Kracauer comments: 'His conversion did not worry him in the least. It was less a change of heart than an external concession, a formality. He never concealed his Jewish origin or spared monastic life in his satire. To him a creed was no more than a backcloth'.[19] In contrast, James Harding writes in his 1980 biography that Offenbach 'did not find it hard to give up the Jewish faith. Though tender, impulsive and moderately God-fearing, he had never been an ardent worshipper in the Hebrew ritual', while Roger Williams states that Herminie and her family insisted on his conversion 'and as Offenbach was indifferent to religion, he readily consented'.[20]

Just as he had set Hebrew psalms and prayers as synagogue chants in his youth, so following his conversion, Offenbach wrote Catholic liturgical music. He composed Masses for the marriages of two of his daughters. The manuscripts have remained in private family archives but two *Ave Marias* and an *Agnus Dei* which have been published probably come from them. He also wrote a soprano aria, *Gloire à Dieu*, and *Litanies de la Vierge* for tenor and organ. There are invocations to the Virgin Mary in two of his stage works, *Les Trois Baisers du Diable*, a one-act operetta of 1857, and *La Haine*, a historic drama for which he wrote the music in 1874. He also composed a sacred song, *Espère, enfant, demain*, which became a choir piece, *Espoir en Dieu*, in an unfinished symphony that he wrote in 1871.

Despite his conversion and his contributions to its liturgy, Offenbach has not been embraced by the Roman Catholic church. A request by the French musicologist and conductor Jean-Christophe Keck to perform one of his works in a German church was turned down by the priest. When Keck asked, 'What about Mozart?', the reply came 'Of course Mozart is allowed', to which Keck responded, 'So you allow music by a Mason who was excommunicated and not that of a Jew who converted to Catholicism?' The priest relented.

On another occasion, Keck asked if he could sing the plaintive and soulful 'Chanson de Fortunio' from the operetta of the same name at the Parisian funeral of one of Offenbach's descendants. He pointed out that it had been sung at Offenbach's own funeral at La Madeleine in 1880 but the priest in charge refused his request with the words 'We are not here for pleasure.'[21]

It is difficult to be sure about the depth and nature of Offenbach's religious faith. He received the last rites from a Catholic priest shortly before his death and that is perhaps enough. What is undeniable is the way that he took his father's syncretism and crossover between 'sacred' and 'secular' music into his own work. It is there in that youthful Rebecca waltz and in the incorporation of the tune of *Espère, enfant, demain* into the finale of his last work, *Les Contes d'Hoffman*. There is a nice illustration of how porous the boundaries between the sacred and the secular were for him in the programme of a 'Grand Sacred Concert' that an enterprising impresario asked him to conduct on a Sunday evening when he was in Philadelphia in 1876. Alongside Gounod's *Ave Maria*, it included from his own works the Angelus from *Le Mariage aux Lanternes*, 'a prayer' from *La Grande Duchesse de Gerolstein* (in fact, the Duchess' declaration of love) and 'a Litany' from *La Belle Hélène* (actually Helen's distinctly pagan lament to Venus). The city authorities smelt a rat and realized that this was an attempt to get round their prohibition on Sunday concerts by making this particular one seem more sacred than it was. They refused to sanction it and it never took place.

Was this just another example of Offenbach's cheeky sense of fun and irreverent insouciance, or did it express something rather more profound in terms of his attitude to the spiritual in music? It was surely no coincidence that at his funeral Jean-Alexandre Talazac, the operatic tenor who had created the title role in *Les Contes d'Hoffmann,* sang both the *Dies Irae* and the *Agnus Dei* set to tunes from that opera. It was a fitting send-off for the son of the cantor who had himself used opera tunes in services in the Cologne synagogue. There is a telling scene in the 1996 film *Offenbachs Geheimnis* (Offenbach's Secret) by the Hungarian director István Szabó in which Jacques is upbraided by his brother, 'Isaac', for incorporating one of their father's synagogue melodies into one of his early 1855 burlesque operettas. He retorts that tunes are universal and that in this case, sacred and profane are meaningless categories.

Overall, while there are undoubtedly both Jewish influences and Catholic expressions in Offenbach's operettas, it is difficult to discern a distinct religious or spiritual dimension to them. There is an undoubtedly soulful

14 MUSIC OF THE NIGHT

quality to some of his music. It is particularly evident, for me at least, in John Styx's aria 'Quand j'étais roi de Béotie' ('When I was king of the Beotians') in *Orphée aux Enfers*, a haunting melody of wistful melancholy which perhaps reflects that sense of a paradise lost noted by Fischer and Selenick. Siegfried Kracauer, who of all critics and biographers is most attuned to Offenbach's spiritual side and most inclined to emphasize it, was especially affected by this song, seeing Styx as the tragic clown and spectre at the feast: 'The sadness of his song is the sadness of the one to whom the present means nothing, the past everything.'[22] It reveals a very different side to the composer from the decadent, iconoclastic satirist portrayed by contemporary critics like Émile Zola and the moralists of the Republican era, one that perhaps drew on that distinctively Jewish mixture of melancholy and melody found both within and outside the synagogue.

Offenbach's Jewish contemporaries

Jacques Offenbach was just one of a group of Jewish operetta composers living in Paris in the middle decades of the nineteenth century. Most of them were German-born and active in their synagogues and in Jewish cultural life. The most prominent was Jacques Fromenthal Halévy (born Jacob Lévy), whose nephew Ludovic became Offenbach's principal librettist. Something of a mentor to his better-known rival, to whom he was twenty years senior, Jacques Fromenthal, too, was the son of a cantor, brought up on synagogue chants, and a graduate of the Paris Conservatoire. An active member of the city's Jewish community, he combined composing religious music with writing stage works for performance at the Theatre Opéra Comique where he was chorus master. He first achieved fame with his funeral march *Mimaamakim* (Out of the Depths), a powerful setting of the Hebrew text of Psalm 130 for bass soloist and chorus commissioned by the French minister of religion and the Israelite Central Consistory of the Departement of the Seine to commemorate the Duc de Berry, nephew to King Louis XVIII and heir to the throne, following his assassination in 1820.

Halévy composed both comic and serious operas, the best known of the latter being *La Juive* about a wealthy Jewish woman living in Constance in the early fifteenth century. It includes a scene featuring a seder with a prayer which seems to focus largely on revenge and secrecy—themes which, as David Conway writes in his study of *Jews in Music*, are 'scarcely consonant with Jewish theology'. Commenting more generally on *La Juive*, Conway notes 'Ironically, it seems very doubtful that the only great opera written by a Jew about a Jew has anything much to say about Jews at all.'[23] Before his death, he was working on an opera about Noah.

Jules Erlanger, a founding member of the Universal Israelite Alliance, wrote several operettas for Offenbach's Théâtre des Bouffes Parisiens, as well as numerous liturgical pieces. In later life, he abandoned operetta composition to concentrate solely on sacred music. Émile Jonas was organist and choirmaster successively of the main Paris synagogue on Rue Notre Dame du Nazareth and the Portuguese synagogue in Rue Lamartine. Along with over thirty Hebrew chants for soloists, choir and organ, he composed operas bouffes and operettas, six of which were produced by Offenbach at his theatre.

The 2020 IEMJ CD, which is entitled 'Jacques Offenbach and Friends' includes religious compositions by Halévy, Erlanger and Jonas as well as one by their contemporary, Giacomo Meyerbeer, who was principally a grand opera composer, although he did occasionally dabble in comic opera. They include settings of the Psalms and verses from the Torah, wedding cantatas, and songs sung at Jewish festivals. Like the liturgical music of Isaac and Jacques Offenbach, they are distinguished by directness and clarity in word setting, a strong lyrical melody line, and lively interplay between soloists and chorus—three features which also characterized golden age operetta.

The subtitle of the IEMJ CD, 'From the Synagogue to the Opera', suggests a direct link between these composers' Jewish upbringing and formation and their later work in the theatre, although it might more accurately have referenced their destination as operetta rather than opera. It is not difficult to find echoes of synagogue chant and of Jewish liturgical music more generally in such features of their operettas as the careful word setting, the clear melodic line, and the exchanges between solo and chorus. Is there, too, a broader Jewish influence at play in the choice of operetta rather than opera as their preferred sphere of composition, deriving in part from a particular blurring of the sacred and secular and from that attraction to wit and wordplay so evident in Rabbinic Judaism? It is tempting to suggest so.

French Catholic composers

Working alongside this group of Jewish composers in mid-nineteenth-century Paris were a number of Roman Catholics who cut their teeth in church choirs and went on to become church organists, while also writing

16   MUSIC OF THE NIGHT

for the stage. One of them, Louis-Auguste Florimond Ronger, is regarded by some musicologists as the true inventor of operetta.[24] His 1848 one-act burlesque on *Don Quixote*, titled *Don Quichotte et Sancho Pança* and billed as a *'tableau grotesque'*, was described by the French composer and critic Reynaldo Hahn as 'a thing for which no name had previously existed: it was an operetta; it was simply the first French operetta.'[25] Ronger's Folies-Concertantes, established in 1854, later the Théâtre des Folies-Nouvelles, was a direct forerunner of Offenbach's Théâtre des Bouffes Parisiens. Indeed, it was at the Folies-Nouvelles that Offenbach's first successful operetta, *Oyayie*, was first performed.

Having been a choirboy at the church of Saint-Roch, Paris, Ronger as a teenager played the organ in the chapel of Bicêtre Hospital, a lunatic asylum from whose patients he formed a vaudeville troupe, a project that was hailed as a pioneering example of music therapy. He later became organist at the prestigious church of Saint-Eustache. Writing sacred compositions under his real name, he adopted the pseudonym Hervé for his operettas and stage works, which numbered more than 120 and which the music critic of *Le Figaro* described as 'spiritual, joyous . . . and wise'.[26] Célestin, the central male character of his most famous work, *Mam'zelle Nitouche*, leads a double life as a reserved and pious organist at a convent by day and an ebullient show-off by night at the theatre where his operettas are performed. It could be taken as a self-portrayal and also as a description of the double lives led by a number of his contemporaries.

Several leading French operetta composers received their musical education at the École de Musique Religieuse et Classique established in Paris in 1853 by Louis Niedermeyer, a Swiss composer who had switched from opera to sacred music and was an enthusiast for plainsong and Gregorian chant. The curriculum in his boarding school for boys from the age of 11 included the principles of liturgical music, organ studies, and sixteenth-century counterpoint. Among his pupils were Edmond Audran, a church organist who wrote a Mass in 1873 and then turned to operettas, and Léon Vasseur, who was organist at two churches in Versailles before switching to writing for the theatre and becoming head of the Folies Bergère orchestra. Vassuer's output included two Masses, two motets, a Magnificat, and several anthems, as well as around thirty operettas, the most successful of which was *La Timbale d'Argent*, first performed at the Bouffes-Parisiens in 1872. Later students at the École Niedermeyer included Victor Roger, composer of successful operettas like *Joséphine vendue par ses soeurs* and *Les Vingt-huit jours de Clairette*, and André Messager, who was organist and choirmaster at St Sulpice church in Paris before becoming stage composer at the Folies Bergère and later musical director of the Opéra Comique. Although not himself educated at the École de Musique Religieuse et Classique, Léo Delibes, who wrote more than a dozen comic operas and operettas, had a similar background in church music, starting out as a boy chorister at the church of La Madeleine in Paris and later becoming organist of St Pierre de Chaillot.

Like their Jewish contemporaries, these Catholic composers regularly crossed over from sacred to secular music, blurring the boundaries between them, none more so than Louis Antoine Jullien, the flamboyant conductor who presided over the band in the Jardin Turc, a Paris pleasure garden decked out in oriental style with chains of coloured lights. Liberace-like, he conducted from a gold music stand wearing yellow gloves, a flashing diamond tie-pin, and brightly coloured waistcoats. It was Jullien who first played several of Offenbach's early compositions, including the Rebecca waltz. He conducted the Jardin Turc orchestra in a piece which coupled the *Dies Irae* with a dance tune, and his life's ambition was to set the Lord's Prayer. Alas, he never got further than designing the title page which announced in bold type: 'Words by JESUS CHRIST—Music by JULLIEN'.

It is not difficult to see how their training in church music equipped and influenced these pioneers of the new genre of operetta. It instilled principles of harmony, counterpoint and choral composition. It also schooled them in the romantic, sentimental sound of mid-nineteenth-century French Catholic music. One can still hear echoes of that sound today in the huge underground basilica at Lourdes, where the liturgy is chanted by ringing tenor soloists accompanied by lots of brass with a lyricism and thrilling emotional power not dissimilar from an operetta performance.

The pioneers of Viennese operetta

It is surely no coincidence that operetta had its origins and found its leading practitioners in Catholic Continental Europe, and not least in the Austro-Hungarian empire, that heartland of central European Catholicism. Like their French counterparts, a number of the pioneers of Viennese operetta trained in church music and continued their involvement in it while writing for the theatre. The one who most clearly straddled both genres was Franz

18 MUSIC OF THE NIGHT

von Suppé, whose *Das Pensionat* in 1860 is generally taken as the first true Viennese operetta, pre-dating those of Johann Strauss by over a decade. Suppé went on to compose around thirty operettas and 180 farces, ballets, and other stage works. He was schooled in church music while singing as a boy in the choir of the cathedral in the Dalmatian city of Zara (now Zadar) where he grew up. Encouraged by the choirmaster, he started writing his first musical work, a Mass, at the age of 13. He extended and completed it three years later following the death of his father, which prompted the family's move to Vienna. An ambitious work, incorporating a *Gloria* lasting twenty-one minutes, it was revised and extended three times before being published much later in his life. Suppé also wrote a *Requiem* following the death of his friend and mentor, Franz Pokorny, director of several theatres in Austria where he had worked as conductor and composer. It was performed at a memorial service for Pokorny in 1855. He later extended it to form an oratorio, *Extremum Judicium*, which could be performed as a concert piece. Towards the end of his life, Suppé returned to sacred music, composing single works for use in church.

There were similar strong religious influences in the upbringing and schooling of Carl Zeller, best known for the enchanting *Der Vogelhändler* which is still regularly performed in Austria. At the age of 7, he was playing the organ and singing soprano solos in the parish church of Sankt Peter in der Au, the small town in Lower Austria where he grew up. Recruited at the age of 11 into the choir of the Imperial Chapel in the Hofburg in Vienna, where he remained for four years, he had a Catholic secondary education as a boarder in the seminary at Lowenburg and the gymnasium attached to the Benedictine Abbey at Melk.

In his teens, Zeller wrote a number of sacred songs, including a *Marienlied* (Hymn to Mary) and a song to St Jacob, although he does not appear to have composed any church music in his adult years. It is suggestive of a continuing faith that he regularly took his family on holiday for three months every summer to the Premonstratensian monastery in Schlägl in Upper Austria, although Thomas Gnedt, director of the Carl Zeller Museum in Sankt Peter in der Au, does not believe that his Catholic schooling had any lasting influence on Zeller and points out that a biography of him written by his son makes no mention at all of religion.[27] It is certainly difficult to discern any distinctly religious or spiritual themes in his operettas, although perhaps his time singing in church choirs did help to mould those beautifully clear, limpid melodies, at once lyrical and soulful, pre-eminent among which is the aria from *Der*

Vogelhändler, 'Wie mein *Ahnl zwanzig Jahr'* (often known in English as the Nightingale Song). I have to say that for me it comes close to the kind of music which I think we may hear in heaven and I have requested it for my funeral.

When it comes to the most famous of the early Viennese operetta composers, Johann Strauss II, there is little to suggest either significant religious influences on his life or spiritual resonances in his work. Nominally Roman Catholic, he had Jewish ancestry through his paternal great-grandfather and converted to Lutheranism in 1887 so that he could marry his third wife, Adele, while his second wife was still alive. About the only time that he mentions religion is in a letter to his brother-in-law, Josef Simon, after his marriage to Adele in which he says; 'Already I no longer know which religion I belong to, although I have become in my heart more Jewish than Protestant.'[28] I share the view of his biographers that he seems to have had no serious engagement with any religion.

If there is anything approaching an underlying spiritual or philosophical theme in Strauss's operettas, it is perhaps a broad benevolence and tolerance, and a plea for belief in the brotherhood of man. We see it expressed in the way that he scores '*Bruderlein und Schwesterlein*' in *Die Fledermaus.* As Lisa Feurzeig comments, at one level, given all the conflicts and tensions which have been brought out, 'this sentimental moment of universal love for humanity is hard to take seriously ... Yet somehow the music carries listeners along, making us want to believe in the wondrous possibilities of reconciliation.'[29] The depiction of the gipsies in *Der Zigeunerbaron* has been read as a similar plea for diversity and tolerance of different peoples and races. For the Austrian historian and musicologist Moritz Csáky:

> Their portrayal can be seen as a direct and deliberate attempt to provide respect and recognition to this particular ethnic group, which was often forced as a despised outsider to the farthest margins of society. This image of the gipsies also contains an indirect invitation to tolerate and respect ethnic minorities in general, and to integrate them into the multiethnic fabric of the monarchy.[30]

Perhaps a key to Strauss' own religion and philosophy is contained in the title of his last operetta, *Die Gottin der Vernauft* (The Goddess of Reason). He certainly comes across as the most secular of the leading practitioners of European operetta in its golden age, albeit one accorded quasi-religious

20   MUSIC OF THE NIGHT

status in cartoons entitled *The Apotheosis of Johann Strauss* and *Johann Strauss in Heaven*, which portray him conducting in the clouds with his violin bow, surrounded by a cherubic orchestra.

Franz Lehár

Operetta's silver age is usually reckoned as beginning with the first performance of Franz Lehár's *Die lustige Witwe* in 1905. Lehár was almost certainly the most religious of all the major operetta composers and also the one whose music has the most evident spiritual resonances. The distinguished contemporary German conductor and musicologist, Ulf Schirmer, was struck by both these features when he was preparing to record seven of Lehár's later works with the Munich Radio Symphony Orchestra and the Bavarian Radio Chorus. 'What I found in Lehár's music', he told me, 'was a great depth and intensity that one occasionally finds in great prayers. There is noticeably no "manufactured" emotionality. I believe that he had more access to his own psychological depths than many other composers of the time.'[31]

A strong Catholic faith is suggested by the number of crucifixes and paintings of the Madonna, the Holy Family, and of saints found on the walls of the villa on the bank of the River Traun in Bad Ischl in Upper Austria which was Lehár's favourite home and place for composition and is now a museum. What his English biographers, Walter Macqueen-Pope and David Murray, describe as its 'strong ecclesiastical flavouring' is further enhanced by the furniture which includes a wooden Madonna and Child from the eighteenth century and a Baroque style Tyrolean sacristy inlaid with painted reliefs of the nativity.[32] His bedroom contains a kneeler and portable altar, above which hangs a portrait of St Ignatius Loyola, the founder of the Jesuit order. It has been suggested that Lehár's veneration of Loyola was such that he actually copied the saint in the way that he signed his name. I have found it impossible to verify this, although there is a striking similarity in the flourishes at the beginning and end of both men's signatures.

The decoration and layout of Lehár's Viennese home, the Schikaneder-Schlössl, was, if anything, even more indicative of a strong Catholic faith. It contained a life-sized statue of the Virgin and Child, a gilded ambo, or lectern, formerly housed in a church, and an embroidered cope spread out on one of the walls. Off the main hall was a fully functioning chapel in which the religious ceremony took place for the marriage of his great friend, Richard Tauber, the tenor who created many of his great romantic leading roles, to the English actress Diana Napier in 1936.

Lehár himself was reticent about his religious upbringing and beliefs and there is little if anything about them in the letters, articles, and papers that form the extensive Lehár archive in Bad Ischl or in the biographies that have been based on it. It is to his brother, Anton, a career soldier, that we owe references to their mother's strong faith and the daily prayers which she led at home. Franz seems rather to emphasize more worldly influences, as in a memoir he wrote, entitled 'my first love', about a girl he met while staying with his grandmother who rapidly put an end to the relationship when she discovered it. He notes that the stirrings that the 'sweet hearted little Budapest maiden' evoked in him 'were the first motive for the operas and operettas of my own life'.[33]

These amorous rather than religious influences are perhaps confirmed by the considerable number of voluptuous nudes that hung on his walls alongside the religious art and by the fact that he chose for his *Ex Libris* bookmark an engraving of a naked and nubile girl sitting under a tree behind which a somewhat predatory-looking Pan is playing his pipes to seduce her. There are shades of *The Phantom of the Opera* here, and maybe a hint of a role in which Lehár rather fancied himself. He engaged in several romantic relationships with younger women and there is a sense of erotic longing as well as spiritual yearning running through his work. The Austrian music critic, Ernst Décsey, noted in his 1924 biography how Lehár's seductive waltzes often feature someone sick with longing, as Danilo is in *Die lustige Witwe* as he dances alone around Hannah Glawari until she finally succumbs and dances with him.

There are, however, occasional suggestions of more serious religious influences and resonances. In a note typed in 1926 reflecting on his work, he seems almost to acknowledge an unseen divine hand, writing that his music 'pours out of every shape and situation' and that it is 'as if the creator of this melody is no longer with us'.[34] In a later reflection, he wrote of his belief 'that music is more than mere entertainment, or earning [a] living; that God has given it for the lifting up of hearts, to exhilarate and to comfort; that the musician's profession serves Man's affirmation of life and joy in life'.[35] Towards the end of his life, in 1944, he reflected on the impact made on him as a young boy by a performance of Franz Liszt's oratorio *Christus*

22 MUSIC OF THE NIGHT

conducted by the composer, in which his father was among the violinists in the orchestra:

> At that moment there was awakened for the first time within my childlike soul the realization that music, the archetype of all the arts, is more than a means of entertainment or livelihood, but a gift from God to uplift, cheer and comfort the heart, and that the vocation of musician means ministering to man's affirmation of life and his zest for life.[36]

This is a powerful affirmation of the spiritual element which exists in operetta as much as in more serious music, and of the sense of divine inspiration felt by one of its leading practitioners. As we shall discover, both Arthur Sullivan and Andrew Lloyd Webber had similar youthful epiphanies which gave them, too, a conviction that their vocation was in some sense God given and involved much more than simply providing entertainment and escape.

Lehár did not write any overtly sacred music, unless one counts the 'Preludium Religioso' which begins his 1893 one-act opera, Rodrigo. Restrained, lyrical, solemn, and ethereal, with much use of solo violin, it is really there to establish the scene which is set in a church from which the heroine is about to be kidnapped while she is praying. However, if one digs a bit deeper, it is not hard to find spiritual resonances in his music, especially around the theme of being alone. His attraction to this theme may well reflect his own lonely soul. Unlike many working in the field of operetta in the early twentieth century, he was not very sociable. He rarely joined his fellow composers and librettists in the cafés of Vienna and Bad Ischl, preferring rather to sit working at home alone.

He went so far as to install a pair of wrought iron gates halfway up the stairs of his villa in Bad Ischl and lock them so that he could work undisturbed in his rooms at the top of the house. This was his favourite place for composing, where he claimed that thirty of his operettas were written. He insisted that his wife sleep in an adjoining house. Was this an expression of the value of solitude, of his own inner loneliness, or even of some deeper spiritual yearning? Ulf Schirmer points out that the gates resemble those found in monasteries where the 'profane' area is separated from the cloisters. For him, this impression is reinforced by the church-like stained glass window behind the gates which casts its coloured light on the stairs: 'Lehár's Catholic background extends into the structural and homely atmosphere.'[37]

Two of Lehár's operettas focus on being alone in both a positive and a negative way. The second act of his 1914 operetta Endlich Allein (Alone at Last) is set on a mountain top where a couple are stranded after getting caught in a storm—they are in fact a Crown Prince and a princess who are both travelling incognito. Their loneliness amidst the beauty and grandeur of nature is contrasted with the stifling society of the hotel where they are staying and is celebrated in the aria 'Schön ist Die Welt'. The entire act is through-sung without dialogue and, with its use of leitmotifs, horns and strings to conjure up the atmosphere, is more reminiscent of Wagner's *Tristan und Isolde* or Richard Strauss's tone poems than of Viennese operetta as it is usually conceived.

Endlich Allein could be said to have had religious influences behind its creation. Its principal librettist, Dr Alfred Willner, was a devout Catholic who, in the words of Macqueen-Pope and Murray, 'found no inconsistency in varying his work as a light opera librettist with the composition of mystical poetry expressing his deeply religious instincts'.[38] The story goes that one 'sultry almost suffocating afternoon' he was summoned by Lehár and told that unless he came up with a libretto by the following morning, the composer would go to his rival, Viktor Léon. Desperate for a storyline, Willner wandered the streets of Bad Ischl and went into the church to pray to the saints for inspiration. He returned to his rooms, resolving to pass the night in solitary meditation. As he sat alone gazing out on the dark mountain peaks that surround the town, an idea came to him at last: a man and woman, both facing arranged marriages that they do not want, climb a peak together to escape the turmoil and frustrations of the world below, find themselves stranded, and gradually fall in love. The next morning, he went to the composer's villa and suggested that an entire act could be devoted to the two characters alone above the world. The composer was enthusiastic and so was born what Lehár later declared his favourite work.

Alfred Willner, who co-wrote the libretti for eight of Lehár's operettas, was highly unusual among his librettists in not having a Jewish background. A trained and practising lawyer, he also wrote for Johann Strauss, being the librettist for *Die Gottin der Vernauft*, and so almost uniquely straddled the golden and silver ages of operetta. Willner almost certainly wrote the Lehár song that most clearly references God: '*Und der Herrgott lacht, weils ihm Freude macht*' (The Lord God laughs because it makes him happy). It initially appeared in the 1916 flop *Der Sterngucker*, of which the original libretto is lost. The melody from this song was resurrected when *Endlich Allein* was reworked in 1930 into an operetta entitled *Schön Ist Die Welt*, where it was given different words, beginning '*Liebste, glaub an mich*' (Dearest, believe in me), and turned from a theological reflection into a love song.

24 MUSIC OF THE NIGHT

Lehár's focus on loneliness and his spiritual yearnings are perhaps most powerfully and movingly expressed in his darkly haunting 1927 operetta, *Der Zarewitsch*, about an heir to the Russian throne who appears to be tortured and conflicted by issues around his sexuality. He does eventually find love with a girl but has to break off the relationship upon becoming the Tsar. There are striking religious resonances in its musical construction. For Paul Seeley, who wrote his doctoral thesis on Lehár's operettas, 'The choral writing in *Der Zarewitsch* recalls the Slavonic church modes heard in the church anthems of Tchaikovsky and Rachmaninoff'.[39] Ulf Schirmer tells me that, following his recording of the work:

> When I listened to the first rough cut, I was increasingly irritated by the fact that the musical progression was carried as if by organ pedal points. After becoming aware of this phenomenon, which, by the way, was not neces-sarily limited to long bass passages, the impression continued. Even when events were flowing quite swiftly on the surface, there was still an under-lying background of slowness—an analogy, perhaps, of the relationship be-tween the temporally moving and the eternal.[40]

The theme of loneliness comes to the fore most directly in the Tsarevich's first aria, the hauntingly stark *Wolgalied*, in which he sings about a soldier on sentry duty on the bank of the Volga River. It begins '*Allein! Wieder Allein*' (Alone, again alone) and ends with a prayer to God:

> Have you forgotten up there too?
> My heart also longs for love.
> You have many angels with you in heaven.
> Send one of them to me too.

The *Wolgalied*, which was later recalled and quoted by the German nov-elist Günter Grass in his chapter on the year 1927 in his 1999 book *Mein Jahrhundert* about the twentieth century, was sung at the requiem for Franz Lehár following his death in Ischl in 1946. Somewhat surprisingly, Maria von Peteani's biography, which goes into immense detail about his final ill-ness, makes no mention of a priest being called at any point to supply spir-itual consolation or administer the last rites.

Lehár had a high view of operetta and its seriousness as an art form, asserting that 'operetta is an artistic genre that deals with human experience in a musical form'. Disturbed that most people perceived it 'simply as a means of entertainment, something to be diverted by and then forgotten', he wanted to enlarge its range and deepen its impact by creating real flesh and blood characters who experienced genuine love and suffering and were not just cardboard cutouts.[41] He did this especially in his later works like *Friederike*, *Paganini*, and *Jusquita*, which are far removed from the frothy gaiety of *Die lustige Witwe*, having a tragic dimension and a much darker and more intense tone, too much so for some of his fellow practitioners. Oscar Strauss commented of *Der Zarewitsch* that 'audiences shouldn't be crying when they watch operetta'.[42]

There is another very different way in which the operettas of the silver age, and those of Franz Lehár in particular, have a spiritual dimension. It is in their cosmopolitan, Bohemian celebration of multi-ethnic diversity and welcome for the outsider at a time when Germany, Austria, and Central Europe were moving towards a narrow nationalism and emphasis on racial purity. It may be that they provided their largely Jewish librettists with a way of expressing both their otherness and their sense of belonging. Micaela Baranello writes that operetta offered Jewish artists 'a haven and community that the government-subsidized theatre and opera did not'.[43] She also points out that, unlike those engaged in 'serious' music, few operetta librettists and composers converted from Judaism. The only major figure from the world of silver-age operetta to do so was Edmund Eysler, who became a Catholic in 1898. Imre Koppstein, educated first in a Jewish school in his home town of Siófok and later in a Christian gymnasium in Budapest, did change his name to the non-Jewish and more explicitly Hungarian Emmerich Kálmán but he remained Jewish, albeit non-practising.

This celebration of multi-ethnic diversity is present in the silver-age operettas from the beginning. It is there in the mixture of Pontvedrins and Parisians in *Die lustige Witwe*, the creation of the Jewish librettists, Viktor Léon and Leo Stein, and of the distinctly cosmopolitan Franz Lehár, whose own genes included Czech, Moravian, Hungarian, Slovak, Italian and Viennese. The message that true love extends over cultural, racial, and religious differences later becomes much more explicit with the coming of operettas with an exotic setting, notably Leo Fall's 1916 *Die Rose von Stambul* (with librettists Julius Brammer and Alfred Grünwald) and Emmerich Kálmán's 1921 *Die Bajadere*, with the same librettists, about the love between an Indian prince and a French singer. It achieves its fullest expression in Lehár's 1929 *Das Land des Lächelns* (The Land of Smiles) where the librettists Ludwig Herzer and Fritz Löhner-Beda convey the tensions in inter-racial relationships while insisting that love is more important than

26 MUSIC OF THE NIGHT

ethnic identity. In Baranello's words: 'What *Das Land des Lächelns* shares with previous exotic operettas is a fundamental belief that the distance conferred by exoticism conceals a deeper common humanity'.[44]

Although the romances between the Chinese prince Sou-Chong and the Viennese Countess Lisa and between his sister Princess Mi and Count Gustav von Pottenstein are both doomed and end because of cultural tensions, they are clearly genuine and that is what makes *Das Land des Lächelns* a tragedy. For the contemporary Viennese composer, Martin Lichtfuss, the irrecon-cilability between Sou-Chong and Lisa reflects the growing *Rassenkonflikt* (race conflict) in early twentieth-century Central Europe. He points out that the operetta never proposes that the two lovers should not be together—the tragedy is that present cultural circumstances mean that they cannot be. For him, *Das Land des Lächelns* is Lehár's plea for tolerance in a precarious world.[45] In that way, it directly prefigures and anticipates the equally intense but doomed relationship between the Tonkinese Liat and Lieutenant Cable in *South Pacific.*

It is appropriate to end this chapter on Continental European operetta with a nod ahead to Rodgers and Hammerstein, who more than anyone else take up and develop some of its elements to create the distinctive genre of Broadway musical theatre. I am conscious that it has been all too brief and that there is more work to be done and more to be said about what is still an unjustly neglected and despised art form. In particular, I hope that others will follow up and develop my suggestions about the Jewish and Catholic influences on both golden- and silver-age operetta. There is more, much more, in play here than shallow sentiment and schmalz. Both in its life-affirming gaiety and in its darker and deeper moments, operetta has a spir-itual quality that deserves to be recognized and affirmed.

Notes

1. Carl Dalhaus, *Nineteenth-Century Music* (Berkeley and Los Angeles: University of California Press, 1989), 228.
2. John Kenrick, 'French Operetta: Offenbach and Company', in Anastasia Belina and Derek Scott (eds.), *The Cambridge Companion to Operetta* (Cambridge: Cambridge University Press, 2019), 17.
3. Richard Traubner, *Operetta: A Theatrical History* (London: Gollancz, 1984), p.xi
4. Micaela Baranello, *The Operetta Empire* (Berkeley and Los Angeles: University of California Press, 2021), vii, 175.
5. Franz Lehár, 'Die Zukunft der Operette', *Die Wage* (10 January 1904), 85.
6. 'Spotlight on John Andrews', *28th International Gilbert and Sullivan Festival Souvenir Programme* (Buxton, 2022), 16.
7. Mark Steyn, *Broadway Babies Say Goodnight* (London: Faber and Faber, 1997), 31–32.
8. Kenrick, 'French Operetta', 17.

JEWISH AND CATHOLIC INFLUENCES   27

9. Laurence Selenick *Jacques Offenbach and the Making of Modern Culture* (Cambridge: Cambridge University Press, 2017), 2–3.
10. Carolyn Abbate, 'Offenbach, Krakauer and Ethical Frivolity', *Opera Quarterly* 33, no. 1 (Winter 2017), 68–86.
11. *Jacques Offenbach et ses Proches: De la Synagogue à l'Opéra* (CD produced by Institut Européen des Musiques Juives, Paris, 2020).
12. Robert Pourvoyeur, *Offenbach* (Paris: Editions du Seuil, 1994), 27.
13. Quoted in sleevenotes to *Jacques Offenbach et ses Proches*, 12.
14. Siegfried Kracauer, *Offenbach and the Paris of his Time* (London: Constable, 1937), 39.
15. Ralph Fischer, *Aus Jacques Offenbach's Kindergarten*, Hefte 169 (Bad Ems: Internationalen Jacques-Offenbach-Festival, 1997).
16. Kracauer, *Offenbach*, 32.
17. Ibid., 85.
18. Ibid., 85.
19. Ibid., 85.
20. James Harding, *Jacques Offenbach: A Biography* (London: John Calder, 1980), 40; Roger Williams, 'Jacques Offenbach and Parisian Gaiety', *The Antioch Review*, 17 (Spring 1957), 119.
21. Donald Fox, 'Scenes with Maestro Jean-Christophe Keck', *Jacques Offenbach Society Newsletter* no. 105 (September 2023), 17.
22. Kracauer, *Offenbach*, 169.
23. David Conway, *Jews in Music: Entry to the Profession from the Enlightenment to Richard Wagner* (Cambridge: Cambridge University Press, 2011), 217, 218.
24. See, for example, Ernest Newman, in Louis Biancolli (ed.), *The Opera Reader* (New York: McGraw-Hill, 1953), 317.
25. Traubner, *Operetta*, 20.
26. Ibid., 22.
27. E-mails to author, 23 July 2023, 8 September 2023.
28. Quoted in Zoë Alexis Lang, *The Legacy of Johann Strauss: Political Influence and Twentieth-Century Identity* (Cambridge University Press, 2017), 118.
29. Lisa Feurzeig, 'Viennese Golden-Age Operetta', in Anastasia Belina and Derek Scott (eds.), *The Cambridge Companion to Operetta* (Cambridge: Cambridge University Press, 2019), 43.
30. Moritz Csáky, *Ideologie der Operette* (Vienna: Böhlau, 1996), 88.
31. E-mail to author, 9 September 2023.
32. W. Macqueen-Pope and D.L. Murray, *Fortune's Favourite: The Life and Times of Franz Lehár* (London: Hutchinson, 1953), 152.
33. *Meine Erste Liebe*, undated typescript, Lehár Glockenverlag Box 152A, Stadtmuseum Bad Ischl.
34. Untitled typescript, Lehár Glockenverlag Box 152A, Stadtmuseum Bad Ischl.
35. Bernard Grun, *Gold and Silver: The Life and Times of Franz Lehár* (New York: David McKay Company, 1970), 27.
36. Franz Lehár, 'Musik - mein Leben', *Neues Wiener Tagblatt*, 23 September 1944.
37. E-mail to author, 9 September 2023.
38. Macqueen-Pope and Murray, *Fortune's Favourite*, 157.
39. E-mail to author, 1 September 2023.
40. E-mail to author, 9 September 2023.
41. Franz Lehár, 'Operetta as I imagine it', *Berliner Tageblatt*, 4 February 1926.
42. Quoted in sleevenotes to *Der Zarewitsch* CD (OEHMS Classics, 2010), 6.
43. Baranello, *Operetta Empire*, 50.
44. Ibid., 145.
45. Martin Lichtfuss, *Operette im Ausverkauf* (Vienna: Böhlau, 1989), 220.

2

A matter of life and death

Darkness and light in Gilbert and Sullivan

The thirteen comic operas on which W.S. Gilbert and Arthur Sullivan collaborated (I am not counting their first joint work, *Thespis*, a burlesque of a different character from the others) are in many ways the direct forebears of the great mid-twentieth century Broadway musicals. Word and story led, with strong characterization and plotting, the Savoy operas, as they are often known, show the clear influences of Anglo-Saxon Protestantism, just as French and central European operettas of the same period bear the hallmarks of their Jewish and Catholic origins.

It is, indeed, important to distinguish Gilbert and Sullivan from Continental operetta, which is a distinctly different genre, although both made their mark on twentieth-century musical theatre. Taking elements from both grand opera and music hall, the British pair put a premium on integrated plot and stagecraft and gave a key role to the chorus to create a new dramatic and musical art form, which largely languished throughout the first four decades of the twentieth century in favour of operetta-style musicals and revues until it was picked up and developed by Rodgers and Hammerstein in the early 1940s.

The Savoy operas do not have any obvious religious or spiritual resonances. Their subject matter is secular—Gilbert's initial idea of making the leading characters in *Patience* two high church clergy vowing with one another in their insipidity was dropped as being likely to cause offence, and they became aesthetic poets instead. There is a noticeable dearth of religious references. It is Minerva, the Greek goddess of wisdom, rather than the Judeo-Christian God who is invoked by the eponymous heroine in *Princess Ida* in her powerful introductory aria, although it is true that Josephine prays to the 'God of love and God of reason' in *H.M.S. Pinafore*. The overall impression that the operas convey is of light-hearted humour bubbling with brilliant wordplay, some sharp satire and much topsy-turvydom, accompanied by stirring and

Music of the Night. Ian Bradley, Oxford University Press. © Ian Bradley 2025.
DOI: 10.1093/9780197699775.003.0003

singable tunes, many galloping along in the 'patter' style or with catchy rum-te-tum rhythms.

There is a more serious side to Gilbert and Sullivan. Igor Stravinsky identified one element of it in remarks that he was reported to have made in an interview with the *New York Times* in 1968. Having praised 'the British team' for never being boring and producing operas that 'gallop along like happy colts, not like cart horses', he went on to say, 'They are also moral. The characters are good and bad, and the moral is always clearly drawn, although I do not overlook the sophistication of the satire.'[1] On the whole, good and bad characters are clearly delineated—the goodies do tend to triumph, and the baddies get their comeuppance. This is in marked contrast to the prevailing amorality of golden-age French operetta. The Savoy operas are altogether more wholesome and respectable than their racier Continental counterparts, eschewing cross-dressing and scantily clad chorus girls. They were calculated to appeal to middle-brow, bourgeois audiences who shunned both the musical hall and the opera house as being decadent and immoral. They had a strong appeal, as indeed they still do, to members of the clergy and proved popular and safe entertainments for church outings and for church choirs to perform. A flyer produced by impresario Richard D'Oyly Carte advertising a provincial UK tour of *H.M.S. Pinafore* in 1879 boasted, 'My theatre in London is visited largely by the clergy, who have given to it a support which they withhold from many others.'[2] Following the success of the same show in the United States, the *American Review* expressed the hope that the work of Gilbert and Sullivan 'might be the means of starting the great work of regeneration of the modern stage in our native land' and approvingly cited wide ecclesiastical endorsement: 'Clergymen have approved it. Church choirs have sung it. Church members have gone to see it and have been conscious of no moral degradation in the act.'[3]

But is there something more than this safe respectability and lack of moral degradation in the religious and spiritual make-up and appeal of the Savoy operas? In this chapter, I want to argue that there is and that it results from the fundamentally different outlooks of Gilbert and Sullivan. The uneasy relationship between the two collaborators has long been a matter of comment by biographers and critics. They differed over the style and tone of their joint works, with Sullivan tiring of Gilbert's contrived topsy-turvy fantasies and wanting more straightforward plots with real human interest. But there were also deeper differences in their philosophy and approach to life. Gilbert, the

30   MUSIC OF THE NIGHT

words man, was more of an exponent of the music of the night with an altogether darker side which bordered on the nihilistic. Pessimistic and cynical in his outlook, he felt that life was governed by the arbitrary decrees of fickle fate. Sullivan, reared in Christianity and continuing to adhere to liberal Protestantism throughout his adult life, was altogether more positive, more trusting and more filled with faith. Their contrasting approaches played out in their joint creations, nowhere more so than in their most popular work, *The Mikado*.

Death in *The Mikado*

When Charles Court Opera performed *The Mikado* in the Arcola Theatre in the East End of London in September 2023, a content warning was issued to the effect that the work contained 'themes of death, referenced in a satirical manner'. It would be wrong to dismiss this and other similar warnings that have accompanied recent performances of this work as simply another example of the extreme wokery that panders to the sensitivities of the snowflake generation and seeks to protect it from any possible offence that might be caused by the robust and for long uncontroversial language of classic literary and theatrical works. There is evidence that young people have been disturbed by *The Mikado*. When the Canadian actress, writer, and comedian Haley McGee was taken to see it at the age of seven, the repeated references to being buried alive lodged in her head. 'I started having these recurring dreams about being buried alive myself', she recalls, 'and so from then on I had this awareness of my own mortality'. Indeed, she attributes the prevalence of the themes of mortality and fear of death in her own work partly to the effect of this youthful encounter with them.[4]

The widely used online opera website, enopera-scores com, highlights this theme when it quotes the Wikipedia entry on the opera: '*The Mikado* is a comedy that deals with themes of death and cruelty'. It goes on to suggest that the darkness and starkness of these themes are mitigated because Gilbert treats them as 'trivial, even light-hearted issues . . . Death is treated as a business like event in Gilbert's topsy-turvy world'.[5] It is certainly true that, as a reviewer of the original production of the opera, which opened in March 1885, noted: 'Things grave and even horrible—decapitation, disembowelment, immersion in boiling oil or molten lead—are invested with a ridiculous aspect.'[6] But this does not necessarily make them less disturbing in their cumulative effect, as mentions of them are piled up both in dialogue and in song after song throughout the work.

It is certainly difficult to read through the libretto of *The Mikado* without feeling that its author has a fixation on death, especially in its more violent and macabre aspects. The theme is introduced in the third musical number where the noble lord, Pish-Tush, recounts that 'our great Mikado, virtuous man' has decreed that 'all who flirted, leered or winked (unless connubially linked), should forthwith be beheaded'. He goes on to introduce the comic lead, Ko-Ko, the Lord High Executioner, 'a convict from the county gaol, whose head was next on some pretext condemned to be mown off'. Ko-Ko has been made Headsman, Pish-Tush explains, on the grounds that, 'Who's next to be decapited [*sic*] cannot cut off another's head until he's cut his own off'.

From then on, the topics of execution and beheading loom large. A letter arrives from the Mikado expressing his concern that no executions have taken place in Titipu for a year and that unless someone is beheaded within a month, the post of Lord High Executioner will be abolished and the city reduced to the rank of a village. This provokes much discussion between Ko-Ko, Pish-Tush, and the enormously self-important Pooh-Bah as to who is to be executed, with the general consensus being that it should be Ko-Ko himself, leading to further dialogue about self-decapitation and suicide and the singing of a trio which ends with the chilling words:

> To sit in solemn silence in a dull, dark dock,
> In a pestilential prison with a life-long lock,
> Awaiting the sensation of a short, sharp shock
> From a cheap and chippy chopper on a big, black block.

The dilemma as to who is to be beheaded is solved when Nanki-Poo, the Mikado's son, who is disguised as a wandering minstrel to escape from the clutches of Katisha, an ageing and unappealing spinster of a kind that Gilbert delighted in portraying, enters with a rope and a dagger in his hand determined to commit suicide because Yum-Yum, the girl whom he adores, is to marry Ko-Ko. A bargain is struck whereby Nanki-Poo can marry Yum-Yum and then, after a month, be beheaded. The wedding duly takes place, but Ko-Ko later learns that by the Mikado's law, when a married man is beheaded,

32 MUSIC OF THE NIGHT

his wife is buried alive—in Yum-Yum's words, 'such a stuffy death'. In the Act II trio, 'Here's a how-de-do!' Yum-Yum, Nanki-Poo, and Ko-Ko sing of slaughter and burial. News that the Mikado is about to arrive prompts Nanki-Poo to ask Ko-Ko to behead him immediately, something which Ko-Ko refuses to do on the grounds that he doesn't 'go about prepared to execute gentlemen at a moment's notice'. He comes up with the idea that he can avoid killing Nanki-Poo by making an affidavit that his execution has been carried out and getting Pooh-Bah to swear to it in the guise of the many high offices that he holds.

The Mikado arrives, and Ko-Ko, Pitti-Sing, and Pooh-Bah regale him with a grisly account of the execution of the criminal 'as he squirmed and struggled and gurgled and guggled'. No detail is spared, whether it be the sabre cutting 'cleanly through his cervical vertebrae' or the trunkless corpse standing on its neck and bowing three times to Pooh-Bah. Katisha reads on the death certificate that it is Nanki-Poo who has been killed, and the Mikado responds by gleefully describing the punishment for compassing the death of the heir apparent (which, as his son, Nanki-Poo is) as 'something humorous, but lingering, with either boiling oil or melted lead'.

Nanki-Poo now reappears and says that he will only end his new existence as a dead man and come to life again if Ko-Ko marries Katisha, leaving him free to be with Yum-Yum. Ko-Ko reluctantly agrees and woos Katisha with a song about a little tom-tit who commits suicide because of blighted affection. He threatens to do the same if she spurns his proffered love. After a capital lunch, the Mikado arrives ready and eager to witness the execution of Ko-Ko, Pooh-Bah, and Pitti-Sing for putting his son to death. However, Katisha intervenes to beg mercy, and Nanki-Poo appears and assures his father that he has not, in fact, been slain. The very last piece of dialogue in the opera returns to the theme of death that has dominated it throughout, with Ko-Ko telling the Mikado that because his will is law, 'Your Majesty says, "Kill a gentleman," and a gentleman is told off to be killed. Consequently, that gentleman is as good as dead—practically, he is dead—and if he is dead, why not say so?', to which the Mikado responds: 'I see. Nothing could possibly be more satisfactory!'

This brisk gallop through the plot of *The Mikado* indicates just how much there is in it about death, particularly in its more grisly aspects. By my calculation, there are in total twenty references in the libretto to death or dying, eleven to execution or executioner, and seven each to beheading and to suicide. Burial alive is mentioned six times and decapitation three times.

Death in Gilbert's other works

The theme of death reappears in several other Savoy operas. Nanki-Poo is not the only tenor lead who comes close to committing suicide on stage. So does Ralph Rackstraw in a dramatic moment towards the end of the first act of *H.M.S. Pinafore*. At the end of *The Sorcerer*, John Wellington Wells, the dealer in magic and spells, yields up his life as a ritual victim to the mysterious and sinister figure of Ahrimanes, in Persian mythology the personification of evil, somewhat analogous to Satan. This is the only way that he can break the spell which he has cast over the villagers of Ploverleigh through his love potion, with its unexpected and unfortunate consequences. The eponymous heroine of *Iolanthe* is condemned to death by fairy law for marrying a mortal but has her sentence commuted to penal servitude for life. In a poignant meeting with her husband, the Lord Chancellor, she begs him to let her die. At the end of the opera, the Fairy Queen announces that the entire company of fairies must die for marrying peers. The female chorus is only saved from this fate by some quick thinking by the Lord Chancellor, who amends the law to read that 'every fairy shall die who *don't* marry a mortal.'

Death figures prominently in *The Yeomen of the Guard*, Gilbert and Sullivan's most serious work. Its hero, Colonel Fairfax, is a prisoner in the Tower of London awaiting execution for sorcery. In his first appearance, he ruminates on death, and whether it is a friend or a foe, first in spoken dialogue, where he reflects that 'it is no light boon to die swiftly and surely at a given hour and in a given fashion', and then in the ensuing ballad, 'Is life a boon?'. In a distinct echo of Yum-Yum and Nanki-Poo's wedding, Fairfax marries Elsie Maynard, a strolling player, on the day that he is to be beheaded. He does this so that his estate will not pass to the detested kinsman who accused him of sorcery, while Elsie enters the marriage for financial reasons so that she may have money to buy medicines for her sick mother. In the Act 1 finale, the executioner's block is brought on stage, and the masked headsman or executioner takes up his prominent place beside it as the death bell tolls.

Everything is thrown into panic when the guards sent to bring Fairfax for his execution find that he has escaped from his cell. He has, in fact, been abducted by sympathetic friends who hold prominent positions in the Tower. After much drama and mistaken identity, Elsie and Fairfax are reunited and find that they are in love, much to the consternation of Jack Point, Elsie's long-term companion who had hoped to marry her. The curtain goes down

34 MUSIC OF THE NIGHT

as he falls inconsolable and insensible on the stage. While his ultimate fate is not made explicit in Gilbert's stage direction, in many productions, Point clearly dies.

Death features in two other Savoy operas. *Ruddigore* has its chorus of ghosts, led by the spectre of the late Sir Roderick Murgatroyd, who sings about the 'grisly, grim goodnight' of the 'ghosts' high noon'. In *The Pirates of Penzance*, the bumbling but well-intentioned policemen, about to go into action against the pirates, are alarmed to be told by the heroine, Mabel: 'Go to death and go to slaughter!' Gilbert's poems and other stage works also frequently reference death. It is a particularly prominent theme in his last play, *The Hooligan*, which opened just three months before his own death in May 1911. Set in the condemned cell of a prison, it presents the thoughts of a young coster-boy who is to be hanged the following morning for killing his former girlfriend. He alternates between terror, fury with the judge for not taking his circumstances into account, and a resolve to be brave. In the final moments of the play, the prison governor, chaplain, and doctor enter the condemned cell to tell him that his sentence has been commuted to penal servitude for life. Asking dazedly, 'Am I to live?', he collapses with a fatal heart attack. It is an unremittingly bleak and harrowing work with a serious message, delivered by Gilbert in several of his writings, about whether those born with no chances in life and all the odds stacked against them should face severe punishment for their misdoings.

Gilbert's death fixation

Some of Gilbert's most cherished possessions provide further evidence of his fascination with death, particularly of a gruesome variety. They include the Japanese executioner's sword, which hung on the wall of his library and may have given him the inspiration for *The Mikado*, although the story that this was when it fell dramatically from its mounting is almost certainly apocryphal. Another macabre piece of furniture which he prized was a large oak sideboard which had belonged to a seventeenth-century murderer who had split his cook's head open with a meat cleaver. When the Savoy Theatre auctioned off its props in 1891, Gilbert bought the executioner's block from *The Yeomen of the Guard* to add to his chamber of horrors. In October 2010, just a few months before his death, he attended the trial of Dr Hawley Crippen, the mild-mannered American physician who poisoned and dismembered his wife in one of the most notorious murders of the early twentieth century.

What was the source of this fascination with death, amounting almost to an obsession? David Eden, the only one of those who have written about Gilbert to highlight it—it is largely missed by both Jane Stedman and Andrew Crowther in their biographies—applies a Freudian analysis and suggests that it is attributable to his infantile ego and the fact that he was essentially a sadomasochist. For Eden, Gilbert's death fixation went along with an obsession with cruelty and sadism, as shown in the characters of the gaoler, Wilfred Shadbolt, in *The Yeomen of the Guard* with his 'racks, pincers and thumbscrews', and the Grand Inquisitor in *The Gondoliers* who revels in the 'persuasive influence of the torture chamber'. Eden sees *The Hooligan* as the ultimate expression of a theme that runs through the dramatist's life's work: 'If one were trying to invent a theoretical culmination for the Gilbertian death instinct, it would be hard to find one more appropriate than this'.[7] It is part and parcel of a warped and flawed personality, which delighted in the macabre and the ghoulish, as expressed in Gilbert's apparent suggestion to Sullivan following the success of *The Mikado* that their next opera should be based on the story of Dr Frankenstein and the monster that he created.

Others have advanced somewhat different explanations for the undoubtedly dark side of Gilbert's character. Although he does not make much of Gilbert's death obsession in his biography, Andrew Crowther does acknowledge the playwright's anger and curmudgeonly misogyny, which he regards as resulting in part from an extremely unhappy and lonely childhood. There was no warmth or affection in his family background and upbringing. In Crowther's words, 'we are left only with a vague feeling of coldness, darkness and isolation'.[8] Perhaps partly because of this unhappy and lonely childhood, Gilbert took a distinctly jaundiced view of the world and the human condition. For him, life was arbitrary, unfair, and unjust, with the world being ruled by the fickle forces of fate rather than a benign and omnipotent deity. His outlook on life was well expressed in Dick Deadeye's utterance in *H.M.S. Pinafore* that 'it's a cruel world' and the Mikado's observation: 'It's an unjust world and virtue is triumphant only in theatrical performances', which precedes the quartet 'See how the fates their gifts allot'. Doubtless influenced, like others of his contemporaries, by Charles Darwin's theory of the survival of the fittest, Gilbert held that 'Man was sent into the world to contend with man, and to get the advantage of him in every possible way'.[9] In keeping with this low view of humanity, he was himself irascible; in his own words, 'an ill-tempered

36   MUSIC OF THE NIGHT

pig—and I glory in it'.[10] The actor and playwright Seymour Hicks wrote that Gilbert 'always gave the impression that he got up in the morning to see with whom he could have a quarrel'.[11] It was perhaps in an effort to escape the grim reality of the world and his own misanthropic musings that he developed his penchant for topsy-turvydom, inverting the usual and expected conventions and inventing ridiculous, surreal characters and situations. In many ways, he was the founding father of the theatre of the absurd.

There is another possible explanation for Gilbert's interest in death, which suggests a more serious philosophical approach. In the context of his generally bleak attitude to life with all its absurdities, vicissitudes, and injustices— a view that many might say is actually very realistic—he saw death as being the one event that sorts things out, bringing an end to conflict and confusion, and establishing order out of the chaos of life. This view is expressed in Katisha's reflection in her aria in Act 2 of *The Mikado* about 'the peace that death alone can bring', and it is summed up in what is perhaps the most profound line that Gilbert wrote, the Grand Inquisitor's observation in *The Gondoliers* that 'Life is one closely complicated tangle. Death is the only true unraveller.'

This perspective on death did not arise from any religious conviction. There is no evidence that Gilbert had a serious faith. Probably influenced, as suggested above, by the theories of Charles Darwin, he shared Thomas Hardy's bleak belief in a Godless world ruled by arbitrary and cruel fate. He was not a churchgoer. When he expressed a wish to be buried in the churchyard of the Anglican parish church near his home because he found its quietness attractive, the vicar declined his request on the grounds that his congregation did not want the churchyard crowded with strangers. In the event, a compromise was reached with Gilbert's widow and his cremated ashes were laid to rest near the church door, guarded over by a white marble angel.

It is not surprising, given all this, that Gilbert's words as they appear in the libretti of the Savoy operas often seem cold, morbid, cynical, and depressing. Take, for example, the chorus of schoolgirls in *The Mikado* ('Comes a train of little ladies') who are wondering what the world will be like and asking:

> Is it but a world of trouble, sadness set to song?
> Is its beauty but a bubble, bound to break ere long?
> Are its palaces and pleasures fantasies that fade?
> And the glory of its treasures shadow of a shade?

There is a similarly gloomy tone in the opening lines of the quartet in Act II of *Princess Ida*:

> The world is but a broken toy,
> Its pleasures hollow, false its joy,
> Unreal its loveliest hue, Alas!
> Its pains alone are true.

Yet when sung, these lines lose their depressing, pessimistic quality and become positively life-enhancing, if still touched with poignancy and pathos. Sullivan set 'Comes a train of little ladies' to an expansive 3/4 melody marked *allegretto grazioso* with a lively tripping semiquaver accompaniment, and he gave 'The world is but a broken toy' a soaring, lyrical melody line with tight harmony and minimal accompaniment, making it affirming rather than depressing, while remaining deeply poignant.

Sullivan's love of life and lack of fear of death

The fact is that Sullivan was incapable of writing a line of music that was pessimistic, cynical, cruel, or morbid. He could not have been more different from Gilbert in his temperament, character, and outlook on life. He was by nature optimistic, positive, trusting, and generous in his assessment of people's motives and character. Far from being death-obsessed, he was in love with life and lived it to the full, despite often being in chronic pain from a severe kidney complaint. He was universally known for his sunny disposition and emollient charm. Edward Elgar described him as 'one of the most amiable and genial souls that ever lived'.[12] His cousin Benjamin Findon wrote: 'He inspired in all who came into contact with him or his work a spirit of tranquil happiness, and an exquisite appreciation of the joy of living'.[13]

Sullivan's love of life owed much to his upbringing. In contrast to Gilbert, he had a blissfully happy childhood, being devoted to his parents and his brother and hugely enjoying both his early exposure to the music of the parade ground at the Royal Military College, Sandhurst, where his father was band sergeant, and his three years as a boy chorister in the Chapel Royal, which gave him his lifelong love of church music and of the Anglican choral tradition in particular. The influence of his genes (he was three-quarters Irish and one-quarter Italian) may perhaps also partly account for both his

38   MUSIC OF THE NIGHT

sensuousness and his spirituality, as well as for his swarthy appearance, as noted by an American journalist when he and Gilbert made their first visit to New York in 1879:

> In his appearance, gentle feeling and tender emotion are as strongly expressed as cold, glittering keen intellect is in that of Mr Gilbert ... he is as dark as his *collaborateur* is fair, with a face of wonderful mobility and sensitiveness, in which the slightest emotion plays with unmistakable meaning, with eyes which only the Germanic adjective of 'soulful' would fitly describe and the full, sensuous lips of a man of impassioned nature.[14]

Sullivan may have been dark in complexion, but he was anything but dark in personality and approach to life. The description of him above as 'soulful' is perceptive. He undoubtedly had a spiritual side to his character, which showed itself in an innocence diametrically opposed to Gilbert's world-weary cynicism and pessimism. It has been well identified by David Eden:

> It seems to me that there is in Sullivan, both as a man and as a composer, a quality one can only call spiritual. This quality is not Christian in the sense that it is not concerned with the dark night of the soul or the mystery of the incarnation. Nor is it pagan, as we currently use the term to mean orgiastic or violent. In terms of the Christian tradition, it is prelapsarian. There is in Sullivan a beautiful quality of innocence and joy which belongs to childhood, or the time in the garden before Adam and Eve became acquainted with sin.[15]

Alongside this quality of innocence, several of his contemporaries were struck by another distinguishing facet of Sullivan's personality—his almost complete lack of fear of death. It was remarked on by his first biographer, Arthur Lawrence, who recalled a conversation where the subject of death had come up and in which Sullivan had simply said, 'Death has absolutely no terrors for me'.[16]

To what was this lack of fear of death attributable? I believe—and here I part company with David Eden—that it came from Sullivan's Christian faith. His cousin, Benjamin Findon, wrote in his 1904 biography: 'Arthur Sullivan was peculiarly sensitive to the subtle and moving influence of the Christian life. The ecclesiastical character of so much of his music is as much a part of the nature of the man as the outcome of his early training and his association with the Church in after years.'[17] Sullivan did not often write or talk about spiritual or theological matters, being naturally reticent in these and other personal areas. But there is clear evidence from his diaries and letters, which has been largely ignored or overlooked by his more recent biographers, that he had a consistent and simple Christian faith, which was shaped in a liberal Broad Church direction partly thanks to his close friendship with George Grove, the Victorian polymath who was a serious amateur Biblical scholar and editor of the music dictionary that still bears his name. I provide more extensive evidence for and discussion of this in my books *Lost Chords and Christian Soldiers: The Sacred Music of Arthur Sullivan* (SCM Press, 2013) and *Arthur Sullivan: A Life of Divine Emollient* (Oxford University Press, 2021).

Sullivan was not frightened of death because he believed in an afterlife, and more specifically, in heaven as a place of eternal rest where family and friends would be reunited. This is demonstrated in his diary entry following the death of his beloved mother in May 1882, 'I was alone in the room, alone that is with dear Mother's lifeless body. Her soul had gone to God.' He noted the words that he had said to her: 'God bless you, and take you to eternal rest.'[18] When his sister-in-law Charlotte died in 1885, he wrote to his young nephews and nieces: 'Now, in your prayers night and morning, pray that your dear mother may have joined your father in God's eternal Rest, and that you all may lead such lives on earth, that hereafter you may be taken to where our hope is they are.'[19]

We can gain much insight into Sullivan's approach to death and how different it was from Gilbert's, from the songs on this theme that he chose to set and the way that he treated it. There are a good many of them, not surprisingly, given that death was such a popular topic in Victorian poetry. They include 'The Lost Chord', his setting of a poem by the devout Roman Catholic, Adelaide Ann Procter, about an organist who strives vainly to recapture a chord which 'links all perplexed meanings into one perfect peace' and concludes that he may hear it again only in heaven. It became the best-selling parlour ballad of the last quarter of the nineteenth century. The way that Sullivan set Procter's poem tells us something about his religious leanings as a composer and something, too, about his own faith. There is undoubtedly a sense of anguished yearning but also a confident belief in death as the final comforter and the solver of all mysteries. This is particularly clear in his setting of the final line, 'It may be that only in heaven I shall hear that Great Amen', to be repeated and sung *'con gran forza'*. There is no hint of the text's

40 MUSIC OF THE NIGHT

conditional 'may' in his triumphal closing chords but rather a ringing sense of certainty and expectancy about heaven and the life to come. Sullivan's other settings of songs about death are cast in a similar mood of assurance and framed in the context of a Christian belief that it is not the end and that beyond the mourning and grieving is the glorious prospect of resurrection, eternal life and the reunion of family and friends in heaven.

Sullivan as a church musician

Like the Roman Catholic French and Austrian composers discussed in the last chapter, Sullivan was schooled in church music—in his case, of an Anglican variety—first as a young boy when he sang in Sandhurst Parish Church, and then during his three years between the ages of twelve and fifteen as a chorister in the Chapel Royal, singing services for Queen Victoria and other members of the royal household in the chapel of St James's Palace in central London. As one of his mentors there commented, on entering the Chapel Royal, 'the future Sir Arthur found himself in an atmosphere of music in accordance with his own spiritual longings'.[20] Church music was his first love and remained so throughout his life. Although it is the Savoy operas for which he will always be primarily remembered, his substantial corpus of sacred works, which included two Biblical oratorios, *The Prodigal Son* and *The Light of the World*; two sacred cantatas, *The Martyr of Antioch* and *The Golden Legend*; three Te Deums; and numerous liturgical settings, anthems, sacred songs, and hymn tunes, meant most to him among his own compositions. More than once, he reiterated the remark that he made in an interview with the *San Francisco Chronicle* in 1885: 'My sacred music is that on which I base my reputation as a composer. These works are the offspring of my liveliest fancy, the children of my greatest strength, the products of my most earnest thought and most incessant toil'.[21]

It is striking and significant that Sullivan's first and last compositions were settings of Biblical and liturgical texts. At the age of eight, he wrote an anthem setting the opening verses of Psalm 137, 'By the waters of Babylon', the manuscript of which is now lost. His first published work, written when he was thirteen, was a sacred song, 'O Israel', based on verses from the Book of Hosea. His last finished composition was the *Boer War Te Deum*, written in 1900 when his strength was ebbing fast and his health waning. He devoted much of the last six months of his life to this sacred piece, which had been commissioned by the Dean and Chapter of St

Paul's Cathedral for what was expected to be the imminent conclusion of Britain's war against the Boers in South Africa. Indeed, he concentrated on it to the detriment of a comic opera, *The Emerald Isle*, which remained unfinished at his death—it was later completed by Edward German. So, in a real sense, church music was Sullivan's first and last love. Sacred pieces, notably the madrigal-like anthems of the Tudor church composers that he fell in love with as a chorister in the Chapel Royal, and the Lutheran choral masterpieces of Bach and Mendelssohn, spoke to his own spiritual side. He once said that it was listening as a boy to Jenny Lind singing solos from Mendelssohn's *Elijah* that made him realize that music was divine. The similar impact on the young Franz Lehár of hearing Liszt's *Christus* comes to mind.

More than any other Victorian composer, Sullivan straddled the worlds of the musical stage and the sanctuary. Some of his many critics suggested that he was much happier in the former sphere and that his comic operas provided a blessed release and escape from the sacred music that he felt he ought to write but which was not really suited to his capabilities. For Erik Routley, the distinguished twentieth-century hymnologist,

> Sullivan's genius was not in the least religious; it was too light for the graver themes. We can imagine the relief with which he escaped from his early occupation with church music, in which he was not at home, into that wholly congenial field of light opera in which, along with his twin genius, W.S. Gilbert, he was to achieve his artistic immortality.[22]

Others have taken the opposite view and seen Sullivan's comic operas as an aberration and distraction from the serious and sacred work that was his true calling. An unsigned article appeared on the day after his death in *The Times* that was almost certainly penned by Fuller Maitland, the paper's music critic who was one of the main proponents of the new English Musical Renaissance associated with composers like Hubert Parry and Charles Villiers Stanford. It noted:

> Many who are able to appreciate classical music regret that Sir Arthur Sullivan did not aim consistently at higher things, that he set himself to rival Offenbach and Lecocq instead of competing on a level of high seriousness with such musicians as Sir Hubert Parry and Professor Stanford . . . If he had followed this path, he might have enrolled his name among the great composers of all time.[23]

42   MUSIC OF THE NIGHT

The truth is that Sullivan was equally happy in the theatre pit and in the church organ loft. Like Isaac Offenbach, he saw no incompatibility between the worlds of so-called secular and sacred music or between lighter and more serious compositions. He expressed his love of church music, his own religious faith, and his spirituality in his comic operas. His nephew Herbert attributed to his uncle's early training in the Chapel Royal 'the note of religious melody which coloured his own composing in later years and often stole, as if unaware, into his operas'.[24] It can be clearly seen in the works that he wrote in collaboration with other librettists who were less death-obsessed and cynical (and, one might add, also considerably less witty and accomplished wordsmiths) than Gilbert. It is there, for example, in his sensitive settings of prayers to the Virgin Mary in his 1898 romantic musical drama *The Beauty Stone*, with a libretto by Arthur Wing Pinero and J. Comyns Carr, and in the haunting Act 1 finale of *The Emerald Isle* (librettist: Basil Hood), which invokes a Celtic other-world with fairy voices calling mortals away to the mythical caves of Carrig-Cleena. The last piece of music that he wrote, it has a numinous, ethereal quality unlike anything else from his pen. It is on my funeral playlist, along with the aria 'God shall wipe away all tears' from his oratorio, *The Light of the World*.

Gilbert and Sullivan together

It is undoubtedly true that Arthur Sullivan did his best work in partnership with W.S. Gilbert. How did the spiritually inclined composer with such a love of life and no fear of death manage to collaborate with the death-fixated, cynical, world-weary librettist, let alone collaborate so brilliantly? There were undoubtedly tensions caused by their different personalities and underlying philosophies of life. Sullivan found Gilbert's cruel portrayal of ageing spinsters particularly unappealing. When yet another one in the mould of Katisha from *The Mikado* and Lady Jane from *Patience* appeared in the person of Lady Sophy in *Utopia, Limited*, he complained that he found her 'unsympathetic and distasteful' and that 'the elderly spinster, unattractive and grotesque . . . is a character which appeals to me vainly, and I cannot do anything with it'.[25] He also made no secret of his longing for less convoluted and more romantic plots and libretti, with less topsy-turvydom and absurdity and more 'human interest and probability'.[26]

A MATTER OF LIFE AND DEATH   43

For his part, Gilbert found Sullivan's music too churchy. He reproached his collaborator more than once for the seriousness of his settings, 'fitted more for the Cathedral than the Comic opera stage', a verdict that would later be echoed by George Bernard Shaw, who found the Savoy operas 'most unexpectedly churchy after Offenbach'.[27] Sullivan conceded to Gilbert, 'I cannot but feel that in very many cases the reproach is just'.[28] The fact was that he could never get away, even had he wanted to, from his upbringing in and deep love of church music. Several of the most characteristic musical features of the Savoy operas derive from the conventions of sacred music. The musicologist Benedict Taylor has convincingly argued that the contrapuntal double choruses found in so many of the operas have their origins in the world of church counterpoint.[29] In their early biography, Herbert Sullivan and Newman Flower assert, presumably on the basis of what the composer told his nephew, that 'many of the unaccompanied quartets, etc., in his Savoy operas' were directly influenced by the church music that he heard during a visit to Russia in 1881.[30] The madrigals that feature so prominently in the operas have something of the character of the Tudor church anthems on which Sullivan had been brought up in the Chapel Royal and that he loved so much. Perhaps even that most characteristic hallmark of the Savoy operas, the patter song, with its frequent repeated notes and careful attention to words, owes something to the tradition of plainchant in which Sullivan was so thoroughly schooled by his great mentor, Thomas Helmore, master of the children at the Chapel Royal and prominent promoter of the revival of plainchant in the Victorian Church of England. Several of the Savoy opera choruses, especially the a capella 'Hail, Poetry!' in *The Pirates of Penzance* and 'Eagle high' in *Utopia Limited*, could, at least in musical terms if not in respect of their lyrics, pass muster as Victorian parish church anthems.

Despite their profound differences, there was undoubtedly a mutual admiration between composer and librettist for one another's skills. We see it most clearly in their exchange of genuine heartfelt compliments in the aftermath of *The Gondoliers*, their happiest collaboration. There are moments in the Savoy operas where one feels that their two creators are completely aligned in articulating a deeply shared conviction. One such is the anthem 'Hail, Poetry!' in *The Pirates of Penzance*, which expresses both librettist's and composer's agreement with the sentiments of the Pirate King's rhetorical question that introduces it, 'What, we ask, is life without a touch of poetry in it?'. Critics have tended to see this as a lampoon or parody of a certain kind

44 MUSIC OF THE NIGHT

of religious sentiment. Arthur Jacobs, Sullivan's late twentieth-century biographer, described it as 'a burlesque of an operatic prayer scene . . . but the words of prayer could not be burlesqued, nor could the Deity be invoked in satire. So the abstraction of "Poetry" takes its place, an awkward substitute.'[31] Gervase Hughes, author of a somewhat scathing mid-twentieth-century attack on Sullivan's music, wrote in similar vein: 'Sullivan's share has been decried as a lapse into "churchiness", and he may or may not have had his tongue in his cheek, but he knew that his audience, steeped like himself in the tradition of English choral singing, would applaud it to the echo.'[32] In fact, I do not think that either librettist or composer had their tongues in their cheeks when they wrote 'Hail, Poetry!'. I believe that Gilbert, accomplished poet as he was, was utterly sincere in his tribute to poetry as 'a heaven born maid', and indeed as 'Divine emollient', which is as near as he gets in any of his writing to directly invoking the Deity. Sullivan was equally sincere in providing a church anthem-like setting for this hymn to the flowing fount of sentiment in which he believed so strongly.

Another song which brings librettist and composer together in an expression of shared belief is the quintet 'Try we lifelong' in *The Gondoliers*, with its philosophy of *Carpe Diem*, its reminder that 'life's a pudding full of plums, care's a canker that benumbs', and its injunction to 'string the lyre and fill the cup lest on sorrow we should sup' and to take life as it comes. It is preceded by the Grand Inquisitor's observation that 'Life is one closely complicated tangle: Death is the only true unraveller', on which I have already commented and which perhaps comes closest to a theological statement in the whole Gilbert and Sullivan canon. The quintet itself leaves death behind and focuses on enjoying, celebrating and making the most of life—Gilbert for once fully espouses Sullivan's philosophy and approach to it. There are several other songs in which Gilbert expresses a Sullivanesque love of life— 'The sun whose rays are all ablaze' in *The Mikado* is one such—and it would be quite wrong to suggest that all of his lyrics dwell on death, although there is no getting around the fact that rather a lot of them do.

How Sullivan responded to Gilbert's death fixation

How did Sullivan approach the death fixation that undoubtedly hovers around so many of his librettist's plots and lyrics? At one level, he treated it with utter sincerity and gave it a spiritual underpinning. There are three

A MATTER OF LIFE AND DEATH   45

pre-eminent examples of this sensitive and sympathetic treatment. The first is another of those anthem-like choruses, 'I hear the soft note of the echoing voice of an old, old love, long dead', from the Act 1 finale of *Patience*. Gervase Hughes describes it as 'a quasi-religious effusion', and Arthur Jacobs brackets it with 'The Lost Chord', the aria 'How many hired servants' from *The Prodigal Son*, and the evening hymn from *The Golden Legend*, in respect of its 'obsessive repeated notes at the opening' which 'no doubt conveyed solemn intensity then as surely as they seem now to be a cliché of such emotion'.[33] It certainly has very close affinities with these much more obviously sacred pieces and, for those of us who do not share the view that Sullivan's repeated notes in these numbers sound clichéd, it works a similar magic in terms of weaving what can only be described as a spiritual aura which is at once both calming and haunting. A sense of death, in this case of the old, old love, is still there, but it is subsumed into a more general gentle wistfulness, accentuated by the Duke of Dunstable's soaring solo, which begins on a high G and floats above the steady pulsating chorus.

The second scene from the Savoy operas in which Sullivan takes Gilbert's focus on death very seriously is the encounter between Iolanthe and the Lord Chancellor towards the end of *Iolanthe*. It begins with the recitative 'My Lord, a suppliant at your feet I kneel', leads into the ballad 'He loves!', and ends with the Fairy Queen appearing and condemning Iolanthe to death. Here, Gilbert provides lyrics of unaffected pathos and genuine feeling, untempered by any satirical jibes or topsy-turvy touches. The death motif is unavoidable—the words 'dead' and 'dies' both occur twice in Iolanthe's opening recitative and ballad; she then asks the Lord Chancellor to let her die, and the Fairy Queen sings: 'Bow thy head to destiny: Death thy doom and thou shalt die'. Sullivan takes these lines straight and gives them a poignant yet simple setting, which does have an unmistakably dark feel, enhanced by the plaintive chromatic wails of 'Aiaiah, Willaloo' from the chorus of fairies, which recur throughout the scene. Some have described it as Wagnerian, and others have sought to find echoes of Weber, but in fact, I think it is Sullivan being true to himself. He began working on *Iolanthe* just three days after the death of his beloved mother. He must often have thought of her as he set this particular number with its references to 'tears—bitter unavailing tears, for one untimely dead' and its line 'sad thoughts of her arise'. Did he write this song in some sense as a memorial to her?

The third example of Sullivan's straight response to Gilbert's death fixation comes in that part of the *Yeomen of the Guard* Act 1 finale, which focuses

46 MUSIC OF THE NIGHT

on Colonel Fairfax's impending execution where the funeral bell tolls as the chorus sings:

> The prisoner comes to meet his doom;
> The block, the headsman, and the tomb.
> The funeral bell begins to toll;
> May Heav'n have mercy on his soul!

Here again, Sullivan sets these lines absolutely straightforwardly, with a heavily accented funeral march spreading out into a much more measured and drawn-out setting of 'May heaven have mercy on his soul'.

In these three cases, Sullivan faces Gilbert's death obsession head-on, as it were, treating it seriously with suitably sombre if still melodic music. But this is not the only way that he responds to it. Let us go back to those songs in *The Mikado* enumerated at the beginning of this chapter in which particularly grisly forms of death are treated in a satirical and humorous manner. Sullivan enhances their comic element while playing down their cruel character, softening the impact of the ghoulish and bloodthirsty words. 'Our great Mikado virtuous man' is turned into an energetic, fast-paced solo and chorus performed *allegro con brio*, while 'To sit in solemn silence' is given a breathtaking, rumbustious rum-te-tum tune full of repeated notes (fourteen to begin with immediately followed by another eleven) which takes away the gloomy foreboding of the words on their own. Slaughter and burial may feature prominently in the text of 'Here's a how-de-do', but Sullivan turns it into a galloping trio with a cracking *allegro vivace* pace. His setting of the song in which Ko-Ko, Pitti-Sing and Pooh-Bah describe Nanki-Poo's beheading 'in most affecting detail' does provide suitable musical accompaniment to the bloodthirsty lyrics, with the phrases 'my snickersnee' and 'cervical vertebrae' being sung in a lower register and repeated for emphasis, and the shriek of the decapitated criminal acknowledged by a rapidly falling scale from the woodwind. Katisha's Act 2 solo 'Alone, and yet alive' is treated seriously and given the same kind of sensitive setting as Iolanthe's 'He loves', dark but sympathetic and soulful. In 'Tit Willow', the echo that arises from the suicide's grave is not morbid or macabre but plaintive and haunting.

It could be said that in dealing with Gilbert's death obsession, Sullivan has resort to the two great formative influences of his musical upbringing: the rum-te-tum of the army parade ground where his bandmaster father drilled his troops and the soulful, sacred strains of the Chapel Royal choir. In both cases, his settings deflect Gilbert's gloom and dark pessimism, softening the harshness of his lyrics and shifting the mood from death to life. It is not too much, I think, to describe this uplifting effect in spiritual terms as having a redemptive effect.

In his biography of the composer, Percy Young writes that 'Sullivan's immediate contribution to English music was recognized as the quality of gracefulness' and notes how this term was used by the *Musical Times* to describe several of his early compositions in the 1860s.[34] Gracefulness, understood in its theological sense as conveying and representing God's grace, as well as in a more general way, remained an abiding characteristic of his work. *The Times* critic hit the nail on the head when he wrote about the performance of *The Golden Legend* in the Albert Hall in November 1886: 'Sir Arthur Sullivan has the rare gift of placing the cynical mind at rest.'[35] There is no doubt that there was at least one troubled, if not perhaps cynical mind, that Sullivan did calm and place at rest. My research has shown just how much he eased the waning faith and theological doubts of his great friend George Grove, particularly with respect to the question of whether there is life after death.[36]

Did Sullivan similarly manage to put Gilbert's cynical mind to rest and help him to overcome his death obsession or at least to manage it in a more positive way? I don't think that he did—that would be asking too much. Gilbert never acquired Sullivan's religious faith or spiritual sensitivity, although he did show a deep compassion and sympathy for the underdog and the disadvantaged, not least in his dealings as a magistrate in the latter decades of his life. He was, in most respects, the dominant partner in their working relationship, not least in determining the plots and characters of their joint works and writing the lyrics. The words came first, as did his name on the playbill.

Sullivan often complained that he subordinated himself to Gilbert and was a mere word-setter. Yet in one crucial respect, he triumphed over him. He ultimately trumped his librettist's gloom and morbid obsessions with his spirituality and love of life. He did this by accentuating Gilbert's humour and softening his cynicism, lifting the depression that is there in the lyrics with his gloriously lyrical, uplifting melodies. This achievement is acknowledged even by Gilbert's greatest supporters. Andrew Crowther is compelled to admit that 'Sullivan's music was able to give Gilbert's words a warmth which they often lacked.'[37] For all his obstinacy and awkwardness, Gilbert was almost always happy to accept Sullivan's settings, even when they did subtly

48   MUSIC OF THE NIGHT

change the colour of his lyrics. A rare exception to this was in the case of Sullivan's original jaunty 6/8 tune for Colonel Fairfax's 'Is life a boon?' from *The Yeomen of the Guard*, one of those songs about death mentioned earlier. Gilbert claimed that it was too similar to previous tenor ballads in the Savoy operas and insisted that Sullivan come up with a new tune, which he did with a more sombre 2/4 setting, marked '*Andante espressione*'. Was the real reason for Gilbert's unease, I wonder, that he found the original tune just too bright and breezy? As the conductor David Russell Hulme writes, 'broadly lyrical and almost nonchalant, it is markedly different in mood to its more contemplative successor'.[38] Here, for once, Gilbert did succeed in suppressing Sullivan's life-enhancing exuberance.

If there are spiritual resonances in the works of Gilbert and Sullivan, and I believe that there are, they come predominantly from the composer rather than the librettist. Gilbert provided biting, caustic wit and satire, wonderfully inventive rhyming schemes and unforgettable phrases, Sullivan a stream of lyrical, life-affirming melodies conveying the promise of Spring and the conviction that the world is new every morning. He softened, brightened, transfigured, and perhaps even redeemed the often rather bleak, cynical, and pessimistic lyrics of his collaborator. In my biography of Sullivan in the OUP 'Spiritual Lives' series, I write that 'it was supremely in the Savoy operas for which he will always be most remembered that he displayed that distinctive if not unique characteristic of divine emollient which made his a spiritual life'.[39] David Eden is quite right to say that 'in Freudian terms one might say that the life instincts of Sullivan overcame the death instincts of Gilbert'.[40] It was a matter of light conquering darkness, and of the music of the day drowning out the music of the night.

Notes

1. *New York Times*, 27 October 1968.
2. Regina Oost, *Gilbert and Sullivan: Class and the Savoy Tradition 1875–1896* (Farnham: Ashgate, 2009), 28.
3. *American Review*, 19 May 1879.
4. Sarfraz Manzoor, 'The show about mortality that will give you a new lust for life', *The Times Saturday Review*, 17 September 2022.
5. Accessed 11 February 2023.
6. William Beatty-Kingston, *The Theatre*, 1 April 1885.
7. David Eden, *The Creative Conflict* (Madison: Fairleigh Dickinson University Press, 1986), 82.
8. Andrew Crowther, *Gilbert of Gilbert & Sullivan* (Stroud: The History Press, 2011), 21.
9. 'Men We Meet' by the Comic Physiognomist, *Fun*, 9 March 1867.
10. Reginald Allen, *W.S. Gilbert: An Anniversary Survey* (Charlotte, Virginia: Bibliographical Society of University of Virginia, 1963), 78.
11. Seymour Hicks, *Between Ourselves* (London: Cassell, 1930), 49.
12. *Strand Magazine*, May 1904, 541–2.

13. Benjamin Findon, *Sir Arthur Sullivan: His Life and Music* (London: James Nisbet, 1904), 3.
14. *New York Herald*, 23 October 1879.
15. *Sir Arthur Sullivan Society Magazine* no. 41 (Autumn 1995), 26.
16. *Masonic Illustrated*, January 1901, 69.
17. Findon, *Sir Arthur Sullivan*, 62.
18. Arthur Jacobs, *Arthur Sullivan*, 2nd ed. (Aldershot: Scolar Press, 1992), 178.
19. Letter from Sullivan to his nieces and nephews, 31 January 1885: Pierpont Morgan Library, New York.
20. Frederick Helmore, *Memoir of the Rev Thomas Helmore* (London: J. Masters, 1891), 73.
21. *San Francisco Chronicle*, 22 July 1885.
22. *Bulletin of the Hymn Society of Great Britain and Northern Ireland*, no. 20 (July 1942), 7.
23. *The Times*, 23 November 1900.
24. Herbert Sullivan and Newman Flower, *Sir Arthur Sullivan* (London: Cassell, 1927), 1.
25. Letter from Sullivan to Gilbert, 1 July 1893, quoted in Michael Ainger: *Gilbert and Sullivan: A Dual Biography* (Oxford: Oxford University Press, 2002), 342.
26. Ainger, *Gilbert and Sullivan*, 230.
27. Sullivan and Flower, *Sullivan*, 187; Jacobs, *Sullivan*, 16.
28. Sullivan and Flower, *Sullivan*, 187.
29. Benedict Taylor, 'Features of Sullivan's Religious Style Found in the Festival Te Deum', *Sir Arthur Sullivan Society Magazine* no. 58 (Summer 2004), 12.
30. Sullivan and Flower, *Sullivan*, 117.
31. Jacobs, *Sullivan*, 140.
32. Gervase Hughes, *The Music of Arthur Sullivan* (London: Macmillan, 1960), 86–7.
33. Hughes, *The Music of Sullivan*, p.151; Jacobs, *Sullivan*, 110–11.
34. Percy Young, *Sir Arthur Sullivan* (London: J.M. Dent, 1971), 74.
35. *The Times*, 16 November 1886.
36. Ian Bradley, *Arthur Sullivan: A Life of Divine Emollient* (Oxford: Oxford University Press, 2021), 68–70.
37. Crowther, *Gilbert*, 119.
38. Sleeve notes to CD of *Yeomen of the Guard*, TER Classics, 1993.
39. Bradley, *Arthur Sullivan*, 204.
40. Eden, *The Creative Conflict*, 196.

3

The fatherhood of God and
the brotherhood of man

Oscar Hammerstein II

Oscar Hammerstein II is a pivotal figure in the history of musical theatre. Uniquely, he straddles the very different worlds of late silver age Viennese-style operetta and the new modernist post-Broadway musical, having provided the libretti for Rudolf Friml's *Rose Marie* and Sigmund Romberg's *The Desert Song*, and gone on to be the chief mentor of Stephen Sondheim. Historians of the genre agree that it was Hammerstein, working in collaboration with Richard Rodgers, who established the integrated musical with *Oklahoma!* in 1943. It broke new ground by integrating book (i.e. plot) and songs, incorporating a greater realism, and giving much more depth to character and motivation. Rodgers and Hammerstein's eleven subsequent collaborations, culminating in *The Sound of Music* in 1959, also brought a new seriousness to musical theatre. In the words of John Bush Jones: 'Rodgers and Hammerstein demonstrated that musicals could be "idea-bearing", socially conscious, and socially responsible, yet still entertain and make money'.[1]

Much has rightly been made of Hammerstein's own considerable involvement in progressive political movements and causes in the mid-twentieth century. He was active in the Hollywood Anti-Nazi League and had a long and close association with the National Association for the Advancement of Colored People, the earliest major civil rights organization in the United States. From around 1950, he was a prominent member of the United World Federalists, a group set up in the aftermath of the Second World War with the aim of preventing another global conflict by advancing the cause of a democratic world federal government. The previous year, in conjunction with their friends and neighbours Pearl Buck and James Michener, Oscar and his wife, Dorothy, founded Welcome House, a child welfare and adoption agency for children of Asian or part-Asian ancestry who were shunned

Music of the Night. Ian Bradley, Oxford University Press. © Ian Bradley 2025.
DOI: 10.1093/9780197699775.003.0004

THE FATHERHOOD OF GOD AND THE BROTHERHOOD OF MAN   51

by existing adoption services. Oscar became its president, and among the first children adopted from the agency was the Hammersteins' first grandchild. In the last years of his life, he lent his support to Martin Luther King's civil rights crusade and joined the board of the National Committee against Discrimination in Housing, having been appalled to discover that homeowners in his own neighbourhood of Bucks County, Pennsylvania, were asking their neighbours not to sell their homes to 'negroes' and thereby lower the area's real-estate values.

Oscar Hammerstein's strong social conscience and liberal political outlook were clearly displayed in the libretti and lyrics of his musicals, and especially in his collaborations with Richard Rodgers, which promoted the themes of community, tolerance, racial integration, and peace-building. For some critics, they had a distinctly preachy and didactic flavour, but that did not diminish their popular appeal. If anyone faithfully obeyed Sheldon Harnick's famous commandment for those involved in musical theatre, 'Enlighten if thou canst, *but entertain thou must*', it was surely Hammerstein.[2] This chapter explores the possible sources of these idealistic liberal values, which so clearly underscore the blockbuster Rodgers and Hammerstein musicals of the 1940s and 1950s, and suggests that they had religious origins.

Hammerstein's representation as secular and Jewish

Most commentators and biographers see Hammerstein as an essentially secular figure without any real religious faith who derived his liberal social and political views from a humanist outlook. Typical is Laurie Winer, in her *Oscar Hammerstein II and the Invention of the Musical*. Having observed that 'the Hammerstein clan was secular', she goes on to say that 'Hammerstein's humanism naturally informed his political activism'.[3] Winer does concede that there was a spiritual element in Hammerstein's makeup and writing. Indeed, she makes a fascinating comparison with William James, the late nineteenth- and early twentieth-century philosopher and psychologist who was strongly influenced by Swedenborgianism and is now best remembered as the author of *The Varieties of Religious Experience*. For Winer, 'they both represent what seems to me a uniquely American way of seeking—one tied to the mystical but at the same time the practical, and one that leaves lots of room for individual interpretation'.[4] Winer even finds herself using theologically loaded language about

52 MUSIC OF THE NIGHT

Hammerstein, noting that he 'was interested in redemption, restoration and renewal'.[5] But there is no suggestion that this mystical/spiritual dimension came from any distinctly religious influence.

This impression of secular humanism is largely confirmed in the substantial collection of Hammerstein's letters edited by Mark Horowitz and published by Oxford University Press in 2022. In an interview with the Jewish magazine *Forward* linked to the publication of the letters, Horowitz asserts: '[Hammerstein] was not a religious fellow, but I think he was a deeply good fellow and I guess a humanitarian, but did not attend services. I think he thought of himself as culturally Jewish. It sort of surprises me that there isn't more Jewishness in any of his major works. . . . The reality is that most of Hammerstein's friends were Jewish. The world he inhabited, the theater world, was largely Jewish.'[6]

When Hammerstein is given a religious label, it is invariably that of being Jewish, as in Horowitz's remarks quoted above. His Jewishness has been especially emphasized in Andrea Most's book, *Making Americans: Jews and the Broadway Musical*. She explicitly lists Hammerstein as a Jewish writer alongside Irving Berlin, George and Ira Gershwin, and Lorenz Hart, brackets him with Richard Rodgers as a Jewish liberal, and argues that *Oklahoma!*, *South Pacific*, and *The King and I* are essentially expressions of Jewish assimilationism, promoting the values of tolerance and egalitarianism and the ideal of a Utopian liberal society in which outsiders are accepted.[7] In an article on the treatment of race in *South Pacific*, she describes Hammerstein and Rodgers as 'assimilated New York Jewish artists'.[8]

Tucked away in a footnote at the end of Most's book is an admission that Hammerstein 'was not technically Jewish, since his father was Jewish but his mother was not'. She goes on to say, however, that 'for the purposes of this book, what is important is that Hammerstein was perceived as a Jew by others and that he recognized the social limitations Jews confronted in the 1940s—not that he was religiously Jewish'. In the same footnote, she states that his background was similar to that of Richard Rodgers and Lorenz Hart: 'second-generation, middle-class upbringing; childhood on the Upper West Side of Manhattan; summers at Jewish boys camps; college at Columbia University'. She also points to the significant roles played by his Jewish grandfather, Oscar Hammerstein I, the opera impresario, and his Jewish uncle Arthur, in determining his choice of career.[9] The message could not be clearer: all the key influences on Oscar Hammerstein II are Jewish, and

THE FATHERHOOD OF GOD AND THE BROTHERHOOD OF MAN   53

to all intents and purposes, he can himself be counted as a Jew. Indeed, he is regularly so described in more popular publications, with a 2023 issue of the online Jewish magazine *Unpacked* proclaiming unequivocally that 'Some of Broadway's most famous musicals—like "The Sound of Music", "Carousel", "South Pacific", and "Oklahoma!"—were created by two legendary Jewish composers: Richard Rodgers and Oscar Hammerstein II.'[10]

I want to suggest, on the basis of evidence from Hammerstein's own autobiographical writings, that this is a serious distortion of the key religious influences on him and his work. It is true that he attended the Weingart Institute's summer camps, which were largely frequented by boys from rich Jewish New York families, including Richard Rodgers, Herbert Sondheim, Larry Hart, and Sig Herzig, who rightly described them as 'a prep school for a Musical Hall of Fame'.[11] But that is the sole specifically Jewish influence that can be discerned in Hammerstein's upbringing and formative years, and one that he makes very little of in his memoirs, in contrast to the considerable emphasis that he gives to the influence of his Christian mother and grandparents and his time at church Sunday School. I wonder if Mark Horowitz is right to say that most of his friends were Jewish. It is true that Hammerstein lived and worked in a milieu, that of Broadway, that was overwhelmingly Jewish, at least in cultural terms if not in practising adherence to the faith. But his social and political activism brought him into close contact and friendship with Christians, and lapsed Christians, from a liberal Protestant background. Among them were the two close friends with whom he collaborated in founding Welcome House—Pearl Buck was a former Presbyterian missionary, and James Michener had been brought up as a Quaker.

The influence of Universalism on Hammerstein

There is clear evidence from his own autobiographical writings that Oscar Hammerstein was deeply influenced by the Universalism to which he was exposed as a boy through regular attendance at the Sunday School of the Church of the Divine Paternity in New York. His youthful encounter with the distinctive beliefs of this denomination, at the extreme liberal end of Protestant Christianity and increasingly closely tied to Unitarianism during his lifetime, had a considerable impact on him and they remained with him

54   MUSIC OF THE NIGHT

throughout his adult years. This chapter will seek to show that Universalism was an important and formative influence on his work, not least in inspiring two key themes in his musicals: the fatherhood of God and the brotherhood of man.

I was first made aware of this largely neglected aspect of Hammerstein's life and beliefs when I was invited to address the General Assembly of the Unitarian Church in Great Britain in Edinburgh in April 2003 and took as my subject the theology and spirituality of musical theatre. A member of the audience came up to me at the end of my talk to tell me that he had been at Oscar Hammerstein's memorial service, which had been led by a Unitarian minister. It had left him with the strong impression that Hammerstein himself embraced Unitarian Universalism even if he had not been a committed adherent or churchgoer.

I duly studied the order for the memorial service, which was held on 24 August 1960 at Ferncliff Cemetery, Hartsdale, New York. It was conducted by the Revd Donald Harrington, senior minister of the Community Church of New York, a Unitarian Universalist congregation. A prominent liberal theologian and political activist, Harrington was chairman of the Liberal Party of New York and ran unsuccessfully in 1966 for Lieutenant Governor of New York on a Liberal ticket with Franklin D. Roosevelt, Jr. Thanks primarily to their joint involvement in the United World Federalists, of which he was president, Harrington was a close friend of Hammerstein's.

The memorial service included Bible readings from Isaiah 52:7 ('How beautiful upon the mountains are the feet of him that bringeth good tidings, that publisheth peace; that bringeth good tidings of good') and 1 Corinthians 13:1–13 ('If I speak in the tongues of men and of angels, but have not love, I am a noisy gong or a clanging cymbal'). There were readings from Walt Whitman's *Leaves of Grass* on the theme of divine immanence and a hymn, 'A Noble Life, a Simple Faith', by Abram S. Isaacs, professor of Hebrew at New York University and editor of *The Jewish Messenger*. It was an eclectic service reflecting Hammerstein's syncretistic Universalist views, as expressed when he signed off a letter to his godson, the actor Stuart Scadron, 'from your affectionate Episcopal, Jewish, Mohammedan godfather', a self-description that is incidentally fully in accord with the current American Unitarian Universalist Association's statement of beliefs and principles: 'We are Atheist/Agnostic, Buddhist, Christian, Hindu, Humanist, Jewish, Muslim, Pagan, and more.'[12] *Forward* magazine noted that there was 'plenty of Yiddishkeit' in the memorial service and that, overall, it was

THE FATHERHOOD OF GOD AND THE BROTHERHOOD OF MAN 55

'a farewell with noteworthy Jewish elements'.[13] But it had as many Christian elements and was essentially a Unitarian Universalist act of worship, surely reflecting Hammerstein's own religious faith, something that was commented on in a tribute that appeared on the day of the memorial service in the *New York Times* by its legendary theatre critic, Brooks Atkinson, who wrote that, like Billy Bigelow in *Carousel*, Hammerstein was 'prepared to be judged by the highest judge of all'.[14]

I first expressed my hunch that Hammerstein was much more the product of liberal Protestant than of Jewish influences in my 2004 book *You've Got to Have a Dream: The Message of the Musical*, where I wrote:

> The most significant religious and cultural influence on Oscar Hammerstein was almost certainly the Presbyterianism of his Scottish mother, Alice Nimmo. His father was a non-practising Jew, and he was not raised with any Jewish culture, traditions or education. Although his first wife was Jewish, Hammerstein did not raise his children as Jewish. In both his genetic makeup and his output, he perhaps comes closer than anyone else from the golden age of Broadway to embodying the Protestant strain, which I have identified as defining the character and especially the moral world order of the twentieth century musical.[15]

I may say that John Bush Jones made a similar observation in his book *Our Musicals, Ourselves* when he noted: 'It's tempting to trace Hammerstein's social advocacy to his Jewish heritage, but his mother was a Scots Presbyterian and he identified himself hardly at all with his Jewish roots'.[16]

To test and develop my thesis, I persuaded one of the best and most engaged students from my Theology of the Musical class at St Andrews University, Kathryn Bradley (no relation, I hasten to say), to embark on a doctoral thesis investigating this neglected aspect of Hammerstein's upbringing and spiritual formation. Her extensive research work in the Oscar Hammerstein II Archives at the Library of Congress in Washington DC unearthed a series of autobiographical reminiscences in the form of letters written by Oscar to his son Bill in the early 1950s 'in answer to your request that I spend one hour a week dictating into a dictaphone all that I can remember about my life'.[17] Strangely, these letters, which contain candid and revealing memories of his childhood and teenage years, have been largely overlooked or ignored by those writing about Hammerstein. Hugh Fordin makes only very limited use of them in his biography *Getting to Know Him*.

Hammerstein's letters to his son

There are three letters in particular that allude to religious influences and are worth quoting in some detail. They make clear that Hammerstein was brought up without any instruction in Judaism and that his early exposure to religion came through his Presbyterian maternal grandparents, his Protestant mother, Alice (or Allie), and his attendance at Sunday School, first at the Episcopal Church of All Saints and later, and more significantly, at the Church of the Divine Paternity.

The first of these letters, undated but almost certainly written in October or November 1952, makes clear the lack of influence that Oscar's Jewish father and grandfather had on him during his childhood. Of his father, William, he writes, 'I didn't really get to know him. He didn't really become a force of any kind in my life until my mother died. I was nineteen then'. He goes on to say: 'My famous grandfather was a vague shadow. He was a presence, but a very remote one for me, because I never saw him during these early years'. By contrast, he describes 'the overwhelming influence exerted by my mother and her family—her mother and father and her sister Annie . . . I was a mother's boy. I adored her. She was my friend, my confidante, obviously my worshipful admirer and also the firmest and strongest person I knew.' He continues: 'The two other people who ran my life in these days, and perhaps influenced me even more than my mother, were her father and mother, my grandparents, James and Janet Nimmo'. Coming respectively from Glasgow and Edinburgh, they were both devout Scottish Presbyterians. From the age of five, Oscar lived with them: 'When we moved to 116th St we took two apartments. Reggie [Oscar's brother] lived upstairs with my mother and father, and I lived downstairs with my grandmother and grandfather'. Indeed, he recalls that for a time he slept in the same bed as his grandmother.[18]

A further letter to Bill, written on 2 February 1953, contains what is perhaps the most explicit statement made by Oscar Hammerstein about the lack of any Jewish influence in his formative years: 'I had no education in Jewish religion. The Hammerstein's [*sic*], the Jewish side of my family, were not religious and none of them ever went to Temple.' By contrast, he emphasizes the Christian influences that were around him thanks to the faith of his mother and grandmother. He writes of the religious language that pervaded the home, noting that his grandmother would regularly exclaim, 'God bless us and save us!', would always say 'Lord have mercy on his soul' when someone died, and when making future plans would add, 'If God spares us'. Although

THE FATHERHOOD OF GOD AND THE BROTHERHOOD OF MAN 57

his mother was only an occasional churchgoer, he recalls her as being 'devout in her way' and reading every day from her prayer book. Oscar adds in his letter to Bill, 'I have the prayer book now. I saw it frequently.' He goes on to write: 'I think my mother had the capacity for religion, but somehow never gave herself to it. Only perhaps in secret, and when she was in the mood.'[19]

However reticent and secret Alice Hammerstein's faith may have been, it was strong enough for her to want to have her two sons baptized by the same Episcopalian minister, Revd Dr Frank Montrose Clendenin, Rector of Old St. Peter's Episcopal Church, Westchester, New York, who had married her and William in 1893. Clendenin was a former Presbyterian minister, and it was perhaps under his influence that Alice moved from Presbyterianism to Episcopalianism. As young boys, Oscar and Reggie were sent to Sunday School at the Episcopal Church of All Angels on West 80th Street. Oscar tried to join the choir there but was put off when, following an audition, he was told by the choirmaster to come back in a year's time.

Following the death of Grandmother Nimmo in 1903 and the family's move to the Aylsmere at Columbus Avenue and 76th Street on the Upper West side of Manhattan, the boys were registered in the Sunday school of The Church of the Divine Paternity, a prominent Universalist congregation in the Central Park West area. It is not clear why Alice made the considerable theological and ecclesiological move from Episcopalianism to Universalism—perhaps it conformed more with her own liberal, slightly unorthodox Presbyterian faith (it was not unusual for Presbyterians to become Unitarians or Universalists), or maybe it was just that this was the church round the corner and the nearest place to park her sons on a Sunday morning.

Oscar's recollections of this Sunday school, and of the impact more generally that the Universalist creed of the Church of the Divine Paternity and its minister had on him, form a significant element in a letter that he wrote to Bill on 8 February 1953, which details his life between the ages of nine and thirteen. Throughout this period, he seems to have been a regular attendee at the Sunday school and an occasional attendee at services in the main church. It is true that his memories focus more on its sporting than its spiritual elements. His nineteen-year-old Sunday school teacher, 'a Yale girl, I guess. She always wore violets, but maybe that was to match her eyes. I have never quite gotten over her', used to spend much of her lessons telling her class about how Princeton, Yale, and Harvard had fared in the previous day's football game to which one of her suitors had taken her. Oscar himself

58 MUSIC OF THE NIGHT

was a member of the Divine Paternity Sunday school basketball team, which played against other church teams, including the Church of the Epiphany, which he remembered because 'I thought it was a funny name'.

But alongside the pretty teacher and the basketball, something of the ethos of the Universalist church seems to have rubbed off on him. Describing the Church of the Divine Paternity to Bill in this same letter, he writes: 'This was a Universalist church. The Universalists admit anyone and are an all-embracing Christian faith.' Having mentioned how much he enjoyed singing hymns in the Sunday school—he quotes one that he particularly liked about 'Easter bells in joyous measure' signalling 'the coming of the Lord'—he goes on to describe the church's pastor:

> The minister was quite a wonderful man—Dr Hall. He had bushy hair. He was a tall man and had a lovely voice. When we went to the church occasionally and heard his sermons, we were never bored. I remember one day hearing him talk about Theodore Roosevelt and how Theodore Roosevelt was many men. He was Teddy, the rough rider, and he was President Roosevelt and he was the African Hunter (maybe he wasn't a hunter yet). He was an athlete, a good boxer. He was many different things and different people thought of him as many different things. This was an eye-opener to me, this sermon, and the theme of it was that the hardest thing in the world to be was to be yourself and to know just who you were. What is yourself? This didn't go over my head at all. It went straight into the middle of it and has never left it.'[20]

Dr Francis Hall

Dr Francis Hall, who served as minister of the Church of the Divine Paternity from 1902 to 1919, and again from 1929 to 1938, was a leading figure in the Universalist General Convention (later known from 1942 as the Universalist Church of America) during the early decades of the twentieth century. His published sermons repeat the message of knowing who you are and being yourself that made such an impression on young Oscar and express other key tenets of the Universalist creed. They emphasize salvation for all souls and the mirroring of divine unity in the unity of humankind, possessed of liberty to believe and practise faith according to the individual experience of divine truth rather than creeds or church doctrines. The final authority for belief lies within the individual conscience. In contrast to a doctrine of

THE FATHERHOOD OF GOD AND THE BROTHERHOOD OF MAN 59

original sin, human nature is viewed positively as being endowed with a capacity for moral and social improvement.

In one of his sermons, entitled 'Making a Soul', Hall asserts that: 'This world is an institution the function of which is the perfecting of manhood.'[21] He goes on to say that it is the responsibility of every individual to discover who they are and to follow the right path. While the raw material of the soul is supplied by heredity and then moulded by environment, humans are ultimately the masters of their own fate with the ability and power to seize upon what has been bequeathed to them and shape it according to their own desires. As he puts it in another sermon, entitled 'Lost Souls': 'Where are you going? Do you want to go to the heights? Or do you want to go wandering round and round in the fog?'[22] In this same sermon, he goes on to say that no one is left to find their own way unassisted but rather is offered a map of life in the form of the Bible and a compass in the form of moral sense or conscience.

Hall's sermons also contain a strong emphasis on cooperative social action and a highly optimistic, if not positively Utopian, sense of what it can achieve. In 'Making a Soul', he argues that 'this world can be saved and saved very quickly and will be as soon as men become sane enough to work together toward the end for which they pray.' He continues:

> When we begin to pray in unison not only with our lips but with our lives, "Thy kingdom come" and really mean what we say and organize the forces of society so that not a single child shall be permitted to grow up amid circumstances which make for cruelty and crime but so that every child shall be nourished physically and psychically into health and hope, love, beauty and intelligence, one single generation will be enough to transform this world into at least a suburb of the Holy City New Jerusalem.[23]

Hall practised what he preached, establishing numerous schemes of social amelioration and improvement for the poor of New York and strongly advocating social gospel issues within the Universalist denomination.

The Principles of Universalism

Hammerstein clearly felt that his experience of Sunday school and his vivid memory of Dr Hall and his sermons were significant enough to include when giving accounts of his childhood to his son. He also felt the need to give Bill

60 MUSIC OF THE NIGHT

a summation of the faith to which he had been exposed during these crucial pre-teenage years: 'The Universalist faith is stated very simply. I will recite it to you. Our faith is the fatherhood of God, the brotherhood of man, the leadership of Jesus, salvation by character, the progress of mankind, onward and upward forever.'[24] In fact, this is a literal word-for-word restatement of the five points of the Unitarian faith as propounded by the transcendentalist James Freeman Clarke in 1886. The Five Principles adopted by the Universalist General Assembly in 1899, and still accepted as the main guiding principles of the denomination at the time Hammerstein was attending the Church of the Divine Paternity, are rather different and somewhat more forbidding: 'The Universal Fatherhood of God; The spiritual authority and leadership of His Son Jesus Christ; The trustworthiness of the Bible as containing a revelation from God; The certainty of just retribution for sin; The final harmony of all souls with God.'

Hammerstein can be forgiven for confusing Universalist and Unitarian statements of faith. By the time he wrote his reminiscences, the two denominations were becoming ever closer—the Universalist Church of America would, indeed, merge with the American Unitarian Association to form the Unitarian Universalist Association in 1961, the year after his death. The statement of faith that he quoted, Unitarian rather than Universalist as it strictly speaking was, clearly represents what he took from the predominant religious influence in his youth, the Sunday school hymns and lessons, and the sermons of Dr Hall at the Church of the Divine Paternity that he could still recall in detail more than fifty years after he heard them. It can also, I think, be taken as a pointer to the beliefs that he continued to hold throughout his life. It is surely not accidental that he describes Universalism as 'our faith', suggesting that it is the faith to which he adhered, in which he reared his own family, and which informed his life and work.

Four of those five 'simple' principles that Hammerstein expounded to his son as lying at the heart of 'our' Universalist faith can be seen being clearly expressed both in later utterances about his beliefs and in the libretti and lyrics of his musicals. They are the fatherhood of God (which must have been reinforced for him by the striking and unusual dedication of the church whose Sunday school he attended), the brotherhood of man, salvation by character, and the progress of mankind onward and upward for ever. The fifth, the leadership of Jesus, is not specifically evoked by him, although it is perhaps significant that when asked to pick a Bible passage expressive of his commitment to human brotherhood, he chose one of Jesus' sayings from the Gospels.

THE FATHERHOOD OF GOD AND THE BROTHERHOOD OF MAN 61

Hammerstein's statements about his own beliefs

Although he was generally reticent about expressing his religious beliefs and did not formally ally himself with any faith or denomination in terms of membership or attendance, Oscar Hammerstein did, on occasions, bare his soul, especially in broadcast interviews. Asked directly about his religious convictions by Mike Wallace in 1958, he replied by recalling a conversation the previous year with a police officer who had stopped him for jaywalking. On discovering who he was, the officer thanked him for *Carousel*, telling him how much his family loved it. Hammerstein continued:

> He said, 'Are you religious?' and I said, 'Well I don't belong to any church' and then he patted me on the back and he said 'Ah, you're religious alright.' And I went on feeling as if I'd been caught, and feeling that I was religious. He had discovered from the words of my songs that I had faith, faith in mankind, faith that there was something more powerful than mankind behind it all. And faith that in the long run good triumphs over evil. If that's religion—I'm religious, and that is my definition of religion.[25]

His statement here that while he has faith in mankind, he also has faith in something more powerful 'behind it all' puts him firmly in the Universalist rather than the humanist camp. In fact, he explicitly referenced God on a number of occasions. In what could be taken as an emphatic if somewhat enigmatic statement of incarnational theology, he once stated that when the curtain goes down, 'God in man must be present'. Quoting this, Winer writes: 'This is a rare mention of a deity for Hammerstein, as he and most of his cohort were deeply secular, art being their one true religion.'[26] Although talk of God is rare in his public utterances, it is not so rare in more private exchanges and when he is being probed by interviewers. In another of his autobiographical letters to Bill in 1953, he suggests that the love and human cooperation that makes the world go round can be referred to as God. Reflecting on his own 'strange, disorderly, unsystematic family', he writes:

> The world is very much like my family, filled with people of unharnessed passions, illogical impulses, inconsistent religions and clashing philosophies. All these whirling atoms are held together loosely and kept going slowly in the same general direction by one element—love. You may substitute another word for this if you please. You may call it God or you may call it goodness.[27]

62 MUSIC OF THE NIGHT

Hammerstein's deepest reflections on God are to be found in an interview with Arnold Michaelis recorded in November 1957. Alluding to his love of humankind, Michaelis asks him if he separates an interest in man from his understanding of the term God. Hammerstein responds: 'That is one and the same thing', and goes on to say: 'Our interest, our belonging to one another, the oneness on earth is the same thing as our oneness with God. God is that oneness in my own conception. He is all of us; we all are Him.' Here is a classic statement of the Universalist/Unitarian emphasis on the oneness of God and the overriding unity which connects all humans with the divine, as promulgated by Hall in his sermons. In technical theological terms, God is both immanent and transcendent, present in humankind and nature but also existing as a separate and higher force. Hammerstein goes on to say that God is not perfect because if He were, and if He were as powerful as we believe Him to be, He would fix the misery and evil found in the world. Michaelis follows this by asking: 'Do you think that we can help God become perfect?' to which Hammerstein responds: 'Oh, yes, indeed, because if, as I say, we are part of Him, He is part of us. It's certainly our function to help Him if we don't get anywhere either. We are all together.'[28]

Theologically, this is an intriguing and complex statement, with echoes both of process theology, the school of thought influenced by the metaphysical process philosophy of Alfred North Whitehead, and of Universalist transcendentalism. It may be significant that Oscar Hammerstein was described by his grandson as 'Emersonian'.[29] Ralph Waldo Emerson, who was himself ordained as a Unitarian minister, envisaged God as a spirit or ideal filling the world and dwelling in every created entity. He became something of a guru and hero to Universalists, and it is quite likely that his ideas were commended by Dr Hall and other preachers whom Hammerstein heard. The idea of human–divine cooperation would come naturally from a transcendentalist outlook reinforced by the Universalist belief in the 'progress of mankind, onward and upward forever'.

The fatherhood of God in *Carousel*

If we turn from Hammerstein's utterances in interviews about the nature of the divine to the libretti and lyrics of his musicals, we find a distinct emphasis on the fatherhood of God. This is particularly the case with *Carousel*, which

THE FATHERHOOD OF GOD AND THE BROTHERHOOD OF MAN   63

could be almost a textbook exposition of the Universalist/Unitarian position. As originally conceived and scripted by him, it included a scene set in heaven in which Billy Bigelow, the errant anti-hero who commits suicide after taking part in a botched robbery, comes face to face with God. It is described by Elliot Norton in an article about material that ended up on what he called 'the Broadway Cutting Room floor':

> The original heaven of *Carousel* was a New England parlor, bare and plain. In it sat a stern Yankee, listed on the programme as He. At a harmonium, playing softly, sat his quiet consort, identified as She. Later, some observers (including Rodgers) referred to this celestial couple as Mr and Mrs God.
> Richard Rodgers, walking back to the hotel with his collaborator afterwards, put it to Oscar Hammerstein bluntly:
> 'We've got to get God out of that parlor!'
> 'I know you're right,' he said, 'but where shall I put him?'
> 'I don't care where you put Him', said Richard Rodgers. 'Put Him up on a ladder, for all I care only get him out of that parlor.'
> So Oscar Hammerstein put him up on a ladder. He discarded the sitting room, too, and put his deity into a brand-new sequence. On a ladder in the backyard of heaven, He became the Star-Keeper, polishing stars which hung on lines strung across the floor of infinity while a sullen Billy Bigelow looked and listened to his quiet admonitions.[30]

In this first draft for the Boston try-out of *Carousel*, God is portrayed in the guise of benevolent and gentle parents, emphasizing divine homeliness as much as holiness. 'He' and 'She' tell Billy that the world needs a mother and a father. Perhaps Hammerstein was thinking of his own relationship with his mother when he gave God both a male and female persona. It is Richard Rodgers, the self-proclaimed atheist and non-believer, who insists that he gets God out of the parlour and out of the show. Many of the attributes of the Divine Father (and Mother) are transferred to the figure of the Star-Keeper, who greets Billy at the back gates to heaven—the mother of pearly gates as opposed to the pearly ones. Along with the Heavenly Friend who accompanies Billy back to earth, where he is given a second chance to redeem himself and act as a dutiful father, the Star Keeper appears as an otherworldly figure exercising divine parenthood and awakening the moral conscience of the childlike Billy.

64 MUSIC OF THE NIGHT

Universalist theology is further reflected in the way that, despite his manifest sins and unrepentant attitude, Billy Bigelow is not consigned to eternal damnation but rather offered a second chance to redeem himself, one that he somewhat reluctantly takes. In this respect, Hammerstein radically changed the original story on which *Carousel* was based, Ferenc Molnar's *Liliom*. As he told Andrew Michaelis:

> The problem of adapting Lilian [*sic*] was the end. The end of Lilian [*sic*] when, after his first visit back to earth, he is offered another chance, he refuses it. And the implication is that he is going to go down unchanged, down through the years in purgatory or wherever he is going to lie with his soul. And I couldn't—it was not the anxiety to have an happy ending that made me shy away from that original ending, but because I can't conceive of an unregenerate soul. I can't conceive of a dead end to any kind of existence.[31]

Hammerstein's self-proclaimed inability to conceive of an unregenerate soul is suggestive of the Universalist belief that no soul remains unchanged and unregenerate for ever and that no existence has a dead end because all will ultimately attain salvation and come to eventual union with God. This is not to say that he does not believe that sin can simply be ignored and carries no consequences. The way that Hammerstein charts Billy Bigelow's journey after death is consistent with the Universalist principle of 'The certainty of just retribution for sin' as well as 'The final harmony of all souls with God'. Billy is made to atone for his sinful actions and go through a period of cleansing and moral reformation. This can be seen as somewhat akin to the Catholic doctrine of purgatory, but it is closer to the Universalist concept of the restoration period of the soul after death, where it is still morally accountable for its decisions and actions. Ultimately, each and every soul is redeemable, and God actively wants the soul to be restored. It is, however, still necessary for it to go through a process of reconciliation and renunciation of previous immoral acts. This notion of a period of restoration of the soul after death was widespread among late nineteenth- and early twentieth-century Universalists, enabling them to hold to the doctrine of universal salvation while still taking sin seriously. There are distinct echoes of it in *Carousel*'s portrayal of Billy Bigelow's post-mortem existence.

Perhaps the clearest expression of the Universalist idea of divine paternity in *Carousel* comes in the contrast between Billy Bigelow's expectation

THE FATHERHOOD OF GOD AND THE BROTHERHOOD OF MAN 65

of what God will be like and the reality of what he encounters with the Star-Keeper. Billy views God as a judge—and a terrifying one at that. This is expressed in his song 'The Highest Judge of All', which portrays an angry deity who will shout and yell and quite possibly send him to hell. In some ways, indeed, this is what he wants. Acknowledging that his sins are 'great big sins', including his suicide and his violence towards and abandonment of his pregnant wife, not to mention his gambling and stealing, he wants to be judged by the Highest Judge of All and not just the equivalent of some inferior police magistrate. Yet when he gets to the gates of heaven and encounters the Star Keeper, instead of being judged, he is shown mercy and infinite patience. He is told that there is plenty of time for him to repent and change his ways. Billy is certain that he will meet the judgemental God of Calvinist New England, but instead, he is brought face to face with the loving, accepting God of liberal Protestantism and of its most liberal expression in Unitarian Universalism. It is tempting to suggest that, as over the portrayal of Mr and Mrs God on stage, Hammerstein was here at odds with his collaborator who, according to his wife, Dorothy, felt that religion was based on fear and 'feelings of guilt'.[32] Rodgers was perhaps more with Bigelow in his view of a frightening, wrathful, judging deity, while Hammerstein believed in one exemplifying the qualities of grace, love, and forgiveness.

Salvation by character and the progress of mankind

If *Carousel* has much to say on the subject of the benevolent fatherhood of God, it also has much to say about that other key Universalist principle, salvation by character. It is by reforming himself, and specifically by showing that he is a good father, as well as through divine mercy and guidance, that Billy attains salvation. He is given the chance to show that he is not a loser and a violent drunkard and that he does care. We are back here to Dr Hall's sermon about being yourself and knowing just who you are that made such an impression on the young Oscar Hammerstein. Billy Bigelow has to work through whether he is the feckless, abusive husband and unrepentant thief or the genuinely repentant loving father who wants to do the best for his widow and daughter. It is this moral challenge and question of identity that the Star Keeper and the Heavenly Friend put to him and help him to confront. He rises to it by changing his character, or perhaps reverting to his true character that was always there behind the bluster and bravado, and so attaining his salvation.

Closely linked in Hammerstein's mind with the notion of salvation by character is his adherence to another of those key principles of Universalist faith that he adumbrates to his son: the progress of mankind, onward and upward for ever. This is something that he makes much of in his 1957 interview with Arnold Michaelis when he says, 'I don't know why I was born, beyond the fact that I know why everybody was born. Everybody was born to advance the life in the universe, the life that we all live'. He goes on to say that his starting point is that all is far from perfect just now. Michaelis then asks him: 'If there isn't any such thing as perfection in the universe or in the world on earth, I wonder where this desire comes from for perfection?', to which Hammerstein responds that perfection is not the goal to aim for, but rather 'I think we should try to do our best all the time, knowing that there is going to be imperfection, certainly in our present state of development, which in the history that is to be written over the next million years is a very short time. And we are, perhaps, very primitive people. I believe we are. We must be. We are so far from perfect that I, myself, don't live with any hope that we are going to get anywhere near perfection.'[33]

The tentative and qualified nature of Hammerstein's belief in human progress shows that he is far from being a naïve optimist who feels that all is for the best in the best of all possible worlds. He acknowledges the brokenness of the world while at the same time feeling a particular mission to accentuate the positive and to encourage a belief in the essential goodness of humanity and in what it can achieve. Hammerstein was at heart an idealist, but he was also a realist. In a guest editorial in *The Saturday Review* advocating world government, he wrote: 'I am tired of listening to self-styled "practical men" patronizing me by calling me an idealist'.[34] His often quoted observation, 'I believe, not that the whole world and all of life is good, but I do believe that so much of it is good, and my inclination is to emphasize that side of life', is amplified in another statement he made in the Michaelis interview: 'I see plays and read books that emphasise the seamy side of life, and the frenetic side of life and the tragic side and I don't deny the existence of the tragic and the frenetic. But I say that somebody has to keep saying that that isn't all there is to life . . . We're very likely to get thrown off our balance if we have such a preponderance of artists expressing the "wasteland" philosophy.'[35]

The brotherhood of man

It is in his adherence to another key plank of the Universalist faith, the brotherhood of man, that Hammerstein most clearly shows himself to be a liberal idealist. This is the single theme which comes across most clearly both in his writings and in his musicals, and it is treated in spiritual as well as in political and social terms. This is in accordance with the way that the notion of the brotherhood of man developed in the theology of both Universalism and Unitarianism. Initially, it had a predominantly spiritual quality, being seen as an aspect of the unity of the divine and the human and as something fostered by the transforming Spirit of God, which altered the relationships between human beings. The growth of the social gospel in the early 1900s gave it a more concrete and worldly focus on moral development, human cooperation, and political and social action.

In 1952, in connection with the annual Brotherhood Week organized by the National Conference of Christians and Jews, *Collier's* magazine asked twenty-five famous Americans to share a favourite Biblical passage that they felt was significant as 'a light and guide for us today'. Hammerstein chose 1 John 2:10–12: 'Anyone who loves their brother and sister lives in the light, and there is nothing in them to make them stumble. But anyone who hates a brother or sister is in the darkness and walks in the darkness.' In a letter to the Revd Ivan Hagerdorn, minister of Bethel Evangelical Lutheran Church in Philadelphia, in 1952, he wrote:

> The Bible passage quoted in Collier's is one of my favorites because it states a truth which could solve so many problems that exist in the world today, and eliminate so much of its strife. We cannot possibly attain security or happiness without really believing and practising brotherhood.[36]

Oscar Hammerstein was not the only leading figure in the world of mid-twentieth-century musical theatre to emphasize this doctrine. Alan Jay Lerner, who was Jewish, wrote in his autobiography that 'To me, the greatest contribution of Jesus Christ is contained in three words, the "Brotherhood of Man".'[37] In similarly linking human brotherhood with the figure of Christ, does Hammerstein come close to acknowledging and invoking the Universalist/Unitarian principle of 'The leadership of Jesus'? For him, human brotherhood undoubtedly did have a religious dimension, being an expression of the outworking of a higher power which might be called God

68 MUSIC OF THE NIGHT

(or goodness), as well as of the fulfilment of that cooperation and mutual respect and harmony for which humans were born and brought into the world to achieve their potential and make it a better place.

It is significant that Hammerstein anchored his commitment to anti-racism in religious principles. In a chapter entitled 'Dear Believer in White Supremacy', written in 1958 for a proposed book on racial prejudice that was never published, he refuted the arguments made by some Christians on the basis of their faith for the inferiority of African Americans. He noted that 'The popular concepts of religion seem to point strongly towards the equality of all men in the sight of God', adding, 'If this is a mistaken idea, and if a closer examination of the Bible reveals a contrary philosophy, we should find out about it'.[38] The book was a collaborative effort with the two friends with whom he had set up Welcome House and who shared his upbringing in liberal Protestant values, the former Presbyterian missionary Pearl Buck and the Quaker James Michener, author of *Tales of the South Pacific* on which the musical *South Pacific* was based. In a draft introduction, the three assert that artificial human barriers have been put in place that keep people apart and that all human beings are equally capable of goodness and evil, wisdom and stupidity. They go on to link the brotherhood of man with that other great article of Universalist faith, 'the progression of mankind onward and upward for ever':

> We are absolutely convinced that the historical tendency of the world leads toward greater communion between races, not less, toward greater equality, not less, and toward greater acceptance of the essential brotherhood of the world, not a retreat from that principle.... We would like to see that brotherhood and equality of opportunity achieved now.[39]

Asked in 1953 by a student who was researching the brotherhood of man motif in his musicals for a statement of his own views on this theme, Hammerstein responded that 'my best personal statements on the subject of brotherhood and tolerance are in the plays that you intend to deal with. None of the references to this theme in my plays is accidental. They are quite deliberate and conscious. I believe that the introduction of this theme in plays is more effective than plays that are written obviously to propagate these virtues'.[40]

It is certainly the case that human brotherhood is a major theme in many of his libretti, not least in his first collaboration with Richard Rodgers,

THE FATHERHOOD OF GOD AND THE BROTHERHOOD OF MAN 69

Oklahoma!, a paean to the values of community, tolerance, and cooperation as emphatically expressed in the chorus 'The farmer and the cowman should be friends' with its insistence that when the territory of Oklahoma joins the union and becomes a state 'the farmer, and cowman and the merchant, mus' all behave theirselves and act like brothers'. Community values and human brotherhood—and sisterhood—are further celebrated in *Carousel*, where they are epitomized by the clambake scene. For Mark Steyn, the song 'This was a real nice clambake' is 'about ritual and sacrament and a secular Yankee communion'.[41] Maybe it is not, in fact, so secular in the context of the musical as a whole.

The brotherhood of man is a central motif in Rodgers' and Hammerstein's three Asian musicals, *South Pacific*, *The King and I*, and *Flower Drum Song*, which assert the unity and likeness of all humankind, transcending racial, cultural, and geographical barriers. Hammerstein had first raised this theme in 1927 in his book and lyrics for *Show Boat*, the first racially integrated musical (some, indeed, would say the first integrated musical). It is, of course, especially marked in *South Pacific* with its critique of American racial prejudice and its argument, made most explicitly in the song 'You've got to be carefully taught', that hatred and racial discrimination are learned rather than natural human attitudes and need to be unlearned in order for humanity to progress. *The King and I* and *Flower Drum Song* similarly focus on coming to terms with cultural difference and celebrating diversity, as does the less well-known *Pipe Dream* with its song 'It takes all kinds of people to make up a world'.

I have argued in this chapter that in his beliefs, his social activism, and his stage works, Hammerstein shows clear evidence of imbibing and applying key tenets of the Universalist faith to which he was exposed as a boy, notably those values that he singled out to his son Bill of the fatherhood of God, the brotherhood of man, salvation by character, and the progress of humanity onwards and upwards. The evidence for this is explored much more fully in Kathryn Bradley's 2013 University of St Andrews doctoral thesis, 'The Liberal Protestant Influence on the Musical Plays of Oscar Hammerstein II circa 1943–1959'. I would strongly recommend anyone interested in pursuing this topic further to read her thesis, which is available online. It demonstrates how Hammerstein's libretti and lyrics display clear religious influences, overwhelmingly of a liberal Protestant nature, as well as clear spiritual resonances.

Hammerstein's religious position

It is important not to overstate Hammerstein's religiosity. He was not a card-carrying Christian, any more than he was a card-carrying Jew. Among the childhood reminiscences in his letters to Bill is one where he recalls strongly suspecting that Santa Claus was, in fact, his father but not wanting to break the magic spell:

> I was striking a fine balance between a kind of half skepticism and a half faith. This seems to have been a pattern which has followed me through life, or perhaps which I have followed through life. I have felt the capacity to be either a religious zealot or a complete cynic, and I have rejected both extremes and seem to have fallen somewhere in the middle. No, not really. I am not a cynic at all, but I do not expect too much of human nature. I am, let us say, one third realist and two thirds mystic.[42]

As we have seen, he had a strong syncretistic streak and did not want to be tied down to any one denominational label, a trait that is characteristic of Universalists. His biographer, Hugh Fordin, is surely correct in his assessment that, although he never joined a formal religious group or attended weekly services, 'Oscar was a "religious" man.'[43]

Not least of the legacies of Hammerstein's grounding in the strenuous, idealistic, character-building principles of Universalism was his desire to create musicals which, if not overtly 'preachy', carried a strong moral message. This is evident in his very interesting observation that 'the goodness of the human spirit must be fighting for its life whether or not it wins the round that is depicted in one play. People must leave the theater, the church or the lecture hall with a deeper faith and a higher interest in mankind than they brought in with them. This must be accomplished if the institutions are to survive.'[44] It is striking, and surely not coincidental, that Hammerstein here brackets theatre, church, and lecture hall as having a common purpose in giving people 'a deeper faith and a higher interest in mankind'. Stephen Citron has rightly observed that *Oklahoma!* 'was the first of the Rodgers and Hammerstein musicals to leave audiences glowing with feeling (and message) while giving them a good time.'[45] Hammerstein had originally planned that he would initially make money out of musicals and then turn to straight plays 'in which I could say and state my reactions to the world I live in'.

THE FATHERHOOD OF GOD AND THE BROTHERHOOD OF MAN   71

Later on, however, I became convinced that whatever I wanted to say could be said in songs, that I was not confined to trite or light subjects . . . The longer I write the more interested I become in expressing my own true convictions and feelings in the songs I write.[46]

Hammerstein's realization that musicals could be highly effective in propagating the values of brotherhood, community building, and racial harmony, in which he so fervently believed and so earnestly wanted to promote, went alongside a passion for sincerity and for finding and being true to yourself. In advice that he gave to the young Stephen Sondheim, he echoed the words that had struck him so much in his own youth in the sermon by Dr Hall: 'Don't imitate other people's emotions. Speak your own.'[47] He returned to this theme in an article in *The Saturday Review*: 'The most important ingredient of a good song is sincerity. Let the song be yours and yours alone. However important, however trivial, believe it. Mean it from the bottom of your heart, and say what is on your mind as carefully, as clearly, as beautifully as you can.'[48]

As we will discover in Chapter 5, Hammerstein tried, and failed, to make Stephen Sondheim, who looked on him as 'the best surrogate father one could wish for, always encouraging, always understanding, always gentle', less cynical, and more idealistic.[49] Did he also try, with rather more success, to do the same with Richard Rodgers, with whom he also had a pastoral relationship, counselling him over his problems with alcohol and women? Can we see him as playing a somewhat similar role to the one I have suggested that Sullivan did with Gilbert, softening and spiritualizing his collaborator's more secular nature?

Hammerstein's influence on Richard Rodgers

Richard Rodgers was subjected to fewer religious influences than his collaborator. Unlike him, he was Jewish and conscious of his Jewish heritage, although he rejected its beliefs. At the beginning of his autobiography, he writes of the rituals surrounding his great-grandmother's funeral, describing them as 'the end of orthodox Judaism in our family'. He continues:

The next step was known as Reform, and even this faded after the bar mitzvah of my brother and me as a gesture to my grandfather on my

72 MUSIC OF THE NIGHT

mother's side. From that time on, my parents, my brother and I were Jewish for socio-economic reasons rather than because of any deep religious conviction.[50]

Hammerstein did pull Rodgers in a more spiritual and religious direction, if only through the nature of the lyrics which he gave him to set. When Cole Porter famously said, 'I can always tell a Rodgers tune. There's a certain holiness about it', he was undoubtedly thinking of the Rodgers of Rodgers and Hammerstein rather than of Rodgers and Hart. There is a world of difference between the music that the composer produced for the two main lyricists with whom he collaborated. In Mark Steyn's words, 'Rodgers and Hart is basically him-and-her romance; Rodgers and Hammerstein is hymns and hearse: all those anthemic exhortations'.[51]

'You'll Never Walk Alone'

There is no more hymn-like number in the entire Rodgers and Hammerstein canon than the soaring anthem that ends *Carousel*. More than any other song from a musical, it has crossed from the stage to the sanctuary, with 'When you walk through a storm' finding a place in several church hymn books sandwiched between 'What a friend we have in Jesus' and 'While shepherds watched their flocks by night'. It has an undeniably spiritual quality—when Irving Berlin heard it sung at a funeral, he said that it had as much impact on him as the 23rd Psalm. There were clear religious influences at work in the construction of the musical's closing scene, of which this song forms the climax. As originally envisaged by Hammerstein, the speaker at the High School graduation, which Billy Bigelow attends as an unseen bystander, was to be the local pastor, the Revd James Reed, played by the same actor who played 'He', or 'Mr God'. In the script of the Boston try-out, he was given a lengthy sermon-like speech which included the line 'Try to stand close together always—as you stand to-day. For, standing so, you are close to God'.[52] This overtly Christian element was removed from the final script, with the graduation address being delivered not by the minister but by the local doctor, Dr Seldon, and being drastically shortened and shorn of its reference to God. One wonders if this change, like the removal of 'Mr and Mrs God', might have been made at the suggestion, or insistence, of Richard Rodgers, the self-proclaimed atheist.

THE FATHERHOOD OF GOD AND THE BROTHERHOOD OF MAN   73

Even in its recast form, the graduation scene which closes *Carousel* retains a distinctly religious feel, as identified by Ethan Mordden, who points to the 'ascetically religious nature of the finale, whose sense of sorrow and ecstasy has the air of a church service'.[53] Dr Seldon reminds Billy of the Star Keeper up on his ladder, and in most productions, the two roles are played by the same actor, reinforcing the doctor's somewhat otherworldly and saintly, if not actually God-like, character. His address retains a sermonic quality, with its call to the graduating students to stand on their own two feet and keep their faith and courage, and Billy urging his daughter Louise, 'Believe him, darling! Believe'. Was Hammerstein thinking back to his own Sunday school days, the hymns that he loved singing, and Dr Hall's inspiring sermons, when he wrote this scene and penned the lyrics of 'You'll never walk alone?' It certainly rings with the sincerity that was his hallmark and with the Universalist principle of salvation by character. Richard Rodgers could not but respond to the sincerity and the religious faith embodied in the song that the erstwhile minister-turned-doctor remembers from his own schooldays, and which Kurt Ganzl in his authoritative history of the musical has no hesitation in describing as a 'rousingly religious piece' expressing 'the maxim that you'll never walk alone while you walk with God'.[54]

Notes

1. John Bush Jones, *Our Musicals, Ourselves* (Lebanon, NH: Brandeis University Press, 2003), 141.
2. Sheldon Harnick in his preface to Bush Jones, *Our Musicals, Ourselves*, ix.
3. Laurie Winer, *Oscar Hammerstein II and the Invention of the Musical* (New Haven, CT: Yale University Press, 2023), 25, 37.
4. Ibid., 8.
5. Ibid., 8.
6. Benjamin Ivry, 'The Jewish Musicals that Oscar Hammerstein never got to do', *Forward*, 29 June 2022.
7. Andrea Most, *Making Americans: Jews and the Broadway Musical* (Boston, MA: Harvard University Press, 2004), 2, 173.
8. Andrea Most, '"You've Got to Be Carefully Taught": The Politics of Race in Rodgers and Hammerstein's South Pacific', *Theatre Journal* 52, no. 3 (October 2000), 309.
9. Most, *Making Americans*, 225.
10. 'These Jewish Harlemites left an indelible mark on American life that persists to this day', *Unpacked*, 10 May 2023, https://jewishunpacked.com/the-jews-of-harlem/.
11. Dorothy Hart, *Thou Swell* (New York: Harper & Row, 1976), 17.
12. Mark Horowitz (ed.), *The Letters of Oscar Hammerstein II* (New York: Oxford University Press, 2022), 732; https://www.uua.org/beliefs/what-we-believe.
13. *Forward*, 29 June 2022.
14. *New York Times*, 24 August 1960.
15. Ian Bradley, *You've Got to Have a Dream: The Message of the Musical* (London: SCM Press, 2004), 72.
16. Bush Jones, *Our Musicals, Ourselves*, 143.
17. Undated letter from Oscar Hammerstein to Bill Hammerstein (1952), 1. Oscar Hammerstein II Collection, Library of Congress, Washington, DC.
18. Ibid., 4, 6, 7, 9, 11.

19. Letter from Oscar Hammerstein to Bill Hammerstein, 2 February 1953, 5. Oscar Hammerstein II Collection, Library of Congress, Washington, DC.
20. Letter from Oscar Hammerstein to Bill Hammerstein, 8 February 1953, 6–8. Oscar Hammerstein II Collection, Library of Congress, Washington, DC.
21. Frank Hall, *Soul and Body: A Book of Sermons Preached in the Church of the Divine Paternity, New York City* (Hong Kong: Forgotten Books, 2012), 33.
22. Ibid., 109.
23. Ibid., 42–3.
24. Letter from Oscar Hammerstein to Bill Hammerstein, 8 February 1953, 8. Oscar Hammerstein II Collection, Library of Congress, Washington, DC.
25. Interview of Oscar Hammerstein II by Mike Wallace, 15 March, 1958. Transcript in Oscar Hammerstein II Collection, Library of Congress, Washington, DC.
26. Winer, *Oscar Hammerstein*, 11.
27. Letter from Oscar Hammerstein to Bill Hammerstein, 18 January 1953, 5. Oscar Hammerstein II Collection, Library of Congress, Washington, DC.
28. Interview of Oscar Hammerstein II by Arnold Michaelis, recorded on Vinyl LP as 'A Recorded Portrait' 1957, reissued by Robins Rare Recordings 5 March 2023. https://www.youtube.com/watch?v=lt1ycOiNjvg.
29. Oscar Andrew Hammerstein, *The Hammersteins: A Musical Theatre Family* (New York: Black Dog & Leventhal Publishers, 2010), 173.
30. Elliot Norton, 'Broadway's Cutting Room Floor', *Theatre Arts* 36 (April 1952), 80.
31. Interview with Arnold Michaelis.
32. Dorothy Rodgers, *A Personal Book* (New York: Harper & Row, 1977), 32.
33. Interview with Arnold Michaelis.
34. *The Saturday Review*, 23 December 1950.
35. Interview with Arnold Michaelis.
36. Letter from Oscar Hammerstein II to the Rev Ivan Hagerdorn, 14 May 1952. Oscar Hammerstein II Collection, National Library of Congress, Washington, DC.
37. Alan Jay Lerner, *The Street Where I Live* (New York: W.W. Norton, 1978), 174.
38. Oscar Hammerstein II, 'Dear Believer in White Supremacy'. Oscar Hammerstein II Collection, Library of Congress, Washington, DC.
39. Oscar Hammerstein II, Pearl Buck and James Michener, Introduction to a book collaboration. Oscar Hammerstein II Collection, Library of Congress, Washington, DC.
40. Letter from Oscar Hammerstein II to Leonard Dinnerstein, 28 October 1953. Oscar Hammerstein II Collection, Library of Congress, Washington, DC.
41. Mark Steyn, *Broadway Babies Say Goodnight* (London: Faber & Faber, 1997), 97.
42. Letter from Oscar Hammerstein to Bill Hammerstein, 25 January 1953, 5. Oscar Hammerstein II Collection, Library of Congress, Washington, DC.
43. Hugh Fordin, *Getting to Know Him: A Biography of Oscar Hammerstein II* (New York, Random House, 1977), 16.
44. Winer, *Oscar Hammerstein II and the Invention of the Musical*, 11.
45. Stephen Citron, *Sondheim & Lloyd Webber: The New Musical* (London: Chatto and Windus, 2001), 30.
46. Carol Brahms and Ned Sherrin, *Song by Song* (Bolton, Lancs: Ross Anderson, 1984), 89.
47. Fordin, *Getting to Know Him*, 241.
48. Oscar Hammerstein II, 'Where the Song Begins', *The Saturday Review*, December 3, 1949, 14.
49. Stephen Sondheim, Introduction to Fordin, *Getting to Know Him*, xi.
50. Richard Rodgers, *Musical Stages* (New York: Da Capo Press, 1995), 20.
51. Steyn, *Broadway Babies*, 97.
52. Boston try-out script of *Carousel*. Oscar Hammerstein II Collection, National Library of Congress, Washington, DC.
53. Ethan Mordden, *Beautiful Mornin': The Broadway Musical in the 1950s* (Oxford University Press, 1999), 95.
54. Kurt Ganzl, *The Musical: A Concise History* (Boston, MA: Northeastern University Press, 1997), 259.

4

Nuns and menorahs

The Sound of Music and *Fiddler on the Roof*

Churches and religious movements have featured prominently in the plot lines of several successful musicals. Indeed, they have supplied some of their best numbers. 'Follow the fold and stray no more', the marching song of the Salvation Army-like 'Save a Soul Mission' in *Guys and Dolls*, the catchy and funky eponymous anthem of the Rhythm of Life church in *Sweet Charity*, and 'Hello' and 'I believe' in the *Book of Mormon* spring to mind.

On the whole, the treatment of religious communities on the musical theatre stage, as in these three shows, has been affectionately satirical, with their characteristics and eccentricities exposed in a perceptive but not antagonistic way. Two classic musicals, however, have majored on religious communities and treated them in a way that borders on the reverential. *The Sound of Music* and *Fiddler on the Roof* portray the dedicated Catholic religious life and Jewish faith and ritual, respectively in a highly sympathetic light, while also finding a gentle, infectious humour at their heart. Their librettists and composers took considerable trouble to research and faithfully represent liturgical and theological traditions.

The Sound of Music

The Sound of Music, which opened on Broadway in 1959, was the last Rodgers and Hammerstein collaboration. Throughout the time that he worked on it, Hammerstein knew that he was terminally ill with cancer. The musical's convent setting and strongly Roman Catholic storyline might seem an odd choice for an atheistic Jew and a devotee of Unitarian Universalism, but both men responded not just to the true-life love story of Maria Kutschera and Georg von Trapp and their stance against the Nazis but also to the warmth and humanity of the nuns and the theme of Christian vocation and God's call which they put at the heart of the musical.

Music of the Night. Ian Bradley, Oxford University Press. © Ian Bradley 2025.
DOI: 10.1093/9780197699775.003.0005

The role of Sister Gregory

Both lyricist and composer took immense care to do justice to the musical's Catholic setting. The role of Sister Gregory Duffy, a Dominican nun who was professor of theatre at Rosary College, River Forest, Illinois, in advising on the show's production, and specifically on instructing Mary Martin, who created the role of Maria, in the details of the dedicated religious life, has long been known. What was not so evident until the publication of Sister Gregory's letters in Hammerstein's collected correspondence in 2022 was the pivotal role she played in determining one of the musical's main themes and its strongly religious dimension.

Sister Gregory was alerted to the fact that Rodgers and Hammerstein were considering turning the Von Trapp family story into a musical by Mary Martin and her husband, the producer, Richard Halliday. In a letter to both of them, which was forwarded to Hammerstein, she signalled her delight in the project, cautioned against sentimentalizing it, and expressed confidence that as 'persons of integrity as well as sensitive artists, if you are true to yourselves, Maria will emerge a flesh and blood woman, radiating simplicity, warmth, generosity, tenderness and humor'. She went on to give her assessment of the nub of the story:

> The whole purpose of life, it seems to me, is pin-pointed in Maria's struggle to choose between two vocations. Like every adult human being, she must find the answer to the question: 'What does God want me to do with my life? How does He wish me to spend my love?'
>
> Many people believe one is attracted to the religious vocation because he or she is either afraid of life or incapable of love. Actually, the majority are drawn to it because they are keenly appreciative of the gift of life and have a tremendous capacity to love. The center of that love is God, and from that center it flows out into all areas of life. Most of us (we lucky ones, at least), were born of love and found great happiness and security in the family of which we were a part. We know from long experience the joy of that particular vocation, and it is natural and right that the majority should choose it because it promises the greatest human happiness this side of paradise. However, for some few, the feeling will persist that another vocation might offer greater scope for the love they feel. In time, such a person usually decides to settle the question by giving religious life a try, and if she is a woman, will enter the religious community that attracts her and for which she is most fitted.[1]

NUNS AND MENORAHS 77

After a lengthy briefing about the nature of the religious life and the various stages that it involves, from postulant to novice to professed sister taking the vows of poverty, chastity, and obedience, Sister Gregory returned in her letter to what she saw as happening to Maria when she is sent while still a postulant as a governess to the Von Trapp family because her superior in the convent recognizes both her deep love for God and her immaturity, more child than woman, not ready to make the choice of her ultimate vocation:

> The very generosity and capacity for love that had attracted her to the religious life in the first place began to deepen and expand. For the first time, perhaps, she knew a man as a friend, and slowly began to be attracted to him, perhaps began to love him.
>
> In other words, she began to mature, and because the experience was new and a little frightening, she ran back to the place that symbolized peace and security for her.
>
> Now Maria was in a position to make an honest choice, because she could understand the power of human love as well as spiritual love. This was the moment her superior had been waiting for, because now Maria could answer the question: 'How does God wish me to use my capacity to love?' And her answer was: to spend it in the heart of the Trapp family. In fact to become the heart of the Trapp family. There was no stigma attached to the choice. It was not a declaration that she loved God less and people more, but rather, a recognition of the road she was meant to travel from the beginning. That sure knowledge was the core of her life from that moment on and helped her to develop into the magnificent woman she was.[2]

What is remarkable about the two extracts above, particularly the second, is that they almost exactly anticipate the dialogue which Hammerstein wrote for the Mother Superior in that key scene in the middle of the musical where Maria comes to her, troubled by the fact that she has fallen in love with Captain Von Trapp. It is clear that Hammerstein lent heavily on what Sister Gregory had written about vocation and finding the path that God has chosen for us.

While he also took note of her comments in other more detailed matters of scripting, he did not always follow her advice. In a letter sent in July 1959 after she had received the draft script, she suggested several small alterations. Some Hammerstein accepted—for example he altered the stage direction to the nuns during the singing of 'How do you solve a problem like Maria', writing to the show's librettists, Howard Lindsay and Russel Crouse: 'Will

78   MUSIC OF THE NIGHT

you please eliminate the direction about giggling to please Sister Gregory'.[3]
However, he did not change the line 'And underneath her wimple she has
curlers in her hair' despite her comment:

> This line bothers me because it drastically changes the image I've formed
> of Maria—that of an untrammelled youngster, something of a tomboy, and
> completely unconscious of her physical beauty and the power that beauty
> could exert. That very unawareness gives impact to a line in the wedding
> scene. Would such a child be vain enough to wear curlers in her hair?
> Would she not be more likely to have uncombed, wind-blown hair?[4]

Another line in the original opening scene, which Sister Gregory particularly
liked, in which Sister Berthe remarks that 'the religious life is no place for the
pious', did not survive into the final script. Overall, however, Sister Gregory's
influence was considerable, both on the script and on the production. It is
significant that Hammerstein maintained a close friendship with her right
up to his final illness.

Richard Rodgers' research at Manhattanville College

Richard Rodgers similarly lent heavily on the expertise of religious sisters
while composing the score of *The Sound of Music*. More than any other
musical, it contains substantial passages of liturgical music, notably the
opening *Preludium* and the complex *Gaudeamus*, *Gloria*, and *Alleluia* sequence that makes up the Wedding Processional in Act II. Rodgers was determined to compose these himself rather than use existing church chants.
He took considerable trouble to make them authentic, as he explained in his
autobiography:

> One musical problem confronting me was the opening piece. Rather than
> begin with the customary overture, we decided to open immediately on a
> scene in Nonnberg Abbey, in which the nuns are heard chanting a Catholic
> prayer, '*Dixit Dominus*'. Since I had been so strongly against a score that
> combined old music with new, I could hardly fall back on using a traditional
> melody for the mass. Writing 'Western' songs for *Oklahoma!* or 'Oriental'
> songs for *The King and I* had never fazed me, but the idea of composing a
> Catholic prayer made me apprehensive. Given my lack of familiarity with

liturgical music, as well as the fact that I was of a different faith, I had to make sure that what I wrote would sound as authentic as possible.

So for the first time in my life I did a little research—and it turned out to be one of the most rewarding music lessons I've ever had. Through friends I got in touch with Mother Morgan, the head of the music department at Manhattanville College in Purchase, New York. She was not only willing to help; she even invited Dorothy and me to a specially arranged concert at which the nuns and seminarians performed many different kinds of religious music, from Gregorian chants to a modern work by Gabriel Fauré. An unexpectedly amusing moment came when Mother Morgan, waving her arms like a cheerleader at a football game, was vigorously conducting a particularly dramatic passage. As the music built to its peak, above the singing could be clearly heard Mother Morgan's booming command: 'Pray it!'[5]

The experience of meeting and hearing the nuns at Manhattanville College made a deep impression on Rodgers. Following their recital, he felt moved to tell the assembled sisters: 'This is one of the happiest moments of my life and I cannot tell you what this means to me. God bless you all', whereupon the choir burst into a resounding rendition of 'Oh what a beautiful morning'.[6] Mother Josephine Morgan, who taught music in the Pius X School of Liturgical Music in the all-female college, later recalled that in the middle of the rendition of liturgical chants by a choir of over seventy nuns from forty different orders attending the liturgical music summer school that she was directing, 'Richard Rodgers beckoned me over and said, "Will you be the abbess?" I laughed and then I said, "You are a scream. No, I am cloistered, I have to stay here all the time." He said, "Oh God," and that was the end of that.[7] In fact, it was not the end of their relationship. They kept up their friendship and Mother Morgan visited Rodgers and his wife Dorothy several times in the 1960s.

Although Rodgers himself made just one visit to Manhattanville College, Trude Rittman, the choral director of *The Sound of Music*, spent a week there studying the nuns' singing. The musical's opening *Preludium* was actually a collaborative effort between her, Rodgers, and Sister Margaret Leddy who taught Gregorian chant at the college. Sister Margaret subsequently assisted in rehearsals and taught the stage 'nuns' how to sing chant properly. Lucinda Ballard, the costume designer, also made several visits to the college to look at more than thirty different habits worn by nuns attending the summer school.

80 MUSIC OF THE NIGHT

'Climb every mountain'

While they took much from their contact and conversations with nuns, both librettist and composer also drew on their own beliefs. There is surely more than an echo of Hammerstein's sense of divine paternity in the way that he makes the Mother Abbess into a wise, benevolent, God-like figure. Indeed, she embodies several of the characteristics of 'Mr & Mrs God', the divine couple in the New England parlour in the original *Carousel* script. This is particularly true in the key scene where Maria is brought into her study having run away from the Von Trapps, terrified of the feelings that she has for the captain. The Mother Abbess gently instructs the confused postulant to go back and find how God wants her to spend her love and find her vocation, telling her that if she does indeed love the Captain and his children, that does not mean she loves God any the less. This is almost word for word what Sister Gregory had expressed in her letter as the essence of Maria's story. In the 1965 film version of the musical, this scene is given added religious atmosphere by being acted out in front of a crucifix standing on an altar with a soundtrack of subdued organ chords.

The Mother Abbess' teaching about the nature of religious vocation is crystallized in 'Climb every mountain', perhaps the most church-like of the great Rodgers and Hammerstein anthems. Hammerstein initially entitled it 'Face Life' and outlined its theme in a note scribbled on the manuscript of an early draft expressing sentiments that could have come straight out of one of Dr Hall's sermons in the Church of the Divine Paternity:

> You can't hide here. Don't think these walls shut out problems. You have to face life wherever you are. You have to look for life, for the life you were meant to lead. Until you find it you are not living.[8]

Early versions of the song contained lines about climbing a hill and getting to the top, 'which doesn't bring you much closer to the moon, but closer to the next hill, which you must also climb'. They also contained the lines beginning 'A song is no song till you sing it' which were later transferred to open the reprise of the duet between Lisl and Rolf, 'You are sixteen, going on seventeen', with their wonderful description of kenotic self-giving love, 'Love isn't love till you give it away'.[9]

In its final form 'Climb every mountain' was pared down to two simple stanzas and given a solemn yet soaring tune by Rodgers which reinforces its anthem-like feel. He marked the score 'with deep feeling like a prayer'.[10] After first hearing it, Sister Gregory wrote to Mary Martin and Richard Halliday:

> It's a beautiful song and drove me to the Chapel, (relax chums, I'm sure it will not effect [sic] your audiences in the same way). It made me acutely aware of how tremendously fortunate are those who find the dream that will absorb all their love, and finding it, embrace it to the end. . . . So I just had to dash into Chapel, give Him a quick but heart-felt "thank-you" and ask that all the youngsters I love so devotedly not only find their dreams but also have the courage to follow them—wherever they lead.

She went on to commend the way that 'the music begins on a low, muted tone and builds toward the exaultation [sic] of the last measures':

> As usual, Mr. Rodgers has done a beautiful job. However, it was the lyric that sent me to the Chapel. Hammerstein lyrics, (even the pre-Rodgers ones), are a unique combination of simplicity, sincerity, a sort of humorous tenderness, and exquisite imagery.[11]

The Sound of Music as an expression of Rodgers' and Hammerstein's faith

The Sound of Music expressed the sincerity and idealism of Hammerstein's Universalist-inspired faith. It also perhaps came as close as anything to breaking through Rodgers' atheism and bringing out a more spiritual side to his character, as hinted at by his reaction to hearing the nuns' choir at Manhattanville College. It was not just 'Climb every mountain' that Sister Gregory enthused over—she was also touched and inspired by the liturgical settings, reporting that she had gathered round the piano with other nuns to sing through the score and that 'after a few practice rounds, that ALLELUIA really orbited and soared all over the place'.[12]

There are other songs in this show which have a religious flavour. Maria's iconic opening number is full of religious language, with its references to 'the chime of a church', 'my heart will be blessed', and a 'lark who is learning to pray'. For one of the students in my Sacred Music class, 'How do you solve a problem like Maria' has the status of a sacred song. He feels that it points to both the inward and outward nature of the dedicated religious life and

82 MUSIC OF THE NIGHT

draws particular attention to the line 'her penitence is real'. I myself see significant spiritual resonances in 'The lonely goatherd', which seems to me a phrase which captures both the loneliness and the task of pastoral ministry and I have used it in training clergy.

Was it in *The Sound of Music* that Hammerstein came closest to softening the cynicism and unleashing the spiritual side of his partner and where Rodgers most clearly displayed the holiness that Cole Porter described as characterizing his tunes? For some critics, the religiosity of their final musical collaboration was its greatest fault. Noel Coward famously complained that 'there were too many nuns careering about and crossing themselves and singing jaunty little songs, and there was, I must admit, a heavy pall of Jewish-Catholic schmaltz enveloping the whole thing', while Kenneth Tynan described it as 'Rodgers's and Hammerstein's Great Leap Backwards'.[13] Responding to similar criticisms of the 1965 film version, Rodgers wrote very much in the idealistic spirit of his late collaborator:

> What I enjoy particularly is what it has done for the un-selfconscious people of the world—the self-conscious ones sneer a little at it. It is sentimental, but I don't see anything particularly wrong with that. I think people have been given a great deal of hope by that picture.[14]

More than any other musical, *The Sound of Music*, particularly in its film version, has taken on the dimensions of a parachurch, being resorted to on a regular basis by people in search of hope, healing, companionship, and moral and spiritual uplift. I have written about this in *You've Got to Have a Dream* and will not repeat myself here beyond saying that when it comes to both religious influences and spiritual resonances, there aren't many other musicals that hold a candle to it. Indeed, there aren't many that end with a direct Biblical quotation. Significantly, it comes from the mouth of the Mother Abbess who quotes Isaiah 55:12: 'For ye shall go out with joy, and be led forth with peace: the mountains and the hills shall break forth before you into singing'.

Other musicals about nuns

A whole series of musicals themed around nuns has followed in the wake of the *Sound of Music. Look to the Lilies* (1970), with lyrics by Sammy Cahn and music by Jule Styne, told the story of a group of German nuns based in New Mexico who persuaded an itinerant African American handyman to build a chapel for them. Despite the catchy choruses, 'Gott is Gut' and 'Follow the lamb', it closed after twenty-five performances. By contrast, *Nunsense*, featuring the Little Sisters of Hoboken in New Jersey, has become a global hit since its off-Broadway debut in 1986 and has spawned six sequels. Its creator, composer, and lyricist, Dan Goggin, who was schooled by Dominican sisters and also spent some years as a seminarian, has written: 'I spent a great deal of time around nuns. And most of my experiences left wonderful memories. I wrote *Nunsense* because I wanted to share what I knew to be the humor of the nun'.[15] The 2006 musical *Sister Act*, based on a 1992 film, has also been hugely successful. Although these shows lack the preachy, theological message of *The Sound of Music*, they present the dedicated religious life in a similarly positive way. When so many are highlighting abuse in convents and Catholic schools, musical theatre presents nuns as hugely engaging, fun-loving figures with whom one just wants to sing along, preferably while dressed in a wimple and habit.

The Jewish background to *Fiddler on the Roof*

Fiddler on the Roof, which opened on Broadway in 1964, five years after *The Sound of Music*, gives an even more sympathetic and idealized portrayal of a religious community than its predecessor, which it easily outstripped in terms of length of opening run. It could have been conceived by any of the host of American lyricists and composers in the first half of the twentieth century who came from Jewish backgrounds and who could relate directly to the persecution and pogroms which had brought their parents or grandparents from Europe to the USA. Indeed, it was a show waiting to be written and it is in many ways surprising that it was not until the mid-1960s that anyone hit on the suitability for the musical stage of the stories of the Jewish communities living in Eastern Europe in the early decades of the century with their combination of poignancy, colourful rituals and traditions, distinctive humour and haunting music.

In fact, some of Broadway 's leading practitioners had been sniffing around this area for several decades. Around 1926 Oscar Hammerstein saw two productions of *The Dybbuk*, the dark and mystical play written by Shloyme Rappoport (known by his pseudonym S. Ansky) set in a shtetl in Eastern

84   MUSIC OF THE NIGHT

Europe in the early 1900s. He toyed with adapting it into a musical but told his uncle that taking up the project would mean casting aside all other plays and studying Jewish lore and tradition which he was not disposed to do. In 1949, he and Richard Rodgers took an eleven-month option on Irving Elman's play *Tevye's Daughters* based on the stories of Sholem Aleicheim, the pen name of Solomon Rabinivitz, who had grown up in a shtetl in what is now Ukraine and emigrated to New York in 1906 after witnessing the pogroms that swept through the Russian Empire. They abandoned the project, apparently because they could not find a producer or director interested. For Benjamin Ivery, it was one of several 'Jewish musicals that Oscar Hammerstein never got to do'. Expressing the usual misconception that Hammerstein was himself Jewish, he comments that 'The lyricist and playwright considered writing about dybbuks but spent more time immortalizing the life of a singing nun.[16]

Maybe it had to take nearly twenty years after the end of the Second World War for what has been described as the ultimate post-holocaust musical to emerge. In the immediate aftermath of the war, the Jewish experience was perhaps too horrendous and raw to explore through the medium of musical theatre. By the mid-1960s American Jews could look back beyond the holocaust and reflect on the communities in Central and Eastern Europe in which their parents and grandparents had grown up. A nostalgic search for their roots was exacerbated by the fact that, thanks to mixed faith marriages, growing secularism, and declining synagogue attendance, they were becoming increasingly assimilated into US society and losing their distinctive identity. This was the background to the creation of *Fiddler on the Roof*, the first work of American popular culture to recall and evoke life in a shtetl. It was based on the stories by Aleicheim that Rodgers and Hammerstein had looked at fifteen or so years earlier.

The team responsible for *Fiddler*, Joseph Stein (book), Sheldon Harnick (lyrics), and Jerry Bock (music), were seasoned Broadway professionals who shared a Jewish immigrant heritage. Although themselves essentially secular and non-practising, they were respectful of their grandparents' adherence to the rituals and tenets of Judaism and would call on their knowledge as they worked on the script. Stein was the only one raised by orthodox immigrant parents in a Yiddish speaking household but 'was never very involved in religion'. Harnick, who grew up in a mostly Gentile neighbourhood, had toyed briefly as an adolescent with the idea of becoming a rabbi but preferred to pursue his passion for music and writing. Bock came from a secular family, although his grandmother's singing of Russian and Yiddish folk songs infused him with what he called his ethnic 'juices'. It was the warmth, humanity, and humour of Aleicheim's stories rather than their Jewishness that appealed to them. In Harnick's words, 'it never entered into our minds that it was Jewish', or, as Stein put it, 'these were stories about characters who just happened to be Jewish'.[17]

Yet for all this, religious faith and ritual came to be put very much in the foreground of the musical that they created. This was partly because of the dominant role given to Tevye, the milkman, and his characterization as a man of unshakeable faith who constantly questions God. Tevye's conversations and arguments with God dominate his dialogue and reach their apogee in his great solo 'If I were a rich man'. This song was inspired by a 1902 Yiddish monologue by Aleicheim, 'Ven ikh bin a Rothschild' (If I were a Rothschild) and Harnick based its 'Ya ba dibba dibba dum' interpolations on Hasidic chants that he listened to while researching life in early twentieth century Eastern European Jewish settlements. There was also a strong emphasis on portraying Jewish religious rituals. The original opening song was entitled 'We've never missed a Sabbath yet' and featured the whole community of Anatevka making preparations for the Shabbat meal.

Fiddler on the Roof—the songs

One of *Fiddler*'s simplest but most affecting songs, 'Sabbath Prayer', is a straight setting of the prayer said round the table at the Friday evening shabbat meal which could be transported straight into liturgical use. Indeed, children on Jewish summer camps regularly sing it on Friday evenings while lighting candles. Like 'You'll never walk alone' from *Carousel*, it has crossed over from the stage to liturgical use. It originated with a tape recording made by Bock which included one of his tunes 'with a certain Yiddish-Russian quality . . . overly sad'. He sang it in the style of a cantor and, as Alisa Solomon remarks, 'maybe that's why Harnick heard something devotional in it and pulled directly from Jewish liturgy—"May God bless you and protect you"— to shape the song Tevye's family would sing around the table on Friday evening'.[18]

There are other songs with significant Biblical and theological resonances. One of my Sacred Music students, a devout Catholic, identifies 'Sunrise, sunset' as her favourite sacred song from a musical. She feels that it conveys the sense that we as creatures are bound by time with the implication that

86 MUSIC OF THE NIGHT

God is timeless. 'Miracle of Miracles', sung by Mostel when he gets Tevye's blessing to marry Tzeitel, compares what has happened to him with the triumph of Daniel in the lion's den, the walls of Jericho tumbling down, Moses softening Pharoah's heart, the parting of the Red Sea, David's slaughter of Goliath, and the manna falling from heaven. He sees his betrothal to Tzeitel as being, like these blessings for the people of Israel, a miracle and a gift from God. Tevye's solo, 'When Messiah comes', originally written to be sung towards the end of the musical, speculates about the eventual arrival on earth of the long-awaited Messiah and has him apologizing for taking so long to come. It was cut in *Fiddler*'s pre-Broadway run in Detroit, perhaps because its humour did not fit with the poignancy and sadness of the ending, or more likely out of a concern that it could potentially offend Christians who felt that the Messiah had already come. There was a concern among *Fiddler*'s creators that the show was too Jewish to appeal to Gentile audiences.

The contributions of Jerry Robbins and Zero Mostel

If Stein, Harnick, and Bock found themselves making more of the religious elements of Aleicheim's stories than they had first intended and were entirely happy about, they were encouraged in this emphasis by *Fiddler*'s director, Jerry Robbins. He was conflicted about his own Jewishness, confiding in an autobiographical note: 'I didn't want to be a Jew . . . I wanted to be safe, protected, assimilated, hidden in among the boys, the majority'. He changed his name from Rabinowitz and noted that his early attraction to ballet was a way of distancing himself from his Jewish heritage: 'I affect a discipline over my body and take on another language—the language of court and Christianity—church and state—a completely artificial convention of movement'. He went on to ask himself 'in what wondrous and monstrous ways would I move if I would dig down to my Jew self?'[19]

Robbins became much more open and sympathetic to his Jewish heritage after a visit he made to Poland in 1959 in search of Rozhanka, the village where his father had grown up and which had been almost completely destroyed in the Second World War. It made a profound impression, leading him to have lengthy conversations with his father about his life there and his escape from it. This fired Robbins' own enthusiasm for the project of portraying the experience of those who had grown up in the East European

Jewish settlements on the musical stage. As director, he showed an almost obsessional concern with ensuring an authentic and correct representation of every detail of life and ritual in the fictional Ukranian shtetl of Anatevka. While insisting that *Fiddler on the Roof* should not be sentimental and schmaltzy, and must avoid 'making all the Jews understanding, philosophic & hearts of gold, wry of expression & compassionate to the point of nausea', he lavished considerable care and attention on making sure that Jewish rituals and customs were accurately portrayed. He visited yeshivas and synagogues, took the costume designer, Patricia Zipprodt, to observe Hasidic and Orthodox dress, hired Dvora Lapson, an expert on Jewish dance and customs, as an adviser, and took the cast to Jewish weddings to observe the rituals and the dance steps. His determination to familiarize the company with Jewish mores and customs even extended to an initial attempt to impose gender segregation in rehearsals, something that lasted for less than a day. Richard Rodgers' concern to do justice to Catholic liturgy and practice in *The Sound of Music* comes to mind, but this was an even more intense effort to honour the subject matter, driven in no small part by the fact that, for all their ambivalence about their Jewish heritage, Robbins, Stein, Bock, and Harnick were affirming their own roots and the experiences of their parents and grandparents, something that was signified by the title originally suggested for the show, 'Where Poppa Came From'.

Another key influence on enhancing the religious emphasis in the musical came from Zero Mostel, who was chosen to create the role of Tevye. He had been brought up in an Orthodox family and community in Brooklyn and although he rebelled against it, becoming a comedian, marrying a girl with an Irish Catholic background, and raising his children without any religion, he clung to several elements of his Jewish heritage, including Yiddish which he regularly spoke. It was Mostel who insisted that Tevye would kiss the mezuzah, the parchment inscribed with texts from the Torah traditionally fixed to the doorpost, as he came into his house. Despite Robbins' opposition, he made this a feature of his performance. He also insisted on keeping the verse in 'If I were a rich man' in which Tevye dreams of sitting in the synagogue to pray and discussing the holy books with the learned men and reflects 'that would be the sweetest thing of all' when there was a move to cut it. He had fond memories of his own father praying devoutly alone every night, poring over a Hebrew text. Mostel unsuccessfully opposed the dropping of 'When Messiah comes' which he declared his favourite song in the show.

88 MUSIC OF THE NIGHT

The importance of the religious dimension in *Fiddler* was acknowledged by the gifts that its creators gave to each other on opening night. Stein presented Harnick with a mezuzah, the first that the lyricist had ever owned; Harnick gave Robbins a shofar, the ram's horn traditionally blown to sound the Sabbath and signal other important religious festivals; and the company gave Robbins a white yarmulke or skullcap. This was more than mere tokenism—it was a sign of how they regarded their joint work as a celebration of Jewishness in its beliefs, rituals, and customs.

Norman Jewison's film version, which came out in 1971, further enhanced the emphasis on Jewish religion and ritual. In its opening sequence images of Hebrew texts on a synagogue wall, the cover of the Torah embossed with the gold star of David, and the distinctive seven-branched candelabrum known as the menorah, flash up on the screen during the chorus 'Tradition', which Robbins had insisted be substituted for the original 'I've never missed a Sabbath yet'. A complete two-storey replica wooden synagogue was made for the film, based partly on the Dubrovnik synagogue, the second oldest in Europe, with its interior modelled on the fittings in an abandoned shul in Targu Neamt, Romania. It featured in several scenes, the most moving one being where the rabbi goes in prior to the expulsion of the community to remove the Torah scrolls.

Fiddler on the Roof's appeal to non-Jewish faith groups and role as a marker of Jewish identity

Fiddler on the Roof's sensitive and sympathetic evocation of a community bound together by religious beliefs, rituals, and traditions has a universal appeal which extends to non-Jewish faith communities, not least Christian ones. The film version was enthusiastically promoted by Protestant and Catholic churches in the USA. Lutheran clergy were urged to tell their parishioners to see it and were offered questions for discussion on the purpose and function of tradition in religion, love, and marriage, and on Tevye's relationship with God. A review in the *Catholic Film Newsletter* praised the film for capturing so beautifully rituals like family prayers, synagogue rites, and religious symbols, and for the respect shown for family and marriage. It went on to suggest that its 'real universality springs from its boundless faith in the providence of God and the resounding hymn it sings to hope and life and the spirit of man'.[20]

I can personally testify to the impact that *Fiddler on the Roof* has had on Irish Catholics. When speaking some years ago in Dublin about musical theatre at a day conference attended by performing groups from across Ireland, I was told that it was their favourite show and that it had been particularly popular among predominantly Catholic musical theatre societies during the period of the 'troubles' in Northern Ireland in the last three decades of the twentieth century. This was because the Catholic nationalist communities identified with the Jewish settlers in the shtetls and saw what they took to be the occupying British troops in a similar light to the Tsarist Cossacks in Anatevka as an unwelcome military presence. This is a good example of the representative role that musicals can have in giving people a way of expressing their identity and concerns.

There is a universality about *Fiddler on the Roof* with its theme of the waning hold of religious and cultural tradition, and of a whole way of life, in the face of pluralism, secular modernity, and the challenging of authority and custom. There are other themes in the musical which make it speak particularly to people of faith, notably religious persecution and the status of minority faith groups. It also, of course, has a broader appeal on the basis of what could be said to be its more secular themes, themselves not devoid of spiritual resonances, such as generational change and love overcoming rules and convention. But alongside this universal character, *Fiddler on the Roof* has served as a signifier and marker of Jewishness. One thinks of Homer Simpson, in need of $50,000 for a heart bypass, going to the local rabbi, pretending to be Jewish in the only way he knows how: 'Now, I know I haven't been the best Jew, but I have rented *Fiddler on the Roof* and I will watch it.' The musical has expressed Jewish identity in a way that has appealed to Jews and non-Jews alike. John Bush Jones recalls seeing the show in Chicago with his non-Jewish fiancée and her saying to him afterwards, 'This is the first time in my life I really wished I was Jewish.'[21] As Alisa Solomon writes in her superb study, *Wonder of Wonders*: '*Fiddler* gave Gentile post-McCarthy America and the world—the Jews it could, and wanted to, love. It gave Jews nothing less than a publicly touted touchstone for authenticity.'[22]

Solomon goes on to chart the show's changing role for successive generations:

In the 1960s, *Fiddler on the Roof* served as an engine of Jewish acculturation in America. For the next generation of assimilated Jews, it became a sacred repository of Jewishness itself. And for the next generation still, it became

90 MUSIC OF THE NIGHT

part of a multi-valent legacy, available as a source of further exploration for those who wish to follow Tevye as he wanders on.[23]

Some Jewish critics of *Fiddler* dispute this narrative and are uneasy about its status as a signifier of Jewishness. For the writer and teacher Dr Yvette Alt Miller, the musical does not make enough of the religious life and faith in a typical shtetl: 'In a real-life shtetl like Anatevka, there would have been much more Jewish learning, and a greater familiarity with Jewish books and wisdom'.[24] Others point to the inauthenticity of building Jewish identity on 'someone else's emotions'. This is the theme of author and musician, Tzvi Glucklin, in his article 'Don't be a Fiddler on the Roof Jew'.[25] While such statements indicate an unease among orthodox and practising Jews about *Fiddler*'s status as a Jewish signifier, it is striking how many secular Jews point to it as having given them a sense of the spiritual meaning of their religious tradition. Typical is the comment by the *Washington Post* chief theatre critic, Peter Marks: 'In the secular Jewish home of my childhood, about the closest we ever came to spiritual sustenance was *Fiddler*'.[26]

Emily Knoppert, a Washington-based freelance editor and educator, has written eloquently on this theme. For her,

> *Fiddler on the Roof* is the base of my Jewish identity . . . Listening to and quoting *Fiddler* was the most Jewish I felt a resolutely secular family could get . . . I never attended Hebrew school but, thanks to *Fiddler on the Roof*, I learned what the Sabbath is and the rules related to its observance. The wedding of Tzeitel and Motel was the first Jewish wedding I ever attended, so to speak. It was the first time I encountered a chuppah, the first time I saw a bride circle her groom seven times, and the first time I heard the groom break a glass with his foot. Years later, at my sister's wedding, I could not help but hear the melancholy tune of 'Sunrise, Sunset' playing in my head while my parents stood by her side.[27]

Knoppert is far from being alone in finding weddings providing a trigger to songs in *Fiddler*. Although it does not happen so often now, there was a time when 'Sunrise, sunset' was almost invariably sung or played in the celebrations following Jewish marriages. I myself turned to *Fiddler* at the reception following my Catholic-baptized godson's wedding to a Jewish husband when I delivered a blessing in the form of a slightly adapted version of 'A blessing on your head, Mazel Tov, Mazel Tov', from Tevye's dream.

NUNS AND MENORAHS   91

Emily Knoppert concludes her reflection on the impact of *Fiddler on the Roof*:

> I'm not a formal part of any synagogue or Jewish organisation, nor have I ever lived anywhere with a sizeable Jewish community. Still, I know that if I listen to the *Fiddler* soundtrack, I feel like I'm part of something tangible in the world, something bigger than my own questioning sense of identity. I may not even know how Jewish I want to be, or what that would look like to me, but it makes me feel like I am part of this diaspora of *Fiddler*-loving, secular Jews around the world.[28]

Like *The Sound of Music, Fiddler on the Roof* has created its own worldwide family of fans who are drawn in no small measure by its spiritual resonances and exceptionally affectionate and positive depiction of a faith-based community. As portrayed on stage and screen, the nuns of Nonnberg Abbey and the settlers of Anatevka may be over-sentimentalized and too good to be true, but they have inspired and given hope to many and taken on the role of religious mentors, guides, and instructors, more real in the minds of those who draw inspiration from them than many actual priests and rabbis.

Notes

1. Letter from Sr Gregory Duffy to Martin Martin and Richard Halliday, forwarded to Oscar Hammerstein, 23 February 1958. Oscar Hammerstein II Collection, Library of Congress.
2. Ibid.
3. Letter from Oscar Hammerstein to Howard Lindsay and Russel Crouse, 29 July 1958. Oscar Hammerstein II Collection, Library of Congress.
4. Letter from Sr Gregory to Richard Halliday, 20 July 1959. Oscar Hammerstein II Collection, Library of Congress.
5. Richard Rodgers, *Musical Stages: An Autobiography* (New York: Da Capo Press, 1995), 301.
6. 'The Sound of Music', *Manhattanville Alumnae Review*, Spring (1960), 9.
7. V.V. Harrison, *Changing Habits: A Memoir of the Society of the Sacred Heart* (New York: Doubleday, 1986), 201.
8. Hugh Fordin, *Getting to Know Him: A Biography of Oscar Hammerstein II* (New York: Random House, 1977), 349.
9. On the theological significance of these lines, see Ian Bradley, *You've Got to Have a Dream: The Message of the Musical* (London: SCM Press, 2004), 16.
10. William Hyland, *Richard Rodgers* (New Haven, CT: Yale University Press, 1998), 254.
11. Letter from Sr Gregory to Richard Halliday, 17 September 1959. Oscar Hammerstein II Collection, Library of Congress.
12. Ibid.
13. Hyland, *Richard Rodgers*, 255.
14. Frederick Nolan, *The Sound of their Music: The Story of Rodgers and Hammerstein* (New York: Walker & Co., 1978), 225.
15. John Bush Jones, *Our Musicals, Ourselves*, 313.
16. Benjamin Ivy, 'The Jewish musicals that Oscar Hammerstein never got to do', *Forward*, 9 June 2022.

92 MUSIC OF THE NIGHT

17. Alisa Solomon, *Wonder of Wonders: A Cultural History of Fiddler on the Roof* (New York: Metropolitan Books, 2012), 1.
18. Ibid., 109.
19. Ibid., 88–89.
20. *Catholic Film Newsletter*, 30 November 1971.
21. John Bush Jones, *Our Musicals, Ourselves*, 215.
22. Solomon, *Wonder of Wonders*, 220.
23. Ibid., 355.
24. Yvette Alt Miller, 'What Fiddler on the Roof Gets Right—and Wrong', *Aish*, 18 December 2022.
25. Tzvi Glucklin, 'Don't be a Fiddler on the Roof Jew', *Aish*, 22 March 2023.
26. Peter Marks, *Washington Post*, 27 February 2004.
27. Emily Knoppert, ' "Fiddler on the Roof" is the Base of My Jewish Identity', *Kveller*, 18 February 2020. https://www.kveller.com/fiddler-on-the-roof-is-the-base-of-my-jewish-identity/. Accessed 27 September 2023.
28. Ibid.

5

God don't answer prayers a lot

The secularism of Stephen Sondheim

As originally conceived, this book was not going to include a chapter on Stephen Sondheim. That there is one is largely thanks to the promptings of one of the two anonymous readers who were sent my draft outline by Oxford University Press for review and comment. He wrote:

> In my opinion, of all the composers of operetta and musicals, the shows of Stephen Sondheim inspire almost a 'cult of spirituality'. Sondheim fans live their lives by his lyrics and music. He also composed what he called an actual operetta in *A Little Night Music*, and that point should be highlighted. Sondheim's partnerships with Hugh Wheeler and James Lapine have produced some of the most spiritually intellectual music I have heard. Readers might question the exclusion of Sondheim, especially since he has recently passed, and his popularity is at an all-time high.[1]

It is in response to that comment that I have included this chapter on Sondheim. While I concede his pivotal position in the development of modern musical theatre, I have to admit that for me he is a distinctly secular figure whose works lack religious influences or spiritual resonances. This impression is confirmed by what he himself has said. His biographer, Meryle Secrest, states on the basis of numerous conversations with him that 'Sondheim said that he had no religious beliefs'.[2] He himself said in an interview, 'Art is as close to a religion as I have'.[3]

I have other issues with Sondheim, one of the biggest being that I feel that he never fully develops a melody but rather leaves it unfinished and cut short, perhaps in keeping with his determination to avoid the 'happily ever after' motif predominant in operetta and musical theatre. His deliberate avoidance of hummable tunes is, of course, part and parcel of his conscious rejection of the whole musical theatre tradition as hitherto conceived.

Music of the Night. Ian Bradley, Oxford University Press. © Ian Bradley 2025.
DOI: 10.1093/9780197699775.003.0006

94   MUSIC OF THE NIGHT

Sondheim has been well described as someone who wrote musicals for people who hate musical theatre. Without a mega-hit, he never achieved the widespread popular appeal of most of the other librettists and composers featured in this book, while at the same time garnering much more attention and acclaim among intellectuals, academics, and those at the cutting edge of the arts—in other words precisely those who on the whole despise musical theatre for its shallowness, sentimentality, and predictability.

Just as I find Sondheim's music frustrating and unsatisfying, I find his lyrics cynical, world-weary and cold. He could be compared in this regard to W.S. Gilbert, whom he greatly admired. Tellingly, he had no time for Sullivan. It is tempting to apply to him the words that the critic uses about Georges Seurat's painting in *Sunday in the Park With George*, 'All head, no heart'.

Witty, intellectual, and brilliantly clever as it undoubtedly is, there is also a dark and depressing quality to much of Sondheim's work. More than any other practitioner of musical theatre, he specializes in the 'Music of the Night' that gives this book its title. In the words of the *Washington Post* theatre critic, Lloyd Rose, 'If he's to your taste, your taste is already dark'.[4] But is this darkness just empty nihilism, or does it have a spiritual dimension, as suggested by my anonymous reviewer?

In probing this question, I have sought to suppress my own prejudices about Sondheim, re-engage with his works, and plough through the morass of academic studies which examine his approach and work from every angle. I have also listened to students taking my undergraduate and masters courses in The Theology of the Musical and in Sacred Music who have sought to convince me that there are religious influences and spiritual themes in his work. This chapter will give space to those who do see Sondheim's shows as having a spiritual quality, as well as to those like me who regard them as essentially secular. It also seeks to analyse where, if anywhere, religious influences on his work are to be found.

Sondheim's upbringing and background

Let us begin with his upbringing and background. Like so many other Broadway lyricists and composers, Sondheim grew up in New York in a non-practising Jewish family. Secrest comments: 'As for religious instruction, Stephen Joshua Sondheim received none at all. He never had a bar mitzvah ceremony, he knew nothing about the observances of the Jewish calendar, and he did not enter a synagogue until he was nineteen years old'.[5] Famously,

Leonard Bernstein had to tell him how to pronounce 'Yom Kippur' (he apparently said 'Yum Kupper') when they were working together on *West Side Story* in 1957. Sondheim described Bernstein as 'the first serious Jew I came into contact with'.[6]

Sondheim's elementary education was at the Ethical Culture School in New York, an emphatically non-religious, progressive establishment committed to inculcating high ethical values in its pupils. This was followed by two years in the New York Military Academy and four years in the George School in Bucks County, Pennsylvania, a co-ed Quaker foundation with a strong provision of art, theatre, and other creative subjects in the curriculum and an emphasis on community service, social justice, environmental concerns, and community-based decision making.

Given this educational background, one might imagine Stephen Sondheim to have imbibed a mildly Protestant liberal idealism not dissimilar from what Oscar Hammerstein gained from his early exposure to Universalism. In fact, in the words of Ethan Mordden, 'Sondheim enjoyed the advantage of private schooling, a wide cultural perspective, and a secular worldview, free of the occult confusions that religion invents'.[7]

The influence of Oscar Hammerstein and Sondheim's childhood

Oscar Hammerstein was a key influence on the young Stephen Sondheim, effectively occupying a parental role soon after his father ran off when he was ten. Sondheim sought escape from his overbearing mother by spending much of his time at the Hammerstein home near to his own in Bucks County. While the librettist of *Oklahoma!*, *South Pacific*, and *The Sound of Music* taught his young protegé the craft of writing musicals, he was not able to inculcate in him his own brand of liberal Protestant idealism. That he tried to is clear from comments that he made on his surrogate son's early scripts. Commenting on Sondheim's first attempt at a musical, *Climb High*, for which he wrote book, lyrics, and music in 1952, Hammerstein expressed his unease with the fact that the characters apparently had no redeeming qualities. As a result, he felt that they would not connect with an audience: 'They all seem shallow wisecracking young people. You know a lot of young people who are nicer than these. I don't think a play should be filled only with nice people, but it is good to have a variety, and some characters who are foils for others.'[8]

96 MUSIC OF THE NIGHT

Hammerstein told his pupil to ditch *Climb High* and regard it simply 'as an important stepping stone in your libretto writing and composing education'. For his next work, he advised him to 'spend a lot of time making up your mind as to its fundamental quality of human interest'.[9] By implication, he was saying that for all Sondheim's genius, he was too detached and sophisticated, lacking the human touch. Arthur Sullivan had used similar words when he complained about the topsy-turvy nature of W.S. Gilbert's plots and told him, 'I should like to set a story of human interest and probability'.

Sondheim acknowledged that his 'surrogate father', as he called Hammerstein, 'taught me how to structure a song, what a character was, what a scene was; he taught me how to tell a story, how not to tell a story, how to make stage directions practical'.[10] What his mentor did not succeed in teaching him was the idealistic, hope-filled, essentially spiritual dimension of musical theatre as he had developed it. When, under his tutelage, young Stephen wrote a romantic song about the wind and the willows, robins, and larks, Hammerstein told him, 'You know, you don't believe in any of this stuff. Write what you feel. Don't write what I feel. I really believe all this stuff. You don't. If you write what you believe, you'll be ninety percent ahead of all other songwriters'.[11] This is a telling observation about the differences between them. Sondheim did go on to write about how he felt—cynical, depressed, and ambiguous. In some ways, perhaps, he took Hammerstein too much at his word. As Mark Steyn has observed, 'all you hear in Sondheim is the voice of the author', in contrast to Hammerstein, who subjugates his own voice and lets his characters speak.[12] What Sondheim later went on to write is not what his teacher would have liked to hear. Steve Swayne is surely right in his observation that 'had he lived, it is likely that Hammerstein would not have always been a willing member of Sondheim's audience'.[13]

More important than Hammerstein's mentorship in influencing the theme and tone of his future work was Sondheim's desperately unhappy childhood. His parents were initially distant, then absent in the case of his father and cold and overbearing in the case of his mother, who would famously tell him that her only regret in life was giving birth to him. Like W.S. Gilbert, he almost certainly inherited his cynical, pessimistic worldview from his father, whom, he recalled, 'always looked at the black side, imagined the worst that could happen'.[14] Like Gilbert, too, he had a strong sense of the arbitrariness and unfairness of life in a world where there was no presiding benevolent deity. His view is encapsulated in the song 'Now You Know' in *Merrily We Roll Along* where, after the reflection that 'thieves get rich and saints get shot', comes the line 'God don't answer prayers a lot'.

Sondheim's unhappy childhood almost certainly explains many of his personality traits, such as his shyness, apparent coldness, and inability to love, and the sense of distance and reserve noted by his friends and colleagues. It also surely lies behind the lack of hope in so many of his musicals. I concur with Meryle Secrest, who feels that he most clearly revealed himself in *Sunday in the Park With George* in ways that went back to his childhood:

> *Sunday in the Park* was the quintessential vehicle for feelings that had been mangled in childhood. And that musical, which on the surface displayed such a clinical dissociation from feeling, perhaps paradoxically revealed the most. Loneliness, the sense of being an outsider, a feeling of continually groping towards something just beyond one's reach—these were themes he knew and had already expressed, always superimposed upon by irony and disillusion, those reliable defences against painful emotions.[15]

Those critics who find Sondheim an essentially secular and cynical figure make much of how far he departed from the model of musical theatre established by Hammerstein. In an article entitled 'Sondheim's Cynicism', published shortly after his death in *First Things*, the magazine of the Institute of Religion and Public Life, the journalist and critic Peter Tonguette writes:

> Sondheim's supremacy in musical theatre owes much to his cynicism about men and women, disenchantment with the American ideal, and enchantment with what is marginal—attitudes that mirror our cultural élites . . . Sondheim seemed to prize that which challenges or provokes rather than that which pleases or nourishes . . . He dissented openly from the sensibility of Hammerstein, a proud left-liberal who nevertheless retained a faith in the eternal verities: God, family values, country, and all that . . . In one generation, the form went from Hammerstein's hymn to indomitability, 'Climb Ev'ry Mountain', to Sondheim's gag about cannibalism [in *Sweeney Todd*], 'God that's Good!'[16]

Cynicism in *Company* (1970) and *Merrily We Roll Along* (1981)

For me, this secular cynicism is revealed most clearly in *Company*, described by Robert McLaughlin as 'arguably the first musical of the postmodern era'.[17] The *New York Times* critic, Clive Barnes, admired its 'sweetly laconic cynicism' but found its sophisticated style to be altogether too slick, clever, and eclectic to make any real emotional appeal to the audience.[18] Significantly, when God is mentioned, it is in a negative way in the couplet in 'The little things you do together': 'It's not talk of God and the decade ahead that/Allows you to get through the worst.'

Company also expresses particularly clearly the assault on the 'happy ever after' theme so prevalent in the golden age of Broadway musicals, which is a hallmark of Sondheim's shows. The song 'Happily ever after' that Sondheim wrote as its concluding number rubbishes marriage and all long-term and close relationships and advocates an aimless, hedonistic life with no real purpose, attachments, or goals, 'ever, ever, ever after in hell'. Director Hal Prince protested that it was just too negative and bitter for the finale, and so the slightly more optimistic and hope-filled 'Being alive' was substituted. This was a rare successful attempt to curb a recurrent Sondheim trope which surfaces again and again in his shows, from the 1971 *Follies* with its jeering at the happy ending of the Rodgers and Hammerstein-type musical to the 1987 *Into the Woods*, whose Act 2 systematically undoes the happy ending of the Act 1 finale. In the words of Sandor Goodhart, who has rightly argued that Sondheim mounts a sustained and full-blown assault on musical theatre as it had hitherto been conceived: 'He stages in full a critique of the one myth that has dominated the musical stage in America and our lives as we live them in accord with that myth—namely, the myth of a happy ending'.[19]

There is a deeper purpose behind this attack on happy endings. Sondheim specializes in shattered dreams and false illusions. He challenges the dream theme that I have argued in my book *You've Got to Have a Dream: The Message of the Musical* is at the heart of twentieth-century musical theatre. For him, in Robert McLaughlin's words: 'the dreams that have historically motivated people . . . have become images, useful nostalgically but no longer connected to any real meaning or real experience'.[20] The theme of dreams not coming true is there in his second Broadway musical, *Gypsy* (*West Side Story* being the first), and it is central to the plot of *Merrily We Roll Along*. At one level, this seems another aspect of his rejection of the idealism of Hammerstein, as summed up in his statement, 'I do like to deal in people's delusions, that is only an inch away from illusions'.[21] Yet it could be said that he is actually calling on us here to face up to the reality of life rather than live in a self-indulgent dream world, and to that extent, making an important ethical statement which has echoes of much traditional religious teaching. There are, indeed, distinct echoes in Sondheim's approach to dreams of what the German Lutheran pastor and theologian Dietrich Bonhoeffer said on the subject:

> By sheer grace God will not permit us to live even for a brief period in a dream world. He does not abandon us to those rapturous experiences and lofty moods that come over us like a dream. God is not a God of the emotions but the God of truth . . . God hates visionary dreaming; it makes the dreamer proud and pretentious.[22]

In a 2019 London University doctoral thesis, published as a book in 2023 with the title *Careful the Spell You Cast*, British dramatist and teacher Ben Francis argues that Sondheim is, in fact, far from being cynical in his insistence that one must let go of illusions, which he distinguishes from dreams. A key text here is the line in Mary's song 'Now you know' from *Merrily We Roll Along*: 'It's called letting go your illusions/And don't confuse them with dreams'. Francis interprets Sondheim's message as being that no one finds happiness by living vicariously through their dream characters. Rather, they have to learn from the failure of their dreams and find something more authentic, perhaps through connection with others. For Francis, this is a motif that comes to the fore particularly in the later shows, which are more positive. In his words: 'A major theme in Sondheim's work is the journey through disillusionment towards maturity . . . the acceptance of the uncertainty of life, and the refusal to give in to cynicism or despair'.[23]

Jewish and Catholic appreciations of Sondheim's spirituality

Others have found a more explicitly spiritual dimension in Sondheim's approach, as my anonymous reviewer does, and even a religious perspective. This has been identified by both Jewish and Christian commentators. In a talk given in 2022 in Temple Israel of Northern Westchester, Lauren Fogelman, currently cantor at Temple Beth Abraham in Tarrytown, New York, notes that there is only one definitively Jewish character in the entire Sondheim canon, Paul in *Company*, who marries Amy, a lapsed Catholic. The music

100 MUSIC OF THE NIGHT

and lyrics surrounding their interfaith Jewish/Catholic wedding are imbued with religious imagery:

> The music—especially the part that Marie will sing—mimics the sound of a church organ and choir in such a stereotypical way that it's almost certainly meant to be a parody. And perhaps that's exactly what it is—a parody of the pomp and circumstance of formal, organized religion.

Fogelman finds it curious that Sondheim incorporates no Jewish elements in the wedding but puts this down to the fact that 'Jewish ritual and practice were never at the forefront of his life'. However, she goes on to say that 'Sondheim may not have been a man of ritual, but he certainly had a spiritual side to him.' To illustrate this, she notes that the three key rules that governed his writing process—Content dictates form, Less is more, and God is in the details—are 'similar to what we observe with regards to Biblical analysis'. This leads her to conclude that: 'For a self-ascribed non-religious person, it seems curious that one of Sondheim's major writing techniques stems from God. Perhaps Sondheim is using God imagery to relate to the idea of transcendence—to creating a moment so meaningful and so beautiful that it almost feels otherworldly.'[24]

I have to say that I find this attempt to give Sondheim's work a religious underpinning unconvincing. There may be moments of transcendence in Sondheim, 'Sunday' in *Sunday in the Park* perhaps being one of them with its evocation of the colours of creation. It is one of four songs that Fogelman takes to support her thesis (the others are 'Getting married today' from *Company*, 'Night waltz' from *A Little Night Music*, and 'No one is alone' from *Into the Woods*). But the notion that Sondheim's writing techniques stem from God because of their apparent similarity to principles of Biblical analysis seems very far-fetched. Nor am I persuaded by Fogelman's suggestion that Sondheim uses God imagery to relate to the idea of transcendence. When God is invoked in Sondheim's shows, it is invariably in a negative way.

The song 'Sunday' is also referenced in an appreciation of Sondheim from a Catholic perspective. Writing in *The Jesuit Review of Faith and Culture*, Fr Jim McDermott, a Jesuit priest and writer, reflects that on the weekend after Sondheim's death, two different groups staged impromptu events dedicated to him in New York's Central Park and Times Square. Both chose to sing 'Sunday', which McDermott views as 'a sort of artist's hymn to the universe, every element of what they see described in the flecks of color for which Seurat was known. It's a choral song that builds from silent reverie to

GOD DON'T ANSWER PRAYERS A LOT   101

passionate adoration, all the while describing what is just a typical Sunday in a park.'

McDermott goes on to speculate why 'Sondheim is a favorite of many Jesuits':

> I think many of us rejoice in his refusal to accept that things are either black or white, wholly good or bad.... Perhaps it is also that sense of the cost of one's art, the sacrifice that comes with dedication to a vocation, that appeals to us Jesuits. Sondheim's stories are populated with characters isolated as a result of their commitments. For much of his life Sondheim himself seemed similar. His life was his art; by his own admission he didn't fall in love until his 60s. But I wonder if we also see in him some of our own sometime loneliness and uncertainty as celibate men. Like Bobby from 'Company', we, too, can look out on the married couples around us both with love and bemusement, and perhaps a little bit of fear. It's certainly not an experience unique to us; from its debut in 1970 the queer community, too, has identified with Bobby's story and wondered whether he shouldn't in the end be gay.[25]

The particular appeal of Sondheim's work to both Catholic priests and the gay community does certainly betoken an empathetic vulnerability at its heart, if not necessarily a distinct spiritual or religious dimension. Those who do detect those latter qualities tend to find them especially in three of his shows, *A Little Night Music*, *Sweeney Todd*, and *Into the Woods*, so let me direct my attention to them in turn.

A Little Night Music (1973)

There have been several suggestions that there are religious influences and references in what is often seen as Sondheim's most operetta-like work, presumably because so much of it is composed in 3/4 time, and which Hal Prince memorably described as 'whipped cream with knives'. Raymond Knapp points to the artwork used for posters, playbills, sheet music, and cast albums of *A Little Night Music*, which shows a panoply of nudes and lovers in the branches of a silhouetted tree:

> While providing a suitable icon for a sex comedy set in Sweden ... the image also invokes the Tree of Knowledge from the Garden of Eden. The bright orb of the perpetually setting sun substitutes for Eve's apple and the

102 MUSIC OF THE NIGHT

serpentine interweaving of the tree's lovers and odalisques proffers, as the tree's forbidden fruit, a knowledge that is specifically sexual (that is, 'knowledge' in the biblical sense).[26]

This interesting attempt to inject a Biblical and theological note seems to me to be stretching things rather too far—and even if the image does have the resonances that Knapp suggests, it would not have been Sondheim who came up with it.

Robert McLaughlin hints at another possible religious reference at the end of *A Little Night Music*. As Frederik and Desirée are about to go off together and apparently confound the Sondheim rule of no 'happily ever after' endings, she announces that she is committed to a week-long engagement in *Hedda Gabler*, and so there is a hitch in their plans to be together. 'What's wrong with Purgatory before Paradise?' asks Frederik, putting emphasis, in McLaughlin's words, 'on the meanwhile, the time in between, rather than the end'.[27] This certainly counts as a very Sondheimian observation, but despite the religious language, hardly as a theological one.

There is undoubted pathos and sensitivity in this show, most obviously and famously in 'Send in the Clowns', although Sondheim himself slightly deflated this aspect with his remark that it could equally well have been entitled 'Send in the fools'. Its darkly cynical mood is expressed in Charlotte's song 'Every day a little death'. If this is, indeed, an operetta, then it is one that expresses the music of the night, as its title suggests, without the infectious *joie de vie* of Offenbach and Sullivan or the soaring tunes and spiritual yearning of Lehár.

Sweeney Todd (1979)

Sondheim's biggest hit, which has enjoyed success on both stage and screen, is surely the ultimate 'musical of the night', described by one critic when it opened in London in 1980 as the darkest musical for sixty years and hailed in the USA by Robert McLaughlin as 'Sondheim's darkest statement of the problem of love in contemporary society'.[28] Intriguingly, Sondheim himself saw it as belonging to the tradition of operetta:

For me, *Sweeney Todd* is not an opera; it's a black operetta in feeling and form. The only thing is it deals with extremely melodramatic material.

GOD DON'T ANSWER PRAYERS A LOT   103

Operettas tended to deal with lighthearted subjects. But if you look at the form *Sweeney Todd* is, let's say eighty per cent sung, and it's almost all songs and arioso singing. Not much recitative. And that is true of operetta.[29]

The most striking religious reference in this 'black operetta' is the repeated use in the score of the traditional plainchant setting of the *Dies Irae*, the medieval Latin sequence used in the Roman Rite Requiem. It first appears in the opening ballad as the melody for the line 'Swing your razor high, Sweeney'. An inversion of its opening bars occurs in 'My Friends', the song that Todd sings about his razors. It surfaces again in the viola accompaniment to his line 'They all deserve to die' in 'Epiphany', the turning point in the story when, having failed to get revenge on Judge Turpin, Todd decides to kill anyone and everyone. In the closing ballad, the *Dies Irae* theme returns in the accompaniment played by flute and oboe under Sweeney's lines 'What happens then, well that's the play, he wouldn't want to give it away'.

What should we make of this interpolation of a tune with clear religious origins and connotations, which is also referenced at other points in the score? Sondheim is on record as saying, 'I always found the *Dies Irae* moving and scary at the same time.'[30] *Sweeney Todd* is not the only work in which he quotes it—it is used as a cantus firmus at the beginning of 'Chrysanthemum Tea' in *Pacific Overtures*. It has, of course, been used as a symbol of death and retribution by numerous composers, perhaps most famously by Berlioz in his *Symphonie Fantastique*, described on a website which lists hundreds of such quotations, although strangely not Sondheim's, as 'the mother of all *dies irae* quotes'.[31] Its use in *Sweeney Todd* is surely primarily to reinforce the frightening and scary aspect of the theme of violent death, which underlies the whole story, rather than to convey any particular religious message.

Overall, it is difficult to discern significant religious influences or spiritual resonances in this show, which, aside from the love between Anthony and Johanna, is irredeemably black and despairing. We get an interesting insight into Sondheim's secularism in the debate that he apparently had with Hugh Wheeler, the British playwright brought in to shorten Christopher Bond's original play to make a lighter book, over how to handle Todd's transition from being 'a private murderer into a serial or public murderer'. According to Sondheim, 'Hugh wanted to have a religious reason, which I thought was not right, so I made up the whole thing and that took me about a month.'[32] Wheeler died in 1987, and I have not been able to find any clue as to what his 'religious reason' for Sweeney's change of direction might have been.

104   MUSIC OF THE NIGHT

Significantly, Sondheim rejected it, although the incorporation of the *Dies Irae* into the song 'Epiphany', which expresses this key turning point in the story could, I suppose, be taken as a suggestion of there being a religious dimension to Todd's consuming thirst for revenge.

It is instructive to make comparisons with *Les Misérables*. As originally presented to us, Sweeney Todd has considerable similarities with Jean Valjean. He has returned to London after spending fifteen years in prison, having been convicted by Judge Turpin on a trumped-up charge. Valjean is similarly consumed by hatred and bitterness following his release on parole after serving a nineteen-year-long prison sentence for stealing bread. But whereas Valjean is redeemed and turned around through his encounter with the Bishop of Digne, Todd remains embittered and becomes increasingly obsessed with revenge. This makes him very similar in outlook and character to Inspector Javert, who is motivated by a crude Old Testament idea of an eye for an eye and a tooth for a tooth. While Javert makes much of following the path of the righteous, Todd does not have recourse to similar Biblical quotations or themes, although we are told in the opening ballad that he 'served a dark and a vengeful God'.

Like Javert, Todd has no sense of forgiveness and no sense of remorse but just an obsessive pursuit of revenge, directed initially at Turpin and then at all humanity. Although he does concede in the closing ballad, after he has risen from the grave in his strange resurrection appearance, that 'to seek revenge may lead to hell', he displays no real remorse or contrition, even when he realizes that he has murdered his beloved wife, Lucy, who has been disguised as a beggar woman. This is something that troubled the directors of both the New York and London revivals, who sought to introduce a note of realization and repentance into what was otherwise a relentlessly bleak and nihilistic ending.

The most theologically charged scene in *Sweeney Todd* is that in which Judge Turpin sits in his house in his judicial clothes, clutching a Bible in his hand and asking God for forgiveness for the lecherous and possessive thoughts that he harbours towards Johanna in the next room. It begins with him singing the words of the *Confiteor*, or confession, in the Catholic Mass, '*Mea culpa, mea culpa, Mea maxima culpa*', and beseeching God to deliver and release him. The subsequent scene shows him alternately whipping and scourging himself and peering through the keyhole at Johanna. His attempts at self-purgation seem to have a strong sexual element. He ends up succumbing to his lusts and resolving to keep Johanna to himself for ever. Can we read this as a genuine, if ultimately failed, attempt to overcome carnal desires, set in the context of a battle between God and the Devil, the spirit and the flesh? There is no sense of God's presence in this scene, and certainly no sense of divine forgiveness or redemption for a character who comes across as a hypocrite and, like others in the musical, as essentially depraved and without redeeming features.

Unlike *Les Misérables*, there is no note of redemption in *Sweeney Todd*. Sondheim himself said of it, 'I wanted just to scare people', and the musical certainly has the shock factor of a horror film as well as the bleak darkness of film noir. It deals with sin and evil but not from a religious perspective. I concur with Ethan Mordden's view that 'It is Todd who frames the show's observation of evil, and he sees it as inherent in humankind, stopping short of the religious concept of a species corrupted by sinful creation.'[33] Religious feelings are equated with madness, as when the lunatics hint of judgment and resurrection in the chorus 'City on fire'. Expressions of Christian belief are generally treated in mocking and dismissive terms. When Anthony tells Todd that it would have been a poor Christian who would not have raised the alarm on seeing him tossing about on a raft, the barber responds, 'There's many a Christian would have done just that and not lost a wink's sleep for it'. Mrs Lovett's remark to Toby that 'God watches over us' is delivered with a cynical wink when more fresh pies arrive to satisfy the appetites of the hordes of customers singing 'God, that's good'.

There are undoubtedly religious references and undercurrents in *Sweeney Todd*, but they are invariably negative, certainly in respect of anything that might be said to come from the Judaeo-Christian tradition. There is, perhaps, a nod to paganism, as Ben Francis suggests in what I find to be a good summation of the musical's overall theme:

> *Sweeney Todd* shows a world where the function of God has been usurped by men. The opening ballad asks the rhetorical question: 'And what if none of their souls were saved?/They went to their maker impeccably shaved'. Todd 'served a dark and a hungry god', a pagan deity that lives on human flesh, not mercy.[34]

Into the Woods (1987)

This relatively late Sondheim show brings together many of his hallmark themes: the pervasive sense of longing and yearning expressed in the constantly repeated refrain 'I wish'; the symbolism of the woods as a place of

106 MUSIC OF THE NIGHT

darkness and confusion in which people get lost, as in the real world; and the message that we cannot remain as children but need to grow up and face the complexities and ambiguities of life.

For many Sondheim fans, *Into the Woods* does contain a significant spiritual message in its affirmation that if we are to face life's vicissitudes, we need to connect with one another and recognize our mutual dependence. It is hinted at in 'Side by side by side' from the much earlier *Company* but perhaps supremely expressed in the song 'No one is alone'. For Laurie Winer, here at last, Sondheim follows his mentor Oscar Hammerstein in spirit as well as in technique: ' "No One is Alone" is a spiritual companion to "You'll Never Walk Alone" from *Carousel*. In it, a lyricist known for wit and wordplay embraces the directness that was Hammerstein's hallmark, a trait Sondheim had always appreciated but not always emulated.'[35] I would not myself go as far as describing it as a 'spiritual companion' to Hammerstein's song. It does not have the same anthemic quality, although I suppose that, at a stretch, the line 'Someone is on your side' could be interpreted in a similar way to 'You'll never walk alone' as suggesting God's companionship.

But as with the rest of Sondheim, there is no religious underpinning or spiritual dimension here. Raymond Knapp perceptively notes of Lapine and Sondheim that 'their woods are to be without a moral compass, lacking especially the ready-made compass of religious devotion' and points out that the first of the two 'lessons' laid out in 'No One is Alone' is 'make no reference to religion, whether through prayer or the earthly authority of the church'. Knapp goes on to say that 'the show is entirely consistent with "secular Protestantism".'[36] I would say just secularism—I can't see any Protestantism there.

Martin Copenhaver's tribute

Stephen Sondheim is a hugely significant figure in the history of musical theatre, having reconfigured the genre in an essentially postmodern direction. For me, his abandonment of overarching metanarrative, moral compass and transcendent value represents its secularization. Yet I concede that there is that repeated refrain of longing and yearning and that conviction that we live in an imperfect world, which could both be construed as spiritual.

There are those whose own spiritual journeys have been helped and even shaped by exposure to Sondheim's shows. One such is the distinguished United Church of Christ pastor and academic, Martin Copenhaver, formerly senior minister of Wellesley Congregational Church in Wellesley, Massachusetts, and president of Andover Newton Theological School. Writing in *The Christian Century*, of which he is editor at large, in the aftermath of the composer's death, he admits that:

> Sondheim's disinterest in religion is reflected in his work. The only character who displays any religious sensibilities—not counting the priest who was baked into one of Mrs. Lovett's pies—is Henrik Egerman, the repressed and tortured seminarian in *A Little Night Music*.
>
> The only explicit reference to God in Sondheim's entire oeuvre is in *Merrily We Roll Along*, in which one embittered character sings: 'It's called flowers wilt,/It's called apples rot,/It's called thieves get rich and saints get shot./It's called God don't answer prayers a lot./Okay, now you know.' This verse, like countless others, demonstrates how far Sondheim departed from the kind of lyrics his mentor Oscar Hammerstein wrote a generation earlier.

Copenhaver goes on to praise Sondheim's 'deep and nuanced understanding of the human condition, particularly the dark side of life', which he attributes to his tough upbringing and his mother's lack of love for him. This, he argues, can illuminate the life of faith. What has specifically helped his own spiritual life is Sondheim's 'inescapable, poignant expressions of yearning'. Sometimes, they can be in the form of nostalgia, as in *Follies* or *Sunday in the Park with George*, but more often, 'the yearning Sondheim evinces is for something that is not yet—for justice, love, and human connection that are elusive'. He points especially to one of Sondheim's earliest songs, Tony's 'Something's coming' in *West Side Story*, with its opening line 'Could be, Who knows?'. For Copenhaver,

> Sondheim's expressions of yearning offer echoes of Augustine's famous prayer, 'Our heart is restless until it rests in you'. Our hearts are traced with yearning—for love, for connection, for the fragmented pieces of our lives to be gathered up into something whole.

108 MUSIC OF THE NIGHT

If Pascal is right that there is a God-shaped void at the heart of each of us, we often try to fill it with anything but God—but no one and nothing else can entirely fill it. And so, at the heart of us, there is yearning.

My spiritual life has been enhanced by having been immersed in this extraordinary artist's expressions of yearning. "God is the answer to the question implied in being," said Paul Tillich. I am grateful for Sondheim, who was able to articulate the question so powerfully.[37]

I am happy to end this chapter with that tribute to Stephen Sondheim's influence on one person's spiritual growth and development. It does not reflect my own experience—I remain as yet unconverted and continue to find in Sondheim cynical sophistication and secularism rather than spirituality. I readily concede, however, that the effect he has on others is very different. Maybe one day, I will see the light in his darkness and join their ranks.

Notes

1. Anonymous review forwarded to author in email 26 September 2022.
2. Meryle Secrest, *Stephen Sondheim: A Life* (London: Bloomsbury, 1999), 305.
3. Abigail Pogrebin, *Stars of David: Prominent Jews Talk About Being Jewish* (New York: Broadway Books, 2005), 114.
4. Lloyd Rose, 'Sunday in The Park: This One's No Picnic', *Washington Post*, 22 April 1997.
5. Secrest, *Stephen Sondheim*, 14.
6. Abigail Pogrebin, 'Stephen Sondheim on West Side Jews, Israel, and Cole Porter', *Tablet Magazine*, 30 November 2021.
7. Ethan Mordden, *On Sondheim: An Opinionated Guide* (New York: Oxford University Press, 2016), 1.
8. Letter from Hammerstein to Sondheim, 6 August 1953, in Mark Horowitz (ed.), *The Letters of Oscar Hammerstein II* (New York: Oxford University Press, 2022), 707.
9. Hugh Fordin, *Getting to Know Him: A Biography of Oscar Hammerstein II* (New York, Random House, 1977), 307.
10. Stephen Sondheim, 'The Art of the Musical', *Paris Review*, no. 142 (Spring 1997), 258–278.
11. Fordin, *Getting to Know Him*, 241.
12. Mark Steyn, *Broadway Babies Say Goodnight* (London: Faber & Faber, 1997), p.144.
13. Steve Swayne, *How Sondheim Found His Sound* (Ann Arbor, MI: University of Michigan Press, 2007), 145.
14. Stephen Citron, *Sondheim and Lloyd-Webber: The New Musical* (London: Chatto & Windus, 2001), 22.
15. Secrest, *Stephen Sondheim*, 406.
16. Peter Tonguette, 'Sondheim's Cynicism', *First Things* (February 2023), pp.7, 8, 9.
17. Robert McLaughlin, *Stephen Sondheim and the Reinvention of the American Musical* (Jackson: University Press of Mississippi, 2016), 65.
18. Clive Barnes, 'Company' Offers a Guide to New York's Marital Jungle', *New York Times*, 27 April 1970.
19. Sandor Goodhart, *Reading Stephen Sondheim* (London: Garland, 2000), 12.
20. McLaughlin, *Stephen Sondheim*, 49.
21. Secrest, *Stephen Sondheim*, 355.
22. Dietrich Bonhoeffer, *Life Together* (London: SCM Press, 1954), 15, 16.
23. Benjamin Francis, 'Careful the spell you cast: Disillusionment and maturity in the musical theatre of Stephen Sondheim' (PhD thesis, Goldsmiths College, University of London, 2019), 7.

GOD DON'T ANSWER PRAYERS A LOT 109

24. Lauren Phillips Fogelman, 'God is in the Details: Jewish and Spiritual values in the musicals of Stephen Sondheim', Lecture given on June 10, 2022 at Temple Israel of Northern Westchester Reform congregation, Croton, NY and posted on the web on 14 June 2022, https://www.tinw.org/cantors-blog.html?post_id=1328590.
25. 'Why do so many Jesuits love Stephen Sondheim? His art was a costly vocation', *America Magazine: The Jesuit Review of Faith & Culture*, 29 November 2021.
26. Raymond Knapp, *The American Musical and the Performance of Personal Identity* (Princeton, NJ: Princeton University Press, 2009), 61.
27. McLaughlin, *Stephen Sondheim*, 104.
28. Robert McLaughlin, 'No one is alone: Society and love in the musicals of Stephen Sondheim', *Journal of American Drama & Theatre* 3, no. 2 (Spring 1991), 35.
29. Secrest, *Stephen Sondheim*, 388.
30. Craig Zadan, *Sondheim & Co.* (London: Pavilion Books, 1987), 248.
31. 'Musical Quotations of the Dies Irae plainchant melody', https://diquotes.victoryvinny.com/quotes/, accessed 20 November 2023.
32. Secrest, *Stephen Sondheim*, 291.
33. Mordden, *On Sondheim*, 106.
34. Francis, 'Careful the spell you cast', 158.
35. Laurie Winer, *Oscar Hammerstein II and the Invention of the Musical* (New Haven, CT: Yale University Press, 2023), 36.
36. Knapp, *The American Musical*, 161.
37. Martin Copenhaver, 'Stephen Sondheim's Expressions of Yearning', *The Christian Century*, 138, no. 26, 29 December 2021.

6

The Reluctant Pilgrim

Stephen Schwartz

If one was to identify the practitioner of musical theatre in the second half of the twentieth century apparently most influenced by religion and with the most evidently religious portfolio of works, then it would surely be Stephen Schwartz with his Biblically based trinity of *Godspell*, *Children of Eden*, and *The Prince of Egypt*, together with the lyrics of Leonard Bernstein's *Mass*, and *The Hunchback of Notre Dame* with its significant religious references.

Yet Schwartz has always denied religious influences in his work. In keeping with the title of his first CD song album, *Reluctant Pilgrim*, produced in response to a challenge from a songwriter friend to stop hiding behind other characters and write about his own life and feelings, he insists, 'I have not chosen religious material. It has chosen me.'[1] Reluctant to discuss or disclose his own religious beliefs, he maintains that the appeal for him in the Bible stories and church liturgies that he has set lies not in their religious elements but in other aspects. He is also emphatic that 'I don't see my works as promulgating any particular religious philosophy.'[2]

Schwartz's upbringing was very similar to that of Stephen Sondheim—upper-middle-class New York secular Jewish. There were no religious influences in his childhood. As he himself puts it, 'I grew up in such a secular environment that when I went to grade school and heard the Pledge of Allegiance for the first time, I thought the phrase "under God" was another way of saying "beneath the sky".'[3] Both Stephens felt somewhat isolated at school and showed considerable early talent as classical musicians, and both developed a passion for musical theatre at a young age.

But there the similarities end. Schwartz's childhood was much happier than Sondheim's, his family more stable and loving. Perhaps because of this, the tone of his musicals is much more positive and idealistic, his lyrics more in the tradition of Oscar Hammerstein and his tunes considerably more lyrical and hummable. For me, he is both a more appealing and a more profound writer and composer.

Music of the Night. Ian Bradley, Oxford University Press. © Ian Bradley 2025.
DOI: 10.1093/9780197699775.003.0007

THE RELUCTANT PILGRIM   111

There is no doubt that in the case of his first major success, *Godspell* (1971), which is discussed in detail in Chapter 8, the religious influence came largely from his collaborator, John-Michael Tebelak, who wrote his musical retelling and dramatizing parables from the Gospel of Matthew from the perspective of a strong Christian faith, coupled with a profound disillusionment with the way Jesus' teachings were presented by the institutional church. For Schwartz, brought in to compose new tunes for the show, the motivation was different: 'I hadn't been brought up as a Christian, and so I was not someone coming in with reverence. I was coming in thinking if you're going to tell this story, how do you make it work?'[4] He has always insisted that for him, *Godspell* is about the characters and the formation of community rather than any deep theological questions. Yet, as we shall see, he ended up having a not insignificant input into its religious and spiritual character—and this was to become a feature of much of his later work.

The Bernstein *Mass* (1971)

Asked by John F Kennedy's widow, Jacqueline, for a piece to inaugurate the Kennedy Center for the Performing Arts in Washington, DC, Leonard Bernstein apparently decided to make it a Mass because JFK had been the first Roman Catholic US president. He got stuck with its structuring and composition and, rather than turning to Stephen Sondheim, with whom he had collaborated on *West Side Story*, he enlisted the help of the younger and less experienced Stephen Schwartz, who had just finished work on *Godspell* and was recommended to him by his sister Shirley. Schwartz has noted modestly that 'I mostly worked with him on shaping the dramatic structure'. He was, in fact, responsible for the numerous English lyrics interpolated into the traditional Latin text of the Roman Catholic Mass, which forms the core of the work.

Bernstein's *Mass* is essentially a piece of musical theatre rather than a liturgical work, as is clear from its description as a 'Theatre Piece for Singers, Players and Dancers'. It follows the order of the Mass exactly, but the liturgical passages are regularly interrupted with commentaries by the Celebrant and the congregation, expressing their religious doubts and concerns. The Celebrant is the central character in the drama. Initially, he displays a straightforward and pure faith, as indicated in his wish to 'sing God a simple song'. However, that faith gradually becomes unsustainable under the

112   MUSIC OF THE NIGHT

weight of human misery, corruption, and the trappings of worldly power. He finds everyone pinning their hopes on him, yet deep down, he is confused and scared. Eventually, it becomes clear that he is losing his mind and experiencing a severe crisis of faith, which culminates in him divesting himself of his robes, jumping onto the altar, and hurling the communion chalice onto the floor, where it smashes into pieces in a scene which Bernstein titled 'Fraction'. The Celebrant's breakdown is countered by the children in the congregation who quietly sing their own simple faith. Their chorus is taken up by the adults who sweep up the shattered shards of the chalice and look around themselves in search of their better natures. In the end, the Celebrant finds that the loneliness of his doubt is no match for the joy of gathering together with other believers in praise.

Mass is often taken to be an expression of Bernstein's own crisis of faith and a commentary on America's crisis of faith in the context of the Vietnam War and the civil rights movement. That is certainly how his daughter Jamie Bernstein interpreted it in a PBS programme in September 2021, and according to Carol de Giere, 'Bernstein wanted *Mass* to express an enduring interest of his: the difficulty of sustaining religious faith in seemingly inhumane times'.[5] For his part, Schwartz has told me that most of the lyrics that he wrote do not represent his own philosophy, having been written, as all his songs are, 'from the point of view of the various characters involved, and thus to have a variety of perspectives'. He does, however, say that 'The Word of the Lord', the Epistle section of the Mass, which is shared between the Celebrant and various members of the congregation and reflects on the creative power of God's word, which cannot be imprisoned, 'is one of the songs that actually fairly closely represents my own point of view'.[6] It has much about the persecution and opprobrium suffered by those who follow the Lord and contains an impassioned statement by a young man: 'We who love our brothers have crossed over to life, but they who do not love, abide in death'. In that song, the Celebrant references both 'forum' and 'follies', which Schwartz described to me as 'Easter eggs', paying tribute to Stephen Sondheim through the titles of two of his early shows.

Schwartz also says that there are two other songs 'that are closer to personal for me': 'World Without End', interpolated into the Credo section, which asks, 'Lord, don't you know it's the end of the World? Lord, don't you care if it all ends today?'; and the Celebrant's riff on the Lord's Prayer, 'I go on', in which he declares that 'the Age of God is dead'.[7] Speaking more broadly about *Mass*, Schwartz has said that 'some of the youthful spirit of *Godspell* influenced the piece and the character of the Celebrant that Lenny and I devised'.[8] This is difficult to discern, beyond perhaps the stipulation in the libretto that the Celebrant should be 'a young man in his mid-twenties dressed in blue jeans and a simple shirt'. There is a world of difference between the anguished, angry Celebrant and the happy, charismatic, clown-like Jesus in *Godspell*. Indeed, he is more similar to the angry, anguished Jesus of *Jesus Christ Superstar*. *Mass* lacks the innocence of *Godspell*, although it does in the end come down on the side of faith and trust, significantly expressed by the people rather than the priest, who comes to the conclusion that he is no different from any of the congregation and has no special authority or supernatural power. Bernstein himself described it as 'a celebration of life', and the *Washington Post* printed its opening night review on the front page under the headline: 'Bernstein's Mass: A Reaffirmation of Faith'.[9]

It is difficult to know quite what to make of this work. Is it a grotesque parody and mockery of the most sacred Christian ritual or an honest interpretation in which the liturgical niceties are interspersed with what people really think in a way which is truly incarnational, with its emphasis on the priesthood of all believers and acknowledgment of the reality of doubt? When it was first performed, many critics found *Mass* nasty, cheap, and vulgar. The Archbishop of Cincinnati called it 'blatant sacrilege'. Yet over the subsequent six decades, perhaps because of growing concern about the negative consequences of clericalism in the Roman Catholic Church, the reaction from both inside and outside the church has become more positive. A performance in David's Hall, Cardiff, in 2000 brought warm praise from the *Church Times* music critic Roderic Dunnett: 'It is a wonderful work: vibrant, alive, visceral, challenging; a piece about faith and trust, and disillusion, and trust (seemingly) betrayed . . . this may be let-it-all-hang-out Christianity, but it doesn't date. The problems were much the same for St Augustine, or Villon or Tippett or Tillich.' Dunnett's verdict was that overall, the Mass is 'theatre, perhaps, but Christian theatre'.[10] Reviewing a fiftieth-anniversary performance in the Kennedy Center in September 2022 for *Broadway World*, Alexander Kafka described it as 'a mad and maddening, flawed but hugely ambitious ecclesiastical fever dream'. He continued:

> Despairing not just over war and environmental degradation but also pretension and sanctimony, it is sometimes more than a little pretentious and sanctimonious itself . . . The Catholic Church blasted the work and then years later embraced it. That combined reaction seems like the right one—a love-hate response to a love-hate Mass that is at once mocking, maudlin, and devotional.[11]

114   MUSIC OF THE NIGHT

I am not going to engage in a detailed analysis of *Pippin* (1972), Schwartz's next musical, because its central message seems to me more psychological than spiritual. Pippin has to learn to curb his self-destructive urge, settle down to a simple life and realize that he has to stop his restless quest for fulfilment in order to find true fulfilment. For Schwartz, 'this is a struggle all of us face in our lives: when to settle and what to settle for. On the one hand, you don't want to stop striving and experimenting, growing and trying to improve yourself. On the other hand, you don't want to spin your wheels so that ultimately you get nowhere.'[12]

Children of Eden (1991)

A fairly straight retelling of the stories contained in the first nine chapters of Genesis, from the creation of the world to God's covenant with Noah following the flood, *Children of Eden* has the strongest religious references and resonances of any of Schwartz's works and takes its place alongside other great Biblically based musicals like *Jesus Christ Superstar* and *Godspell*. For me, it is his best musical by quite a way (he was responsible for lyrics and music), both for its original and nuanced approach to the subject matter and for its score, which provides an exuberant mixture of soft rock, vaudeville, blues, gospel, and calypso, in some ways reminiscent of *Godspell* and *Joseph and His Amazing Technicolor Dreamcoat*, but with its own distinctive feel. Significantly, it is the only one of Schwartz's shows where he took the initiative in pursuing an idea when it was first suggested to him rather than simply agreeing to an offer to be involved in an ongoing project. In that respect, it is the closest of all his works to being his own baby.

The original conception for the show came from Charles Lisanby, scenic designer for the annual Christmas spectacular at Radio City Music Hall. He envisaged a pageant called 'The Glory of Creation' based on the Biblical book of Genesis to be staged at the Crystal Cathedral near Disneyland in Garden Grove, California, where he had staged Easter and Christmas pageants. Lisanby was struck by televised talks by Joseph Campbell, the scholar of mythology and comparative religion, about the way that young people brought up in a world of discipline and obedience have to learn to be independent, transcending their early dependence and becoming self-responsible. For Lisanby, this became a dominant theme in the book that he wrote for the musical, which he re-titled *Family Tree*, emphasizing the theme of intergenerational tensions and conflicts. In his words, 'It started with God having

THE RELUCTANT PILGRIM   115

a problem with Adam, or Adam having a problem with his Father' and went on to explore Adam's relationship with Cain and Noah's issues with Japheth.

It was this aspect of Lisanby's book, and of the Genesis story more broadly, that appealed to Schwartz. He has told me that he saw it as 'a story about families, the relationships between parents and children, and generational conflict, not a story about religion'.[13] He certainly made much of this theme in the lyrics and music that he wrote for the show, not least in the wonderfully infectious calypso style number 'Generations' which opens Act 2 and has the chorus bellowing out that distinctive and ubiquitous Biblical word 'begat' with its connotations of one generation following another. It is also emphasized by the double casting that has the same actors playing both Adam and Noah, Eve and Mrs Noah, Cain and Japheth, Abel and Ham, and Seth and Sham. In a fuller explanation of his attraction to Lisanby's subject matter and approach, quoted in Carol de Giere's biography, Schwartz says that it 'had themes I've always liked: personal freedom versus authority, the quest for self-definition in a universe without definition, and parent–child relationships, in particular those between father and son'.[14]

Family Tree was first performed in the summer of 1986 at Youth Sing Praise, an annual musical event in Belleville, Illinois, which had been established four years earlier to bring young people from every Roman Catholic diocese in the United States together to learn and perform new liturgical music. Following *Godspell*, Schwartz had been approached by the organizers, the Oblates of Mary Immaculate at the National Shrine of Our Lady of the Snows, to write a new religious choral piece. He offered *Family Tree*, with its cast of Old Testament characters and a large choir fulfilling the role of a classical Greek chorus. So, for all his protestations about its non-religious nature, the show that would become *Children of Eden* effectively began life as a Christian musical.

When Radio City Music Hall turned down *Family Tree*, Schwartz and Lisanby decided to abandon thoughts of a Broadway opening and try it out in London's West End instead. To this end, they brought in John Caird, the British theatre director who had co-directed Cameron Mackintosh's original London production of *Les Misérables* and was at the time directing its first US national tour. Caird proved to be very much more than a director. He substantially re-wrote Lisanby's original book and changed the show's title from *Family Tree* to *Children of Eden*. He brought to it not just his considerable theatrical experience but an inherited familiarity with the Bible from his father, George Caird, an English Congregational minister and formidable Biblical scholar, who had ended his distinguished academic career as

116 MUSIC OF THE NIGHT

Dean Ireland's Professor of the Exegesis of Holy Scripture at the University of Oxford.

One of the most important changes introduced by Caird was a significant alteration in the characterization of God. In Lisanby's original *Family Tree*, God made his presence known through thunderclaps and was an off-stage voice. Caird insisted that an on-stage actor should appear in the role. In his words, 'In the mediaeval mystery plays, God was always a character who came on and related to the other characters—even chatting with the audience. He was always played by an ordinary working man. Our God derived from the same idea.'[15] Schwartz has echoed this, insisting that he approached God as he would any other character, as a person rather than as a type or historical figure. He is called 'Father' in the musical and there is an emphasis on his relationship with his first son, Adam, as well as with his broader family of children. John Caird told me: 'Curiously enough, as I was writing the character of Father, I found myself writing as if my own father was speaking. It just came out that way. Not that my dad was an authoritarian patriarch, quite the opposite, but he talked in the same short sentences, with lots of space for ironic interpretation between the lines.'[16]

Although there is a human side to the God of *Children of Eden*, there is also a deeper portrayal of His divine character, which, consciously or unconsciously, introduces some significant theological concepts. As re-worked by Schwartz and Caird, the musical begins with the chorus singing the opening words of Genesis: 'In the beginning, God created the Heaven and Earth'. God appears, and His first words are 'Let there be', indicating both a generous creativity and also an openness to its consequences. He is portrayed as having just woken up from a dream of a perfect garden with whirling shapes and swirling sounds and, indeed, as dreaming the world into creation. This rather attractive presentation of the idea that, in the beginning, it was not so much the word as the dream, which is accompanied by the repeated refrain 'Let there be, let there be', has certain similarities with the portrayal of Aslan singing the world into existence in C.S. Lewis' Narnia tale *The Magician's Nephew* (1955). Caird confirms that 'Lewis' Narnia was certainly a source for us'.[17]

One of the key aspects of God's dream of creation is His realization that 'I wasn't lonely any more'. He sings that by creating a world teeming with all sorts of vibrant, living forces and beings, He will still His own hunger and fill His emptiness. He comes back to this theme again several times, perhaps most movingly in His song 'Father's Day' when He sings of the children He has created in His own image: 'They will keep me company, they will keep me young'. There is a profound sense here of divine loneliness being the first cause of the creation of the world. This is accompanied by a suggestion that God gives away something of Himself in order to create, making space for others to live and flourish in what is essentially an act of self-sacrifice, withdrawal and humility. This is expressed in the scene in which Adam and Eve are expelled from the Garden of Eden, where God says, 'All that I had to give, I gave to you'.

There are distinct echoes here of the notion of *zimzum*, God's withdrawal into Himself to make space for creation, found in the kabbalistic Jewish tradition as described by Rabbi Lionel Blue: 'Before God created the universe, He abandoned a part of himself to leave an emptiness in which we and the world could exist in freedom'[18] This idea was taken up by the twentieth-century Reformed theologian, Jürgen Moltmann, who has written:

> God 'withdraws himself from himself to himself' in order to make creation possible. His creative activity outwards is preceded by this humble divine self restriction ... God does not create merely by calling something into existence, or by setting something afoot. In a more profound sense he creates by letting be, by making room, and by withdrawing himself.[19]

This notion of creation as a sacrifice, initiated by God partly in response to His own loneliness and involving a fundamentally generous and self-giving 'letting be', is explored in much more detail in my book *The Theology of Sacrifice*. It may not have been explicit in the mind of Stephen Schwartz, but it is surely suggested in his repeated use of the phrase 'let there be' and in the way that he emphasizes the risk God takes in giving His human creatures free will. It also reflects input from his collaborator John Caird, drawing on his father's Biblical and theological scholarship.

Caird himself has told me that the most important element that he developed from ideas he had discussed with his father before his death in 1984 was that of the silence of God:

> If God is an all-caring and all-loving father to his children, why is he so relentlessly silent in the face of such obvious global suffering? For Stephen and myself, this became the central dramatic destination for the events of the second act of *Children of Eden*. The final song makes it clear to characters and audiences alike that they will not be hearing from God

118   MUSIC OF THE NIGHT

again. Rather, they must take responsibility for the world they are living in and all the creatures with whom they share it.

Stephen and I were a little worried that such a strong statement would stop people of faith wanting to perform the show. But the opposite happened. They took on the show as if it belonged to them and perform it as if the character of Father is their own actively living deity.[20]

In many ways, this conception of God anticipates His characterization as 'the great allower' by Richard Rohr, the American Franciscan priest and writer on spirituality, in his book *The Immortal Diamond*. Rohr sees God as almost being too generous in stepping back from creation, letting us make our own mistakes and not wanting to control anything. There are other suggestions of quite sophisticated theological ideas in Caird and Schwartz's portrayal of Father/God. The song 'Father's Day' hints at maternal as well as paternal feelings about God's children and suggests divine motherhood as well as paternity, which we have already encountered in Oscar Hammerstein's Unitarian Universalist-inspired writing. There is also an interesting take on the Biblical idea of humans being created in the image of God. In 'Father's Day', God explicitly states that He is passing on His genes to His children. They are more than His creatures, being directly related and in some senses His own flesh and blood. There is a hint here of the neo-platonic emanationist theology developed by the ninth-century philosopher John Scotus Eurigena, which sees all creation as flowing directly out of God's very being and eventually returning there. Alongside a clear statement of the Thomist idea of the pleroma, or fullness, of creation, expressed in the song 'The Naming', which enumerates all the creatures beginning with an 'a', there is also an emphasis on the special place of human beings, a little lower than the angels and uniquely bearing the imprint of God's image.

Characteristically, as ever wanting to play down the theological and religious resonances of his work, Schwartz himself has focused in his reflections on this work on the more human side of Father's relations with His children, although in this revealing remark on his website, he does concede a religious element in the development in God's character:

The only time I have used God as an onstage character in any of my shows is the character of Father in CHILDREN OF EDEN. In that work, because the Bible story is used as a metaphor for a story of dysfunctional families and how the problems of one generation are perpetuated by the next, the

THE RELUCTANT PILGRIM   119

character of Father begins as the Old Testament jealous and vengeful God, and then changes during the course of the show to the more forgiving and loving God of contemporary religious belief. But he is depicted in that show more as an autocratic Father who learns to let his children go than as 'God' per se.[21]

In fact, the character of God was further changed by Schwartz and Caird between the original London production in 1991 and subsequent North American productions. They continued to make much of His relations with Adam and to portray Him in human family terms as a parent struggling with recalcitrant children. But they further emphasized the transition towards a more forgiving, understanding Father, as suggested by Schwartz above in his analysis of the difference between the Act 1 and Act 2 portrayals. This change of character was similarly reflected in Noah, who also became a gentler and more understanding father to his sons. The song 'The Hardest Part of Love', originally written as a solo for Noah, was changed to be a duet for Father and Noah. It is a clear statement of the Judaeo-Christian idea of free will as the supreme gift of God with all its attendant risks. God sings that the one thing that His children most treasure is to make their own mistakes and that the hardest part of love is letting go. This is echoed by Noah, and so we come back to the theme of 'letting be' with all its kenotic, self-giving, sacrificial overtones.

This is far from being the only religious message in *Children of Eden*. It is not just Father and Noah who have the theological punchlines. Schwartz makes much of the character of Eve as an independent thinker. In her solo, 'The spark of creation', she sings about the need to be curious, to discover, and to express her questioning nature, traits that later show up in her son, Cain. This vibrant anthem introduces and explains the theme of the fall as being all about making choices. As God says to Adam, 'Where there is choice, there is pain'. Eve, who, like God, is portrayed as something of a dreamer, also sings the show's title song, 'Children of Eden', in which she laments the loss of an innocence that cannot be regained. This theme is picked up after her death when Noah asks his children, 'Can we give Eden back to you?'. The whole musical is suffused with yearning for the lost Eden of primal innocence and purity and the sense felt by each succeeding generation that they owe their children an apology for having fouled things up and handed over a more tainted world than they themselves inherited.

Overall, *Children of Eden* provides a fascinating and richly nuanced take on the key Biblical themes of creation and the fall. Resolution and

120   MUSIC OF THE NIGHT

redemption come not through Christ but through an acceptance by Noah, and, indeed, by God, that their children must be free to make up their own minds, lead their own lives, and let be. It also comes through the sacrificial actions of Yonah, a descendent of Cain and servant of Noah, who falls in love with Japheth and becomes his wife. She is the one character not found in the Bible and totally invented by Schwartz and Caird. In answering a question which I put to him about viewing the show through the prism of a Christian musical, Schwartz shared a thought about her which he said had never occurred to him before:

> Yonah is actually a Christ figure—the outcast who is willing to sacrifice herself to save the rest of humanity. In *Children of Eden*, she doesn't actually die, but in her speech to Father before she sends out the dove, John Caird wrote this dialogue for her: 'If it will save the ark, I'll drown myself in the flood'. And at the critical moment, it is her interposing herself between Japheth and Ham that changes the actions of the other characters from vengeance to forgiveness.[22]

This sacrificial element provides a Christian undercurrent, which is also present in the understanding of free will both as God's great gift and as the great burden for humans to bear, leading to sin, alienation, and the loss of innocence. There is, too, an emphasis on the importance of forgiveness. The final number, entitled in a rather Sondheimian touch, 'In the beginning', has the children of Eden asking their own children for forgiveness and Father/ God singing:

> There is no journey gone so far,
> So far we cannot stop and change direction.
> No doom is written in the stars.

This comes very close to the classic Christian message of redemption and forgiveness, whereby there is always the possibility of wiping the slate clean and of a fresh start and a new beginning. There are shades here too of Hammerstein, as critic Chris Gladden saw when he wrote of 'Schwartz's brand of open-armed optimism and sense of brotherhood'.[23] For all Schwartz's insistence that it is not at root a religious work, *Children of Eden* has considerable theological depth. Peter Filichia described it in the *New Jersey Star-Ledger* as 'one of the most intelligent and profound musicals ever written'.[24] I agree.

The Hunchback of Notre Dame (1996)

There are clear spiritual resonances in the two Disney animated musicals for which Stephen Schwartz provided the lyrics and Alan Menken the music in the mid-1990s. In a paper given to the American Academy of Religion in 1998, Donald Fadner sees both *Pocahontas* and *The Hunchback of Notre Dame* as offering an 'alternative' religious vision to that of Disney's conservative Christian critics, with 'the first of these films articulating a generalized spirituality, loosely based on Native American animism, which was given a Christian setting and presentation in the second'.[25]

I am going to focus on *The Hunchback of Notre Dame* as it is particularly replete with religious references and allusions. In his book, *The Gospel According to Disney*, Mark Pinsky describes it as 'the first Disney feature to put traditional religious faith—in this case, pre-Reformation Catholicism—at the centre of the narrative'. He goes on to say that 'it would be difficult to find a more thoroughly Christian film, one which stands the devoutly anti-clerical novelist Victor Hugo, the author of the book on which it is based, on his head' and to note that belief in a loving, forgiving God anchors the story, that the words 'God' and 'Lord' are spoken and sung more frequently than in all previous animated Disney features combined, and that 'there are crosses everywhere'.[26]

The religious element in this musical is clearly evident in the treatment of Claude Frollo, the bigoted zealot who is the Archdeacon of Notre Dame in Victor Hugo's original novel but made into the Minister of Justice in the movie musical because of Disney's concern about Roman Catholic reaction to having a priest as the arch-villain. In the song 'Hellfire', Frollo obsesses over the gipsy Esmerelda, much like Judge Turpin does over Johanna in *Sweeney Todd*, but if anything in an even more evil and frenzied way. He is determined that if he is not to have her, she will die in the fires of hell. The song begins with monks chanting '*Confiteor Deo*', the beginning of the Confession in the Latin Mass, and their chanted lines of Latin liturgy continue to punctuate it. Frollo frames the song as a prayer addressed to *Beata Maria*, the Blessed Virgin Mary, and asks God to have mercy on him and on Esmerelda, but the overall impression is of someone consumed with lust and hatred. There is an interesting theological observation contained in Frollo's line that it is not his fault if, in God's plan, 'He made the Devil much stronger than a man'.

Stephen Schwartz has described Frollo both as 'probably the most despicable human being in anything I've done' and also as his favourite creation: 'I

122   MUSIC OF THE NIGHT

love him as a character. He was so totally self-justifying and in such denial of his own true motives. It was really fun to go to dark places in myself I would never let myself do in real life.'[27] 'Hellfire' thus stands as his own deepest and darkest expression of the music of the night. It can also, perhaps, be read as a portrayal of the hypocrisy and evil found at the heart of the institutional church, where sexual longings and abuse are sublimated and covered up by fierce judgmentalism. Schwartz was surprised that Disney did not ask him to tone down the song's lyrics, although the original visual depiction of Frollo's fantasies of Esmerelda was re-animated to make it less overtly sexual.

Quasimodo's song 'Heaven's light' was written as a deliberate counterpart to 'Hellfire'. In it, the hunchback uses religious imagery to describe the experience of being in love. He sings of an angel smiling on him and touching his face so that he experiences the glow of heaven's light.

The clearest articulation of religious belief in *The Hunchback of Notre Dame* comes in Esmerelda's anthem, 'God help the outcasts'. Sung as the gipsy girl gazes at a statue of the Virgin Mary and baby Jesus, it is couched in the form of a prayer to a deity whom the gipsy is not even sure is there and whom she asks in a highly significant line: 'Were you once an outcast too?'. It is tempting to take this as a Christological reference to Jesus, the one who is despised and rejected and lives his life on the margins among tax collectors and sinners before being condemned to die on a cross. It could also be taken as an allusion to the loneliness of God, as explored at the beginning of *Children of Eden*. Esmerelda's song goes on to ask for blessing from God and the angels and to make its central heartfelt plea: 'Please help my people, The poor and down-trod, I thought we all were children of God'. Like 'God save the people', the Chartist hymn in *Godspell*, and 'Do you hear the people sing?' in *Les Misérables*, 'God help the outcasts' could easily be transported from the screen to the sanctuary and serve as an anthem invoking divine favour and mercy on the oppressed and marginalized.

The Prince of Egypt (1998)

When he was approached by DreamWorks to provide both lyrics and music for a projected animated film entitled 'The Ten Commandments', Schwartz was hesitant as he felt he had done enough Bible-based musicals. However, when the project was changed to major on the life of Moses and his role in leading the people of Israel out of slavery, with the title *The Prince of Egypt*,

THE RELUCTANT PILGRIM   123

he agreed as he felt this allowed him to focus on a particular character. 'What was interesting to me', he wrote, 'was finding the personal, human story that we can all in some way relate to. It can be a metaphor, in some way, for all our lives'.[28]

Before any artwork existed or the film had been fully planned, Schwartz set to work on what he felt must be the opening number, 'Deliver us':

> Almost as soon as I heard that we were doing *The Prince of Egypt*, I knew how to do the opening. It seemed to me so obvious that if this whole show was going to be about somebody changing his entire life in order to deliver these people from bondage, we had to feel what the bondage was like ... we really had to experience it emotionally.[29]

His inspiration for the song came from a scene that he recalled from the epic Cecil B. DeMille film *The Ten Commandments*, which he had seen as an eight-year-old in 1956. He had been particularly struck by an incident in the film in which Moses' mother caught her garment between stone blocks being manoeuvred by Hebrew slaves while Egyptian guards stood looking on heedless of the fact she could be crushed to death. 'Deliver us' begins with the Egyptian guards exhorting the Hebrew slaves to work harder and faster in their back-breaking task of turning mud, sand, and water into bricks. It then becomes a chorus of slaves praying directly to God (referenced as Elohim) for deliverance, in many ways reminiscent of the opening chorus 'Look down' sung by the chain gang of prisoners in *Les Misérables*, even down to the similar descending chords towards the end.

Described as 'the first spiritual animated film', *The Prince of Egypt* had the prominent conservative evangelical preacher Jerry Falwell, co-founder of the Moral Majority, as one of a large team of Christian and Jewish religious advisors. Schwartz did considerable research before writing his lyrics, going on a field trip to Egypt, where he explored Cairo, sailed up the Nile, and travelled through the Sinai Desert, as well as visiting temples, tourist sites, and 'the crummy little towns with the kind of ancient tenements where the Hebrews would have lived'.[30] He included authentic Hebrew verses in several of the songs.

Two key songs with strong religious and spiritual resonances caused Schwartz some headaches in their conception and composition. The first was 'Through heaven's eyes', which is sung by Jethro, the priest of Midian and father-in-law of Moses. Both Schwartz and the directors felt that a song was

124   MUSIC OF THE NIGHT

needed to cover the period of around twenty years which Moses had spent in the Midian desert in Sinai after leaving behind his early life as a prince. It would locate his character in the wider context of the Exodus and move from the particular to the universal. In Schwartz's words:

> We needed to take a human passage of time and give it a huge philosophical context. A man spends twenty years becoming part of a tribe, falling in love, taking a wife, et cetera. But these very human events needed a broader context. This was great to think about from a theoretical point of view, but I had no clue what to do.[31]

He tried out various approaches and drafted four different versions of the song, which would reflect Moses' change of status and set up his role in leading the Exodus. None of them worked. Then Steve Hickner, the film's co-director, showed Schwartz an anonymous poem entitled 'Measure of a Man'. This gave him the inspiration that he needed:

> What I did was take the poem and translate the idea into 'Midianease'. I basically took the idea that the measure of a man is not what he owns or how much he's worth monetarily but how much he gives to other people. Then I translated it with images that were appropriate to that tribe—stones on top of a mountain, or water in the desert, or tending a sheep. All the imagery of the song is appropriate to the life of that tribe. So, all the metaphors that they use are things that they know in life.[32]

Although Schwartz characteristically describes this song as having an essentially philosophical meaning, it is actually profoundly theological. The key theme of the song, a power ballad with a strange little 'lai-la-lai' chorus, which could have come straight from *Fiddler on the Roof*, is the need to look at your life, not through human eyes but through heaven's eyes. This message, with its very clear religious connotations, is repeated three times in the text.

There is even more theology in the stand-out hit song in *The Prince of Egypt*, 'When you believe', a soft rock number about miracles sung by Miriam and Tzipporah. According to Steve Hickner, the inspiration for this song came when he and Schwartz were riding out to St Catherine's Monastery at the foot of Mount Sinai.

THE RELUCTANT PILGRIM   125

What we discussed was to try to create a signature song that would be both the anthem for the Hebrews as well as for the entire movie. We also discussed that it would be great if it could accomplish all that and end up being an anthem of sorts for DreamWorks as well, the way 'When you wish upon a star' is for Disney.[33]

Schwartz wanted to make a transition in the song from the mournful lament of the Hebrew slaves to their triumph at the end. He felt that this could best be expressed by using Hebrew lyrics:

I called one of the religious advisors on the project, Rabbi Robbins in Los Angeles, and asked him if he knew of any Hebrew poetry that might be appropriate. He suggested the song of the sea, which the Hebrew tribes were supposed to have sung after they crossed over the sea of reeds. He thought it would be alright if I used some of the words for the beginning of the Exodus, and I selected the ones I thought were most appropriate for the situation, and then set them to music, trying to use a simple folk like melody.[34]

So in the middle of Miriam and Tipporah's song, a children's chorus sings in Hebrew the words from Exodus 15.1: 'I will sing to the Lord, for He has triumphed gloriously'. Their singing gets faster and faster, ending in a wonderfully exuberant and joyous rhythmic chant.

Several quite profound theological questions are raised in this signature song. Miriam's opening lines, 'Many nights we've prayed/ With no proof anyone could hear', introduce the idea of the absent or unresponsive God, so prevalent in the poetry of the Welsh Anglican priest, R.S. Thomas. They also raise the vexed question of unanswered prayer, to which Tsipporah returns in her solo verse when she reflects that 'prayer so often proved in vain'. Interestingly, it was not these potentially troubling theological speculations about God which disturbed the more conservative Christian advisers involved in vetting the film but rather the line that Schwartz wrote proclaiming 'you can work miracles when you believe'. They objected to it on the grounds that only God can work miracles. He told me:

I was asked to change it to something like 'God will work miracles when you believe', and needless to say, I declined for both aesthetic and philosophical reasons. But ultimately it was so important to DreamWorks to

126   MUSIC OF THE NIGHT

have the imprimatur of approval from these religious leaders, or at least not have them urge their followers to boycott the film as had happened with other films in the past, that I acceded to the request to change the line and came up with the more innocuous 'There can be miracles when you believe'.[35]

He has said that this was the only occasion when he has ever been subjected to religious censorship. He refused to change a later line in the song, 'Who knows what miracles you can achieve', and somehow got away with it.

What is fascinating is the way that Stephen Schwartz enters so fully into the Biblical story of the Exodus in *The Prince of Egypt*, just as he had with the story of the creation in *Children of Eden*, while seeing both essentially as philosophical and ethical rather than religious or theological. Carol de Giere quotes him as saying, 'I like thinking about the larger issues that are contained in shows like *Children of Eden* and *The Prince of Egypt*—about the ethical and philosophical issues that concern me and others. I'm interested in the themes in those pieces'.[36] Although, in my reading at least, he actually engages in his lyrics with some of the knottier theological and religious issues raised in these stories, he himself, true to his stance as the Reluctant Pilgrim, sees these elements as something of a barrier and impediment. He writes on his website that doing religious subjects decreases audience appeal because 'many people just don't want to see something about religion' and that 'there is no question in my mind that, despite the relative popularity of *The Prince of Egypt*, it would have been a far more successful film commercially, given its quality, if it had been about something else'.[37]

Wicked (2003)

When it comes to Stephen Schwartz's mega-hit musical, I have to say that for once I am with him in not finding spiritual or religious themes prominent. It is much more about social and cultural paradigms and stereotypes. Students taking my classes on the spirituality and theology of musical theatre beg to differ. They have sought to persuade me that *Wicked* does have religious themes and messages, among them the motif of revelation by which hidden things become revealed, the suggestion that worldly perception does not grasp the truth, and the overarching sense of destiny and figuring out

THE RELUCTANT PILGRIM   127

what you are meant to be. They also point to the possible God-like character of The Wizard.

Elphaba could, I suppose, be said to have a kind of spiritual persona, as an outsider who is somehow changed and transfigured. Schwartz has written of his own identification with her:

> Anyone who is an artist in our society is going to identify with Elphaba. Anyone who is of an ethnic minority, who is black or Jewish or gay, or a woman feeling she grew up in a man's world, or anyone who grew up feeling a dissonance between who they are inside and the world around them, will identify with Elphaba.[38]

I struggle to find any deep religious or spiritual themes in the show's signature song, 'Defying gravity'. Although it is about being changed, this is not conceived in terms of the metanoia of religious conversion. Its central message that everyone deserves the chance to fly is, rather, expressed in broad humanistic terms. For me, *Wicked* stands apart from much of Schwartz's other work in not having strong religious resonances.

Stephen Schwartz continues to maintain his lifetime's refusal to discuss his own religious beliefs. Perhaps the nearest he has come to hinting at them is in a response on his website to an impassioned and committed Catholic questioner who accuses him of relativism and argues that 'Without God, without a recognition of transcendent Truth and Reality, talking about morals and personal responsibility and what's right and wrong becomes nothing more than vague speculation and opinion, subject to whim, fads, and worse: New Age rubbish'. Schwartz replies:

> You are quite right that I don't discuss my own personal religious views, and I will continue to refrain from doing so. However, I strongly disagree with your contention that belief in God is a requirement for strongly held and valid ethical philosophies. Nor is a moral philosophy that is not based on belief in a Supreme Being necessarily 'new age' or relativistic. I cite, for instance, the existentialists, or going much further back in history, the Greek philosophers. I am not saying that I necessarily agree with them but I don't think their way of looking at the world was any less valid than, say, Thomas Aquinas'. And it is certainly empirically true that the followers of the non-religious philosophers have caused a great deal less bloodshed,

128 MUSIC OF THE NIGHT

cruelty, and violence throughout history than the followers of Jehovah, Jesus, or Allah.

I can think of other philosophies which do not acknowledge the existence of a deity per se but have proven valid for millions of people, specifically those of the Asian philosophies of Confucianism and Buddhism. While I'm not a big fan of the conservatism and rigid class structure of Confucianism, I do like a lot of what Buddhism has to say.[39]

This is probably as near as the Reluctant Pilgrim is going to come to making a personal confession of faith. Buddhism appeals, it seems. So perhaps does Greek philosophy. His extraordinarily empathetic and nuanced treatment of stories from the Hebrew Bible in *Children of Eden* and *The Prince of Egypt* suggests that there is also a residual identification with Judaism and its foundational stories and legends. What is undeniable is the existence of a genuine spiritual and religious awareness, which has shown itself again and again in Stephen Schwartz's work, however unconscious it may be and however reluctant he may be to acknowledge it.

Notes

1. Email to the author, 2 July 2002.
2. Stephen Schwartz, *Comments about Religion as It Relates to musicals like Godspell, Children of Eden, The Prince of Egypt, and Bernstein's Mass*, from the archive of the StephenSchwartz. com Forum, 2, https://stephenschwartz.com/wp-content/uploads/2017/05/SchwartzOnRelig ion.pdf.
3. Schwartz, *Comments about Religion*, 4.
4. Carol de Giere, *The Godspell Experience* (Bethel, CT: Scene 1 Publishing, 2014), 78.
5. Carol de Giere, *Defying Gravity: The Creative Career of Stephen Schwartz* (New York: Applause, 2008), 71.
6. Email to the author, 28 January 2024.
7. Ibid.
8. De Giere, *Defying Gravity*, 71.
9. *Washington Post*, 9 September 1971.
10. 'Blatant Bernstein', *Church Times*, 2 June 2000, 28.
11. *Broadway World*, 16 September 2022.
12. De Giere, *Defying Gravity*, 103.
13. Email to author, 2 July 2002.
14. De Giere, *Defying Gravity*, 205.
15. Ibid., 213.
16. Email to the author, 16 February 2024.
17. Ibid.
18. Lionel Blue, *Blue Heaven* (London: Coronet, 1987), 27.
19. Jürgen Moltmann, *God in Creation* (London: SCM Press, 1985), 88.
20. Email to the author, 16 February 2024.
21. Schwartz, *Comments about Religion*, 3.
22. Email to the author, 28 January 2024.
23. '"Children of Eden": A stylish, entertaining look at Genesis', *Roanoke Times*, 30 November 1991.
24. De Giere, *Defying Gravity*, 222.

THE RELUCTANT PILGRIM   129

25. Donald Fadney, 'Disney gets religion', conference paper from 1998 national convention of the American Academy of Religion, Orlando, Florida, posted in June 2020, https://www.researchg ate.net/publication/342182716_DISNEY_GETS_RELIGION.
26. Mark Pinsky, *The Gospel According to Disney* (Louisville, KY: Westminster John Knox Press, 2004), 167.
27. De Giere, *Defying Gravity*, 245.
28. Ibid., 252.
29. Ibid., 253.
30. Ibid., 256.
31. Ibid., 259–60.
32. Ibid., 260.
33. Ibid., 262.
34. Ibid., 262.
35. Email to the author, 23 September 2003.
36. De Giere, *Defying Gravity*, 262.
37. Schwartz, *Comments about Religion*, 1.
38. De Giere, *Defying Gravity*, 275.
39. Schwartz, *Comments about Religion*, 5.

7

Spiritual yearning and
High Church aesthetics

Andrew Lloyd Webber

At first sight, it may be difficult to discern an obvious spiritual element in either the life or work of Andrew Lloyd Webber, the man who almost single-handedly moved the centre of gravity in musical theatre from the United States to the United Kingdom and who has been a dominant figure in the genre on both sides of the Atlantic for the last half-century. Undeniably gifted as a composer, producer, and impresario, he has been dubbed the King Midas of Musicals.

Yet dig below the surface and there are clear religious influences and spiritual resonances in the work of the composer of *Evita*, *Cats*, and *The Phantom of the Opera*. His father, William (Bill) Lloyd Webber, was a serious church musician, organist at one of London's foremost Anglo-Catholic churches and at the 'cathedral' of English Methodism, and composer of religious cantatas and oratorios. Young Andrew grew up steeped in the Anglican choral tradition and developed an early passion for churches and ecclesiastical architecture. He won a scholarship at Westminster School on the basis of an essay on how Victorian 'improvements' associated with the Gothic Revival improved medieval church architecture and an exhibition to read history at Oxford University by impressing the medieval history tutor at his chosen college with his knowledge of the date and details of the nave of Westminster Abbey. He has written about seeking solace and inspiration by visiting churches, sometimes just to be on his own in an empty sanctuary and at others for the characteristically Anglican service of Choral Evensong. Disturbed at finding so many churches locked, he set up the Open Churches Trust to assist congregations to keep their buildings open for several hours a day so that others could experience the sense of spiritual peace that he finds in them. His earliest musicals had religious themes—the life of the Christian philanthropist Dr Thomas Barnardo and the Biblical stories of Joseph and

Music of the Night. Ian Bradley, Oxford University Press. © Ian Bradley 2025.
DOI: 10.1093/9780197699775.003.0008

the passion of Christ, and he returned to spiritual themes in two later shows, *Whistle Down the Wind*, about the possible return of Jesus during a religious revival in Bible-belt Louisiana, and *The Beautiful Game*, which focused on attempts to heal the sectarian divide between Protestants and Catholics in Northern Ireland. He has written sacred and liturgical music, notably his 1985 *Requiem* and, more recently, his anthem 'Make a joyful noise to the Lord' for the coronation of King Charles III in 2023.

Critics, fellow composers, and members of the musical establishment have often been scathing in their denunciation of the commercial vulgarity, shallow populism, and derivative character of Lloyd Webber's music. Some of the more discerning and perceptive, however, have picked up and identified a spiritual dimension, although you have to search quite hard to find their acknowledgement of it, and even they can find it difficult to define. Buried away in the middle of Michael Coveney's biography, *Cats on a Chandelier*, is the statement, 'If there is one theme running through all of Lloyd Webber's works, it is a quest and a yearning for the spiritual dimension of life. I hear church bells in the rock and roll, the liturgy in the levity and the agony in the ecstacy'.[1] Coveney comes back to this point at the end of his book, where he portrays Lloyd Webber as characterized by 'unfulfilled potential and spiritual yearning'.[2] In among the brickbats hurled at *Jesus Christ Superstar* came recognition from some critics of its genuine spiritual power—*Time* magazine compared it to Bach's St John and St Matthew Passions, and Derek Jewell in the *Sunday Times* described it 'as every bit as valid as (and, to me, often more moving than) Handel's *Messiah*'.[3] A somewhat surprising convert to the spiritual quality of Lloyd Webber's theatre music was Malcolm Williamson, the Australian classical composer who had earlier rubbished it when he learned that the composer of *Cats* rather than himself, as Master of the Queen's Music, had been invited to write something for the fortieth anniversary of Queen Elizabeth II's accession in 1992. Complaining that Lloyd Webber 'fails to touch emotion and has used every meretricious trick from Jesus Christ downwards to make a fast buck', he continued, 'the difference between good music and Lloyd Webber is the difference between Michelangelo and a cement mixer', adding cuttingly, 'the comparison only breaks down to the extent that there is an element of creativity in a cement mixer'.[4] However, having seen *Sunset Boulevard* in London the following year, he dramatically changed his tune, conceding that not only was it 'technically musically marvellous' but 'it also has spiritual and philosophical depth'.[5]

This chapter seeks to identify and explore the religious influences and spiritual resonances in Andrew Lloyd Webber's music. They are most

132 MUSIC OF THE NIGHT

predictably and obviously evident in his *Requiem* and the scores of *Jesus Christ Superstar*, *Whistle Down the Wind* and *The Beautiful Game*, if only because of the nature of their subject matter and the words of their lyrics. But some of the clearest expressions of that 'quest and yearning for the spiritual dimension of life' that Coveney characterizes as the underlying theme of all his work are to be found in the show-stopper power ballads from his seemingly more secular musicals, 'Don't cry for me, Argentina' from *Evita*, 'Memory' from *Cats*, and 'All I ask of you' and 'The Music of the Night' from *Phantom of the Opera*.

Andrew Lloyd Webber's faith

Andrew Lloyd Webber has not spoken or written much about his own faith, displaying an understandable and characteristic reticence in keeping with his own shy and diffident personality, but he has given enough hints to reveal someone who has considerable spiritual awareness and sensitivity. Keith Richmond quotes him as saying, 'I'm religious, but not part of a church'.[6] Perhaps his most revealing remark on this subject came when he was the subject of BBC Television's flagship religious programme, *Songs of Praise*, on the occasion of his fiftieth birthday in March 1998. Asked by the presenter, Pam Rhodes, whether he prayed, he said 'Yes'. In answer to her follow-up question, 'Who do you pray to?' he responded, 'I don't know but I do believe there is something we don't understand'.[7] The interview was filmed in front of the Grade II-listed Victorian church, which stands in the grounds of his country house at Sydmonton in North Hampshire. He bought it from the Church of England for £1, and it has been the venue in which he has tried out every show since *Evita* as part of the annual Sydmonton Festival to which he invites friends and performers. The festival has embraced sacred works as well as musicals—a typical double bill in 1978 featured an afternoon performance of Fauré's *Messe Basse* followed by a late-night showing of the newly released movie *Grease*. The festival includes a regular Sunday morning service of worship, held either in his own church in the grounds of Sydmonton or in the parish church of Kingsclere, the neighbouring village, followed by an afternoon cricket match.

The very fact of Lloyd Webber being made the subject of an edition of the BBC's flagship religious programme, which usually features hymns and devotional songs, on the strength of his musicals—included were extracts from

Joseph, Jesus Christ Superstar, Evita, Cats, and *Whistle Down the Wind*—could be taken as an acknowledgement of their significant spiritual dimension on the part of the religious department of the national broadcasting corporation. Nor was it just the BBC that turned Lloyd Webber's fiftieth birthday into a quasi-religious event. A journalist attending the celebratory birthday concert in the Royal Albert Hall, in which performers included the London Community Gospel Choir, noted that 'the first half of the evening, with songs from *Jesus Christ Superstar, Joseph, Evita* and the *Requiem,* seemed almost like an evangelist's meeting'.[8]

There was an even more emphatic endorsement of Lloyd Webber's spiritual standing and influence in the service that was held in Kingsclere parish church on the day of his fiftieth birthday. Following an opening hymn-like chorale, 'The keys to the vaults of Heaven', from *Whistle Down the Wind,* and the 'Sanctus' from his father's *Missa Princeps Pacis* which segued into the 'Hosanna' from his own *Requiem,* his good friend, Canon Don Lewis, a Welsh Anglican clergyman who functioned almost as a private chaplain, preached on the text of 2 Kings 3:15: 'The Prophet Elisha commanded, "Send me a minstrel!" And when the minstrel played, the power of the Lord came upon him.' Lewis' sermon depicted Lloyd Webber as a minstrel similarly sent from God and his 'irresistibly hummable' tunes as 'a powerful vehicle for carrying themes of the spirit of God throughout the world'. Lewis singled out specifically *Joseph and the Amazing Technicolor Dreamcoat* and *Jesus Christ Superstar* for 'introducing Biblical themes to a Biblically illiterate age', and 'Love changes everything' from *Aspects of Love* for 'proclaiming in an idiom we all understand the centrality of love'.[9]

Upbringing and early influences

If Andrew Lloyd Webber's music does have a spiritual and even a religious dimension, then where does this come from? He was not specifically schooled and trained in church music like Arthur Sullivan or the Continental operetta composers discussed in Chapter 1, but it was an ever-present influence on him as he grew up. Michael Walsh, the distinguished former music critic of *Time* magazine and the *San Francisco Examiner,* rightly acknowledges it among other influences in his significant study of the composer's life and work. Locating him in a quintessentially English musical tradition stretching back to the eighteenth-century *Beggar's Opera,* via Sullivan's parodies of

134   MUSIC OF THE NIGHT

Verdi and Donizetti in the Savoy operas, Gustav Holst's and Ralph Vaughan Williams' use of folk song, and the Anglican church's choral tradition, Walsh writes: 'opera, opera parody, folk music and church music: it is precisely from this tradition that Lloyd Webber emerges'.[10]

His father was his earliest and most important mentor. One of the earliest extant photographs of Andrew shows him at the age of twenty months poring over the score of one of Bill Lloyd Webber's choral works, which included *The Saviour*, a meditation on the death of Christ for chorus and organ, *The Divine Compassion*, a sacred cantata for tenor, baritone, chorus, and organ, and *St. Francis of Assisi*, an oratorio for soprano, tenor, baritone, chorus, string orchestra, and harp. The main focus of Bill Lloyd Webber's work as a composer was church music. As well as these big choral works, he wrote anthems, carols, two Latin masses, and numerous liturgical settings, most of them conceived and expressed in a lush, romantic style that was out of favour by the time that he wrote them. In his 2018 autobiography, *Unmasked*, Andrew describes his father as 'steeped in the late High Church nineteenth century choral tradition beloved by the Anglo-Catholic "smells and bells" establishments'.[11] He was organist and choirmaster at two of those establishments, St Cyprian's, Clarence Gate, near London's Hyde Park, and All Saints, Margaret Street, in nearby Marylebone, before becoming organist and director of music at Westminster Central Hall, London, the headquarters of the Methodist church in England.

The High Church Anglo-Catholic tradition that he associated with his father was to have an abiding influence on Andrew, initially as much in terms of its aesthetic and architecture as of its music. He also admired and was later to draw on his father's unfashionable Romantic style of composition, shown most dramatically in the orchestral tone poem 'Aurora' written in 1948, the year of Andrew's birth. Of all his compositions, it was the one of which Bill was most proud, and Andrew had it specially recorded in 1986 by the Royal Philharmonic Orchestra under Lorin Maazel as a companion piece to his own *Variations*. He also played it to Ken Russell, the flamboyant and controversial film director, who proclaimed it an erotic, supercharged minimasterpiece. It is, indeed, a soaring, sensual, seductive work, hardly spiritual in the usual sense of the world but not a million miles away in its effect from 'The Music of the Night' written by his son nearly forty years later.

As a boy, Andrew Lloyd Webber regularly attended services of worship at Methodist Central Hall when his father was playing there. He recalls that, 'apart from the occasional blood and thunder sermons or rousing free-church

SPIRITUAL YEARNING AND HIGH CHURCH AESTHETICS 135

hymns, the ray of sunshine in the colourless services that Julian and I were now dragged to every Sunday was the moment Dad goosed up proceedings with one of his organ improvisations'.[12] More satisfying and more formative were the choral services that he attended at Westminster Abbey during his ten years as a pupil at Westminster Under School and Westminster School next door. The Abbey effectively functioned as the chapel for both schools. In later life, he recalled particularly the London premiere there of Benjamin Britten's *War Requiem*. A somewhat frightened child, he developed an early fear of the military and was terrified during the Suez conflict of 1956 that he might be conscripted into the army, a fear that he later said first led him to pray at bedtime.[13] He found solace in church music and architecture, on which he wrote several detailed treatises. At the age of seven, he sent a letter to the Dean of Westminster Abbey enclosing his pocket money to help conserve the building's fabric and declared that his ambition was to become chief inspector of ancient monuments in Britain.

Andrew Lloyd Webber's overwhelming childhood passion was for musical theatre. His baptism came at the age of ten when, in the space of 'four game-changing weeks' in the 1958 Christmas holidays, he saw *My Fair Lady* and *West Side Story* in the West End and *Gigi* and *South Pacific* in the cinema. *South Pacific* made the most impact and initiated a love affair with Rodgers and Hammerstein. His father encouraged this youthful enthusiasm. Just before taking him to *South Pacific*, Bill played Mario Lanza's recording of 'Some enchanted evening'.

> Three times, he played it, tears streaming down his face. The third time around, he muttered something about how Richard Rodgers' publisher told him that this song would kick off the post-war baby boom. When the record finally stopped, he looked at me straight in the face. 'Andrew', he said, 'if you ever write a tune half as good as this I shall be very, very proud of you.' On that evening my love affair with Richard Rodgers' music began. I went to bed heady with melody.[14]

In May 1961, at the age of thirteen, Andrew attended the first premiere of *The Sound of Music* at the Palace Theatre, London (which he would later buy), at the invitation of Richard Rodgers, to whom he had written a sycophantic fan letter. He was overwhelmed by the melodies and defended them staunchly against school contemporaries who found them sickly sweet and cloying. He built himself a model theatre on which to perform his own musicals. While

136   MUSIC OF THE NIGHT

his contemporaries were listening to the Beatles, he remained steeped in
Rodgers and Hammerstein and determined to write musicals in their idiom.

Dropping out of Oxford after just one term, having realized that what he
wanted to do more than anything else was to compose musicals, he was put
in touch with Tim Rice, just a couple of years older, who was keen to write
song lyrics. The two men were temperamentally very different, Rice more
confident and assured, but they shared an early enthusiasm for musicals—
Rice's favourite was *My Fair Lady*. They also shared the peculiarly English
upper-middle-class experience of private education with its central compo-
nent of compulsory Christian worship. While Lloyd Webber had fallen in
love with Anglican choral music and medieval church architecture during
his hours sitting in the pews of Westminster Abbey, Rice had more equivocal
memories of this aspect of his education. He spent a formative year, aged
eleven, when his family was based in Japan, at an international school run by
'a bunch of rather aggressive Canadian monks, whose order, the Brothers of
Christian Instruction, clearly regarded corporal punishment as an essential
stop en route to heaven'.[15] He had less negative feelings about the strong religious ethos of Lancing College, the High Church boarding school in Sussex
on the English south coast, where he spent the first four years of his teens:

> The Chapel dominated Lancing's architecture and timetable—a gargan-
> tuan nineteenth-century Gothic Revival masterpiece in which we had eight
> compulsory services a week. Lancing was about as High Church as it is
> possible to be without being Catholic. Most prayers were sung, there were
> banners, robes, processions, and, on Saints' Days, incense. If one has to go
> to church that often, it was at least a good show, rather like a musical being
> saved by its set.[16]

Joseph and the Amazing Technicolor Dreamcoat (1968)

The first joint project on which the seventeen-year-old budding composer
and the twenty-one-year-old aspiring lyricist collaborated was *The Likes
of Us*, a musical about the Victorian Christian philanthropist, Dr Thomas
Barnardo, who founded over 120 homes for orphaned and deprived children. Lloyd Webber was undoubtedly drawn towards this subject through
the influence of his Methodist mother, Jean, who was an enthusiast for social
reform and helping underprivileged children. The musical, which cast the

SPIRITUAL YEARNING AND HIGH CHURCH AESTHETICS   137

Victorian philanthropist as a Christ-like figure and had an uplifting moral feel, never reached the stage. Much more fruitful was the project suggested by Alan Doggett, a music teacher in whose choir Andrew's brother Julian had sung. Impressed by what he had heard of *The Likes of Us*, he asked for a short cantata to be sung at an end-of-term concert by the boys of Colet Court, the preparatory school for the prestigious St Paul's School in London. The requirement was for a short piece which would appeal equally to the eight- to thirteen-year-old pupils who would perform it and their parents and grandparents who would form the audience. Doggett suggested a Biblical theme. In previous years, he had performed Herbert Chappell's *The Daniel Jazz* and Michael Hurd's *Jonah Man Jazz*, two of the many popular upbeat contemporary 'pop cantatas' for schools written in the mid-1960s and based on Bible stories. Rice, whose favourite Bible story from school was that of Joseph and his coat of many colours, dug out his well-thumbed childhood copy of *The Wonder Book of Bible Stories*, which became his principal source text.

The earliest public performances of *Joseph and the Amazing Technicolor Dreamcoat* following its initial outing at Colet Court in March 1968 were in ecclesiastical settings—first at Westminster Central Hall and then in St Paul's Cathedral, as part of a festival entitled 'Pop into St Paul's' devised by the progressive and self-consciously 'trendy' New Zealand-born Dean, Martin Sullivan, who had achieved notoriety by parachuting down from the Cathedral dome to the nave. Its first staging in the USA was a production in May 1970 by the Cathedral College of the Immaculate Conception in Douglaston, Queens, New York City. Gradually expanded, it was performed at the 1972 Edinburgh Festival as a forty-minute show paired in a double bill with excerpts from medieval mystery plays from Wakefield in West Yorkshire. It was subsequently combined with a short singspiel entitled 'Jacob's Journey' with additional songs by Rice and Lloyd Webber and dialogue by the comedy writing team, Alan Simpson and Ray Galton, famous for BBC comedy hits such as *Steptoe and Son* and *Hancock's Half Hour*. This combination did not really work, and the idea of a double bill was dropped in favour of extending *Joseph* to be a full length show. It had its West End premiere in this form in February 1973 and since then has seldom been off the stage, either in amateur school performances or ever more glitzy and over-the-top professional productions.

Tim Rice has written of *Joseph* that 'this great tale has everything—plausible, sympathetic characters, a flawed hero and redeemed villains ... It

138 MUSIC OF THE NIGHT

is a symbolic, spiritual, religious and human story—even in our light-hearted re-telling of it the presence of God is inescapable'.[17] In truth, its spiritual and religious resonances are sparse. It sticks fairly closely to the Genesis story of Joseph, Jacob's favourite son, his cruel treatment by his jealous brothers and his time as a slave in Pharoah's court only to emerge as the ruler's trusted adviser on the basis of his ability to predict dreams. However, contrary to what Rice says, God is effectively airbrushed out of the musical. Instead of being the divine messenger and interpreter that he is portrayed as in Scripture, Joseph is more of a hunky superstar. The message of the prologue: 'If you think it, want it, dream it, then it's real—you are what you feel', reinforced in its best-known song, 'Any dream will do', is very far from the one that the Bible gives. Terence Copley, a professor of religious education at the universities of Exeter and Oxford, has argued that the musical has done serious harm by distorting generations of children's view of Joseph through portraying him as 'an opportunist who strikes lucky . . . the epitome of a secular westerner in the late twentieth century'. For him, 'The themes, though distantly biblical, caught a mood of assertive individualism which was sweeping Europe and continues to dominate western society'.[18]

In marked contrast, Michael Walsh has written that *Joseph*'s huge success on Broadway, where it opened in January 1982, owed something to the fact that it perfectly caught the zeitgeist of the times when 'the pendulum of American culture had swung away from faux-Nietzsche God is dead pessimism toward a renewed interest in religious subjects'.[19] I suspect that is much more applicable to the altogether more serious *Jesus Christ Superstar* and that the appeal of *Joseph* on both sides of the Atlantic has more to do with its freshness, energy, and feel-good vibes than any religious resonances it may have. If there is a spiritual dimension to the show, it is not so much in its subject matter as in the way it is almost always performed, whether in professional or amateur productions, with an on-stage choir of school children providing a kind of innocence and sense of wonder. This aspect is superbly conveyed in the 1999 video version starring Donny Osmond, which is set in a school assembly hall. The wide-eyed children initially form the audience and then follow Joseph on stage to join in 'Any Dream Will Do', that seductively simple soft rock ballad in C major. They return later in procession carrying candles to accompany the more Biblically accurate and theologically nuanced ballad 'Close every door to me' with its repeated assertion that 'children of Israel are never alone'. Here is a moment of genuine spirituality, albeit sentimental and slightly cloying, propelled by a classic Lloyd Webber simple, soaring, diatonic melody calculated to stir the emotions and stick in the memory.

For all its dodgy theology and distortion of the Biblical message, *Joseph* remains a favourite show for church and school groups to perform and attend. Its appealing, caricatured Biblical characters with their infectiously catchy songs, many of them pastiches, cast a sufficiently warm quasi-spiritual glow to shine through the campery and leave audiences feeling uplifted and moved by the theme of forgiveness, which does at least come through relatively unscathed from the original Bible story.

Cats (1981)

Jesus Christ Superstar, the next Rice-Lloyd Webber collaboration after *Joseph*, is treated separately and in some depth in the following chapter. It is the most daring, original, and theologically thought-provoking of all Andrew Lloyd Webber's musicals, but it is not the most spiritual. There are more clearly spiritual passages in the score of *Cats*, as is appropriate given that, for the most part, it sets the poems of T.S. Eliot, whose devout Anglo-Catholicism embraced the High Church architecture, ritual and theatricality so appealing to Andrew Lloyd Webber. They also shared a love of cats. 'Memory' is one of those melodies which expresses the spiritual quest and yearning identified by Michael Coveney as the underlying theme in Lloyd Webber's music. *Cats* also includes three anthem-like numbers which could have been written for the church choir at All Saints, Margaret Street, where Bill Lloyd Webber had been organist or, indeed, at the equally High Church St Mary the Virgin, Graham Street, and St Stephen's, Gloucester Road, where Eliot had worshipped. The first is in the passage in the opening number, 'Jellicle songs for Jellicle cats', about 'the mystical divinity of unashamed felinity', which Lloyd Webber set as an ecclesiastical-like chorus with organ accompaniment. The second is the journey to the Heaviside layer, and the third is Old Deuteronomy's song, with accompanying chorus, 'The ad-dressing of cats', which ends the show and has a distinctly hymn-like quality, beginning in B flat major and modulating to B major, while maintaining a steady foursquare 4/4 tempo marked 'moderato'. As Michael Walsh puts it, 'What was Old Deuteronomy if not some High Church cantor . . . squarely in the tradition of such operatic holy bores as Mozart's Sarastro or Verdi's Padre Guardiano?'[20] It provides a distinctly churchy-sounding finale to the show.

140 MUSIC OF THE NIGHT

Cats is essentially a parable of redemption, resurrection, and rebirth. Seeking something to give a narrative structure to what would otherwise be a series of unlinked character sketches, Lloyd Webber and director Trevor Nunn hit on a reference in an unpublished letter of Eliot's to 'the Heaviside Layer', a feline heaven to which deserving cats are transported to be-reborn and enjoy a better life. At the annual Jellicle Ball, the cat deemed most worthy to ascend to it in a giant balloon is selected by Old Deuteronomy, whose Old Testament name signifies his position as a kind of spiritual guru and God-like figure. Both in Eliot's original conception and in its depiction in the musical, the Heaviside layer is clearly intended to represent heaven. Indeed, in the Japanese version of *Cats*, it is translated as 'heavens' and in Chinese productions as 'the ninth layer of the sky', reflecting the ancient Chinese view of there being nine heavens.

The 2019 film version, directed by Tom Hooper, which (in my view, totally unjustly) was almost universally panned by critics and shunned by audiences, made more of the heavenly nature of the 'Heaviside layer' and also emphasized the Christian Gospel message of radical inclusion and the last being first by the introduction of a new character, Victoria, an abandoned cat. In the newly added song 'Beautiful Ghosts', with lyrics by Taylor Swift, Victoria sings of being 'born into nothing' and being frightened to stalk the streets of London, reflecting that 'All that I wanted is to be wanted'. In the film's gritty urban setting, it is impossible not to feel that she is personifying the capital's marginalized and homeless. Yet she is not the one who is ultimately portrayed as the victim and the outcast. That status is reserved for Grizabella, the Glamour Cat, who was once beautiful and 'haunted many a low resort' but is now mangy and unloved, living through her memories with the withered leaves collecting at her feet.

As portrayed in the film, Grizabella has something of Mary Magdalene about her. Befriended by Victoria, whose innocence, vulnerability, and compassion give her an almost Christ-like quality at times, Grizabella is literally brought in from the cold and is subsequently chosen as the one to ascend to the Heaviside Lair by Old Deuteronomy, played by Judi Dench, who tells the bumptious and opinionated Rum Tum Tugger that she is looking for 'a cat with soul'. Having befriended Grizabella, the abandoned Victoria is welcomed into the fellowship of the Jellicle cats and finds her own redemption through being accepted by them and included in their company. Overall, this much-maligned film conveys a deeply spiritual message about inclusion, the power of forgiveness, and the importance of the soul. As with

SPIRITUAL YEARNING AND HIGH CHURCH AESTHETICS 141

Carousel and *Les Misérables*, the cinematic version of *Cats* has considerably more religious resonances than the original stage show.

Requiem (1985)

Andrew Lloyd Webber's most obviously spiritual work is his *Requiem*, which he describes as 'the most personal of all my compositions'.[21] Although a setting of a liturgical text, it warrants serious consideration in a book about the spiritual dimension of musical theatre because of its evident theatricality, its influence on the composer's later works, and what it tells us about his motivation and beliefs. The initial trigger for it was the death of his father in October 1982 at the age of 68, and the work is dedicated to his memory. But it was not just inspired by filial grief. He had been approached in 1978 by Humphrey Burton, Head of Music and Arts programmes at the BBC, to write a *Requiem* for the victims of terrorist attacks in Northern Ireland, and he found himself increasingly moved by the deaths inflicted on the British mainland by IRA bomb attacks, especially the one near Harrods in London in December 1983 in which six people were killed, including a young journalist with whom he had had a long discussion at a party about the Burne-Jones windows in his Oxford college. He was also moved by a story that he read in the *New York Times* about a young Cambodian boy who was forced by Khmer Rouge terrorists to choose between killing his mutilated sister or being killed himself—in the event he killed his sister. It was with this particular tragedy in mind that Lloyd Webber decided that the specific focus of the *Requiem* would be on the manipulation of children in war. He was taken back to his own childhood fear of war and the military, which had first led him to pray, and to his memory of attending the London premiere of Britten's *War Requiem* in Westminster Abbey, which had made such a profound impression on him as a teenager. He also had a broader agenda, writing, 'I feel great anger at what humans have done to one another in the twentieth century and I hope that comes across'. [22]

There was another more personal motive for writing the *Requiem*. He freely admitted that it was conceived in part to showcase the vocal talents of Sarah Brightman, with whom he had become infatuated and for whom he left his wife of nearly twelve years and his children. In his words: 'I was confused personally. I felt really guilty about my kids. Dad's death had affected me much more than I realised. I truly was in love with Sarah B and of

142   MUSIC OF THE NIGHT

course her voice enthralled me'.[23] He goes on to suggest in his autobiography that it was a visit to a church at the end of 1983 that finally and decisively inspired him:

> As I invariably do when I am depressed I turned to architecture. I hobbled on my broken toe into Winchester cathedral for advent evensong. I don't remember what the choir sang but I do recall my tears and they weren't only about my toe. The combination of uniquely English architecture and the equally unique English choral tradition overwhelmed me with a combination of inadequacy and a burning need to compose something that would really stretch me.[24]

This is a revealing statement on a number of levels. It suggests a frustration, perhaps even guilt, that the composer was not really stretching himself with his musical theatre work—the theme of spiritual quest and yearning raising itself again. It also shows the huge importance for him of churches, not just in terms of their music and architecture but as places to find peace at times of stress. It was his own experience of their healing power that led him in 1994 to set up the Open Churches Trust to assist congregations to keep church buildings open to the public for several hours each day. He had found himself in Manchester with some time to spare and tried to get into some of the city's Victorian churches but found them all locked. The Trust pays for closed circuit cameras and other security devices and in some cases also for caretakers.

Lloyd Webber also explicitly acknowledges in the statement above the influence on him of the English choral tradition. It was the experience of attending Anglican Evensong that moved and inspired him. What is interesting is that he chose to write a Latin Requiem rather than an oratorio, extended anthem, or something else more clearly in the Anglican choral tradition. Bill Lloyd Webber had never written a *Requiem,* and perhaps that was part of the reason why his son decided to compose one. We get another strong hint of why he went for that particular form in a subsequent entry in his autobiography describing the process of composition of the *Requiem.* It takes us back to his love of church architecture and to his fascination with all things Anglo-Catholic:

> I found it impossible to set the Latin words sitting at the piano. Thanks to my elementary school Latin and a good English translation I puzzled over the text and its meaning during long walks and days when I gorged myself

SPIRITUAL YEARNING AND HIGH CHURCH AESTHETICS   143

on the wealth of church architecture that is Britain's most undervalued asset. I would go over phrases time and time again in my head, take them to the piano, conclude they were rubbish, go and see another building and try again. The English choral tradition with its unique dependency on boy 'treble' soprano voices was my bedrock. Latin obviously is not the language of the Church of England but that's never been a bother in the Victorian Tractarian incense-toting Anglo-Catholic churches I love.[25]

Lloyd Webber's *Requiem* is set, unusually, for soprano, boy soprano/treble, and tenor, for reasons that he explained:

> I wanted the boy to represent uncorrupted childhood, that no child was born to hate, any more than a child is born with a specific religious faith. We may have Jewish, Muslim, Protestant or Catholic parents—we can't change our ethnicity—but we are not born Jewish, Muslim, Protestant or Catholic. I visualised the soprano as an idealistic young woman repelled by violence committed in the name of religion, and the tenor as a world weary everyman who had seen it all.[26]

In many ways, that statement echoes Hammerstein's Universalist idealism as expressed particularly in *South Pacific* and *The King and I*. Lloyd Webber has a particular aversion to intolerance, animosity, and violence displayed in the name of religion. He mentioned it in his interview on *Songs of Praise*, and it is the theme of his musical *The Beautiful Game*, considered below. There are further hints of his own religious views in his comments about the way that parts of the *Requiem* are set. '*Fac eas, Domine, de morte transire ad vitam*' (Lord, make them pass from death to life) in the *Offertorium* section is made a bold unison statement for the full choir because 'I liked its words and its plea for salvation'.[27] The *Requiem* ends with the boy soprano singing the '*requiem aeternam*' section, 'with its suggestion that the child sees infinite light— "*lux perpetua*". But the repetition of the word "*perpetua*" implies that the needless violence that was the catalyst to the requiem will never go away'.[28] There is a lingering sadness here, of a kind that re surfaces at the end of *The Phantom of the Opera*, *The Beautiful Game*, and *Whistle Down the Wind*. Is it another expression of that trademark unfulfilled spiritual yearning?

How do we assess the *Requiem*? Is it essentially a theatrical work, an operetta dressed up in a cassock, to paraphrase Hans von Bülow's famous comment about Verdi's *Requiem*? That might be suggested by the range of stars

144   MUSIC OF THE NIGHT

assembled for its premiere on 24 February 1985 in St Thomas' Episcopal Church, New York: Sarah Brightman, Plácido Domingo, Paul Miles-Kingston, and the choirs of Winchester Cathedral and St Thomas' Church conducted by Loren Maazel. Lloyd Webber himself treated it as a theatre piece, programming it in his own Palace Theatre for a week in a double bill with his *Variations*. Yet the exuberant syncopated 'Hosanna' in 7/8 time is the only Broadway touch in what is otherwise a conventional romantic classical score. In that respect, it is much less of a musical theatre piece and much more of a sacred work than the altogether edgier and more irreverent Bernstein *Mass*.

Hostile critics savaged the *Requiem* for its cheap populist vulgarity, just as an earlier generation had savaged Sullivan's sacred oratorios. For Martin Berheimer in the *Los Angeles Times*, 'It aspires to the pure fragrance of churchly incense, but it ends up reeking of cheap perfume.'[29] Similar comments were made about those lush Romantic nineteenth-century French Catholic settings of the Mass for soaring tenor cantor and trumpets, which I have suggested are close cousins of the operetta tradition and which still resound around the vast underground chapel at Lourdes. More discerning critics recognized the genuineness and accessibility of the *Requiem*'s emotion and sentiment. Andrew Porter described it in *The New Yorker* as 'a "felt" work and an honest one. The effects are obvious, but they are effective.'[30] Imants Cepitis, chorus master of the Latvian State Choir, who performed it in Moscow in January 1989 with the Moscow Philharmonic, said, 'What I like is the work's obvious emotion. Today, composers of choral music are usually too afraid of writing tunes which express emotion so openly.'[31] It is the emotion of the *Requiem* which ultimately makes it a deeply spiritual work, as shown most perfectly in the *Pie Jesu*, written in A flat and combining the two soprano voices in thirds. Carefully crafted but seemingly without artifice or contrivance, its effect is ethereal, soothing and undoubtedly spiritual. Of course, it is also shamelessly populist, and it climbed to the top of the pop as well as the classical charts. Lloyd Webber confesses in his autobiography that he would love it to have been recorded by the Everly brothers.

The Phantom of the Opera (1986)

Several of those writing about Lloyd Webber's overall corpus of work have seen the *Requiem* as paving the way for his later more complex and classically

SPIRITUAL YEARNING AND HIGH CHURCH AESTHETICS   145

inclined musicals. Stephen Citron notes that some of what he learned from composing it 'is apparent in the extensive part and choral writing in *Aspects of Love* and *Sunset Boulevard*'.[32] More immediately, as Michael Walsh states, 'it had given Andrew the technical tools that he would need for his next major work in the theater'.[33] That work was *The Phantom of the Opera*, of all his musicals the most successful and the most spiritually charged.

The original story of the Phantom of the Opera is, of course, intrinsically spiritual as well as haunting, scary, and tragic. The musical milks all those aspects for all it is worth. There is the unambiguously religious referencing in the phrase 'Angel of Music', used both by the Phantom about Christine and by her about him. She is portrayed throughout as an angel, dressed in virginal white, and he as a fallen angel, if not the Devil himself, with his black coat and hat. The scenes where he seduces and tempts her are played out in an almost Biblical way reminiscent of the serpent's interactions with Eve, most notably in 'Past the point of no return' and in 'Stranger than you dreamt it' when he slithers across the floor towards her. Then there is the central ambiguity surrounding the Phantom's character. Is he a tragic outcast who has never been loved or understood and is condemned to a life of loneliness and despair? Has his soul been twisted and corrupted so much that he cannot be saved or welcomed back into the human world, or is he just an evil and manipulative seducer?

If the theme of temptation looms large, so does that of redemption. The Phantom begs Christine to see through his deformed face into his soul, and she responds, addressing the 'pitiful creature of darkness', asking God to 'give me courage to show you, you are not alone', and turning him from loathing to love with a kiss. It is through her forgiveness of the Phantom that she is able to rescue herself and Raoul, and indeed the entire opera house, from the 'dominion of darkness' that is the Phantom's Lair. She also rescues him from the hatred that has consumed him throughout his life. Yet her Christ-like action in reaching out to him in love and forgiveness is not enough, and it is ultimately the Phantom who is the sacrificial figure, indeed the sacrificial victim. In 'Past the point of no return', Christine sings 'Our Passion Play has now, at last, begun'. The Passion is completed only when the Phantom sacrifices his life and love as well as his dream and obsession for Christine, knowing that she needs to be free, even though it will kill him to let her go. Christine's kiss in some senses saves him, but only for him to disappear at the end. What exactly has become of him as the curtain falls remains a mystery, but there is a sense of the Unquiet Spirit departing and an echo, albeit in a

146   MUSIC OF THE NIGHT

much more intense and tragic vein, of the self-surrender of John Wellington Wells as he yields up his life to Ahrimanes at the end of Gilbert and Sullivan's *The Sorcerer*.

A somewhat cheeky critic once wrote of Lloyd Webber musicals that the audience comes out 'humming the sets'. This is perhaps especially true of *Phantom*, where the sets, props, and costumes are particularly sumptuous and contribute hugely to its emotional power and appeal. The monkey music box, the crashing chandelier, the opera house stage, and the grand staircase for 'Masquerade' all add enormously to the atmosphere. There are two sets which particularly enhance the show's spiritual dimension—the Phantom's lair and the graveyard, which Christine visits to sing at her father's tomb. In the case of the subterranean lair to which Christine is lured by the Phantom across a lake, there is a distinctly ecclesiastical as well as a darkly Gothic aura. Indeed, it resembles one of Lloyd Webber's beloved Anglo-Catholic church interiors with its proliferation of candles, prominently situated organ, and Gothic pillars. Writing about how she conceived the lair set and the route to it across the subterranean lake, the show's designer, Maria Bjornson, acknowledges this similarity while also invoking elements of ritual and sexuality:

> There are three things that we share and whose symbols touch everyone's lives: the church, the theater, and the brothel. And certain objects that we might connect with these experiences—like candles, drapes, an organ, even smoke—we associate with ritual, and it makes things seem more important, more underlined, somehow. And then there are even older symbols and associations that go back to ancient myths and stories. These are also part of our common vocabulary. *Phantom* touches on a lot of them: Beauty and the Beast, Leda and the Swan, Pandora's Box, stories of nymphs and satyrs. When Christine and the Phantom go down to his lair, I draw on many of these. First of all there's the water that surrounds them. Water is always used to represent sexuality, particularly a woman's sexual feelings. And candles, of course, are very male. So as they descend and they're enshrouded by all of this, I was trying for a feeling of ritual — that he was taking her as part of a ritual and there was nothing she could do about it. But I don't want the audience to think at all about any of this. I just want them to feel it.[34]

An even more explicitly religious atmosphere is conjured up by the sculpted angels and cold monuments in the graveyard that Christine visits in Act 2,

SPIRITUAL YEARNING AND HIGH CHURCH AESTHETICS   147

dressed in a blue cloak, reminiscent of that worn in many classic portrayals of the Virgin Mary and reinforcing the sense that her father is in some sense a benevolent God-like figure.

The simplest and most powerful costume/prop, which provides the distinctive icon for the musical's unmistakable marketing and merchandise, is, of course, the Phantom's mask. It acts as a visual pointer to some of the show's moral and spiritual messages. One of these is about our reaction to those who are disfigured and disabled. In Lloyd Webber's words, 'People normally recoil from those who are deformed. But they are just like you and me. Behind his mask, our Phantom is a man capable of giving love but he can never receive it.'[35] Another is about the way we wear masks to hide our true identity, so well expressed in the chorus 'Masquerade' with its words about 'paper faces on parade', which 'hide your face so the world will never find you', acting as a reminder that hiding the truth about ourselves can never make us free. A student in my Theology of Musical Theatre class constructed a highly imaginative service of Christian worship around the story and songs of *Phantom*, with the congregation wearing masks and sitting in a darkened church. The first half of the service focuses on the seductive appeal of the Devil-like Phantom and the temptation we face to hide from the truth about ourselves and succumb to our darker desires. In the second half, the emphasis moves from darkness to light, with the congregation discarding their masks and seeing themselves as God sees us.

Important as the sets and costumes are, it is the music of *Phantom* that ultimately provides its spiritual quality and ambiguity. In keeping with the church-like character of the Phantom's lair, there is a distinctly ecclesiastical touch, reminiscent of the 'mystical divinity' sequence in *Cats*, in the descending chromatic triads on the organ, which introduce the Phantom and provide his *leitmotif*. Lloyd Webber's quest and yearning for the spiritual dimension in life, as noted by Coveney, is evident in the innocence and intensity of 'All I ask of you', which provides such a counterpoise to the darkness and devilry of the Phantom's lair. It also underscores 'Wishing you were somehow here again', sung by Christine when she visits her father's tomb. This is a song that I have used regularly in pastoral care classes for trainee ministers of religion and medical doctors because its lyrics so powerfully and beautifully convey the classic stages of grief, as chronicled by bereavement experts like Elizabeth Kubler-Ross, from the early pangs of denial and anger to the final necessary letting go. Indeed, it provides almost a textbook guide to healthy grieving.

148   MUSIC OF THE NIGHT

Which leaves us with 'The Music of the Night', with its overwhelming sexual tension and disturbing Jungian undercurrent of venturing into our darkest dreams, to that murky but appealing underworld where our fantasies unwind and we let our darker sides give in to the music of the night. It is a song of such a dark and demonic character that it seems almost blasphemous to categorize it as spiritual. In Lloyd Webber's own words, 'the sexual tension, the passion and the yearning in the song was like nothing anyone had seen in one of my musicals before'.[36] He wrote the melody for Sarah Brightman in the first flush of their romance, and it was initially paired, rather appropriately, with a text by Trevor Nunn entitled 'Married Man' about a girl having an affair with a married man. It was performed with different lyrics, although not those that would feature in the final stage production, when *Phantom* was given its initial run-through in the church at Sydmonton in the 1985 Festival there. The gallery at the west end of the church housed the musicians, and it was from there that the crashing chandelier was first launched, with the Phantom's boat sailing away under the bell tower. To that extent, at least this song of seduction and abandoned moral senses had ecclesiastical origins. Alongside its sexual tension and atmosphere of diabolical temptation, there is an undeniably spiritual element in the notes of ecstasy and release in the melody. It is ultimately undefinable and, like the ritualistic set of the phantom's lair, something to be felt rather than analysed or thought about.

The oft-made accusation that 'The Music of the Night' plagiarizes the tenor aria 'Quello che tacete' from Giacomo Puccini's 1910 opera, *La fanciulla del West* (*The Girl of the Golden West*), which led to the Puccini estate filing a lawsuit against Webber, seems to me misplaced. One phrase is very similar, and possibly derivative, but Lloyd Webber's melody is more shaped and developed than Puccini's, with greater light and shade and changing dynamics, and altogether more subtly seductive by modulating more and not staying at one level. It is much more reminiscent of late Lehár than of Puccini. Indeed, this is true of *Phantom* as a whole, which is more of an operetta than any of Lloyd Webber's other works, echoing Lehár in its lush, bittersweet quality and soaring romanticism. It is not an imitation of late Italian grand opera, as often suggested, but rather a late silver age operetta. It was singularly appropriate that Alan Jay Lerner, librettist of *My Fair Lady*, perhaps the last of the great Broadway operetta-style musicals, was brought in to fix the lyrics. Sadly, he had to pull out when diagnosed with terminal cancer. 'Dark operetta', the phrase that Sondheim used to describe *Sweeney Todd*, seems a particularly apt label for *Phantom*.

Whistle Down the Wind (1998) and *The Beautiful Game* (2000)

Post-*Phantom* Lloyd Webber musicals, including its sequel, *Love Never Dies*, have never quite achieved either its spiritual depth or audience appeal, perhaps indicating that these two aspects are, indeed, related. Two, however, *Whistle Down the Wind* (1998) and *The Beautiful Game* (2000), did tackle serious religious issues. *Whistle Down the Wind,* for which the lyricist was Jim Steinman—memorably described by the *Los Angeles Times* as 'the Richard Wagner of rock' and best known for his Meat Loaf album, 'Bat out of Hell'— was based on a short story by Mary Hayley Bell about a murderer on the run sheltered by a group of children who believe that he is Jesus. The musical transported the setting from sleepy Sussex on the south coast of England to 1950s Bible belt Louisiana in the throes of a religious revival, creating an atmosphere of steamy intensity and revivalist fervour. More than either the book or Richard Attenborough's 1961 film version, the musical explores the nature of religious faith by pitching the children's trust and credulity against the sceptical cynicism and harsh judgmentalism of the adults. This theme is introduced in the opening number, 'The keys to the vaults of heaven', where the adults sing about the nights growing darker, 'even darker now than sin', and the children counter with 'One sweet day when the whole world's ready, we'll awake to a glorious sight'. The subject of prayer looms large in the musical. 'The Man', as the central criminal/Christ character is called, has a long, anguished soliloquy, 'Unsettled Scores', in which he bemoans the fact that while there is a prayer for everyone and everything else, 'you haven't got a prayer for me'. In the show's best-known song, 'No matter what', a lilting soft rock ballad in the style of 'Any dream will do', which became a chart hit when recorded by the boy band Boyzone, the children express their simple faith in contrast to the cynicism and scepticism of the adults. *Whistle Down the Wind* never took off in either the UK or the USA despite radical revisions being made to the book and the score, but it was rightly hailed by critics for engaging with deep spiritual subjects. Charles Spencer welcomed it in the *Daily Telegraph* as 'a commercial musical with the courage to take Christian faith, mortality, racism and the problem of suffering as its subject matter', while for Michael Coveney, it signalled that Lloyd Webber had 'come full circle to the primal questions of faith, belief and friendship that he and Tim Rice had first addressed in *Superstar*.'[37]

150 MUSIC OF THE NIGHT

These themes were taken further in *The Beautiful Game*, on which Andrew Lloyd Webber collaborated with left-wing English comedian Ben Elton to explore the subject of sectarianism in Northern Ireland in the early 1970s. The first Lloyd Webber work to tackle a near-contemporary subject, it follows firmly in the wake of those dark, gritty, realistic musicals of the 1980s and 1990s like Willy Russell's *Blood Brothers* and Jonathan Larson's *Rent*. *The Beautiful Game* is based on the true story of Bobby Sands, who played as a teenager in the 1960s for the Belfast-based Star of the Sea football team, which had both Catholic and Protestant players. He went on to become a member of the Irish Republican Army and deliberately starved himself to death in the Maze Prison in Belfast in 1981. Another player in the team became a loyalist paramilitary and also ended up in prison. Lloyd Webber and Elton had both been captivated by a BBC television documentary about the non-sectarian football team, which showed how a shared love for the game of football briefly eclipsed sectarian rivalries until the onset of the troubles in Northern Ireland in the early 1970s broke up the squad.

The Beautiful Game provides a chilling insight into the strange combination of idealism and cynicism that makes up the terrorist mind and into the power of violence to corrupt and deaden all those caught up in its spiral. There is not much sense of redemption or hope, and the overall mood is one of bitterness, despair, and the needless waste of so many young lives. Its most moving song, which does undeniably have a spiritual quality, is the anthem 'Let us love in peace' sung by the girlfriends of the boys in the football team who have ended up either dead or in prison. It was sung at President George W. Bush's inaugural gala in January 2001 and at the first major interfaith service at Ground Zero, remembering the victims of the 9/11 terrorist attack on the World Trade Centre.

In the programme note for *The Beautiful Game*, Lloyd Webber returned to one of his abiding concerns, writing that 'it deals with the issue of bigotry and hatred and what religions can stir up'. He also confessed to another motivation for writing a work so different from his usual output: 'I've been worrying about where musicals are going. This one will tackle issues and will very much have a contemporary feel and sound'. In proclaiming that he had become a convert to the issue-based musical and moved away from the romantic escapism of some of his earlier works, he was keen to point out that this latest work still lay very much in the great tradition of twentieth-century musical theatre, noting 'It was the kind of story that Rodgers and Hammerstein in their early days would have seriously thought about

SPIRITUAL YEARNING AND HIGH CHURCH AESTHETICS 151

setting'.[38] He was absolutely right that Hammerstein might well have tackled this kind of subject, but he would have done so with his trademark optimism and idealism and not in the deeply pessimistic way that Lloyd Webber and Elton did.

The sparse seriousness and starkly depressing message of *The Beautiful Game* was surely a major contributor to its failure at the box office. It was set too near home and demanded too much of an audience who expected an evening out to a Lloyd Webber musical to be an escape from real life into up-lifting romantic tunes and glorious sets. When I saw the show, which ran for just twelve months in the West End and never transferred to Broadway, sev-eral of those sitting around me chatted throughout the performance, clearly bored with the substantial dialogue, which makes it very different from the usual through-sung Lloyd Webber score, and unprepared to engage with its serious attempt to grapple with the mentality of the terrorist mind, some-thing one might expect from a late-night television documentary but not from a musical by the creator of *Starlight Express*.

Lloyd Webber returned to another gritty near-contemporary subject in 2013 with *Stephen Ward*, built around the central figure in the Profumo af-fair that rocked the British establishment in the early 1960s, but it, too, was a box office flop. Was he striving too hard to be serious, political, and rele-vant? Whatever the reason, the Midas touch had gone and his more recent musicals, *School of Rock* and *Cinderella* (later re-named *Bad Cinderella*), have similarly lacked box office appeal.

More recent compositions—a return to the sacred?

Like Arthur Sullivan, Leonard Bernstein, and the French operetta composers mentioned in Chapter 1, although to a more limited extent than any of them, Lloyd Webber has straddled the worlds of musical theatre and sacred music and occasionally crossed over from the stage to the sanctuary. Aside from the *Requiem*, his religious compositions have been few in number and small in scale. He wrote a version of the Lord's Prayer for his first wedding at a Gloucestershire church in July 1971 and toyed with incorporating it into *Jesus Christ Superstar* as a solo beginning 'Hey, Father' for Jesus after his entry into Jerusalem but dropped the idea. In 2000, he set lines written by a fourteen-year-old schoolgirl who won a national competition which he had initiated with the Open Churches Trust for a new prayer for the millennium.

It was performed in a somewhat bizarre three-way mix as the climax to a BBC *Songs of Praise* special broadcast from the Cardiff Millennium Stadium on the first Sunday of the new millennium. A soprano soloist sang the title song from *Whistle Down the Wind*, with a Welsh male voice choir interjecting extracts from 'No matter what' and a rather truncated version of the millennium prayer, shorn of its opening line, 'Dear Lord and heavenly Father' and of its closing intercessions, leaving a rather bland set of humanist aspirations.

The most high-profile and successful recent excursion by Lloyd Webber into the world of sacred music is the anthem that he wrote for the coronation of King Charles III and Queen Camilla in Westminster Abbey in May 2023. It was written at the king's request—Charles said that he wanted something 'hummable' for the ceremony—and makes much use of boys' voices as well as of trumpets and drums. 'Make a joyful noise to the Lord', based on Psalm 98, is a thrilling choral piece, which for me was easily the best of the many new works commissioned for the coronation. Accessible and theatrical, it displays the influence of the English choral tradition and of Lloyd Webber's particular love of high church liturgy and architecture. In the words of Serena Davies, chief culture writer for *The Daily Telegraph*:

> This piece is a fine example of the intelligent populism that he has made his signature. The anthem communicates a childhood wonder, which conjures the image of Lloyd Webber himself as a small boy sitting in the Abbey, as he did many times as a pupil of Westminster Under School, awed by this building that he has called the greatest gothic architecture in the world.
>
> Lloyd Webber has a love of the numinous. After the cascade of catchy notes that accompany the main refrain, there comes a more mystical passage that reaches towards the sublime. You could sense here a nostalgia for the mid-twentieth-century flowering of English music led by William Walton and Ralph Vaughan Williams. Nevertheless, the end of the piece feels very much like Lloyd Webber the showman, with a flourish that is strangely reminiscent of 'Love Changes Everything' from his 1989 musical *Aspects of Love*.[39]

On the strength of this anthem, I hope that Andrew Lloyd Webber writes more church music. I have gone on record in a letter to *The Times* as saying that a collection of Lloyd Webber hymn tunes would do more to bring people back to church than any amount of mission planning. In fact, as he has become older, he has shown a growing interest in writing religious

SPIRITUAL YEARNING AND HIGH CHURCH AESTHETICS   153

compositions. He alludes briefly in his autobiography to a conversation with Jonathan Sacks, Chief Rabbi of the United Hebrew Congregations of the Commonwealth from 1991 to 2013, 'who discussed with me the possibility of combining elements of the Christian and Jewish faiths into a text that I could set to music'.[40] Sadly, nothing came of this, and Sacks died in 2020. Lloyd Webber has said more than once that he would like to return to his *Requiem*, which he feels needs further work. In an interview following the death of his son in early 2023, he is quoted as saying, 'One of the things with the death of my son is that I have been wondering whether I should rewrite my *Requiem*. I think that is what I am going to do next.'[41]

If Andrew Lloyd Webber does turn more to sacred music in his later latter years, he will perhaps finally be acknowledging the power of that spiritual high church aesthetic that I have argued in this chapter has been an inspiration throughout his life. He has expressed this sometimes rather hidden side to his personality and faith most openly in relation to what has been his other great consuming passion apart from music: the art, architecture, and artefacts of the Victorian period, and in particular of the High Church Anglo-Catholic movement and the Pre-Raphaelites, of whose paintings and designs he has a world-leading collection. There is undeniably a slightly camp, affected, and precious aspect to both these worlds, from which Lloyd Webber is not totally immune, as shown by his enthusiasm for giving his children names like Parthenope and Proserpine, a proposal that was sensibly vetoed by his second wife, Sarah. But Victorian Anglo-Catholicism and the Pre-Raphaelite movement also had a strong spiritual side, seeking to bring beauty, purity, and high aesthetic standards into worship and everyday life, and championing medieval virtues of faith and chivalry against what they took to be the ugliness and moral and spiritual bankruptcy of their own age. William Alwyn, the twentieth-century composer and near contemporary of Bill Loyd Webber, who also collected Pre-Raphaelite paintings, loved them for what he called their 'spiritual sensuality'.[42][43]

Among the Pre-Raphaelite pictures that Andrew Lloyd Webber has bought, many have religious themes, like William Holman Hunt's *The Morning Prayer*, which shows a girl with her hands clasped standing beside her bed (shades of Andrew as a boy). It is one of his most prized possessions. Another of his most valued treasures is John Millais' design for a Gothic window in All Saints, Margaret Street, in the form of a stone model made up of pairs of winged angels bent over and embracing each other to form arches. They could be models for the sculpted angels that Christine sings about in

154 MUSIC OF THE NIGHT

the prelude to 'Wishing you were somehow here again' in *Phantom*. Michael Coveney has rightly observed, 'The Millais window demonstrates a deep-seated passion not just for the churches themselves but for what goes on inside: spirituality, music, decoration, design. Lloyd Webber buys the whole package.'[44]

This whole heady High Church aesthetic package played a central role in a moment of musical epiphany which came to Andrew Lloyd Webber at the age of thirteen and can be compared in its impact to Arthur Sullivan hearing Jenny Lind singing arias from Mendelssohn's *Elijah* and Franz Lehár hearing Liszt's oratorio *Christus* at much the same age. Driving home from the Christmas morning service at Central Hall Westminster, his mother put on the car radio. The 'Te Deum' from *Tosca* was playing and absolutely bowled him over. He has since written: 'I realise now why that "Te Deum" hit every nerve in my body. My love of Victorian church architecture equalled an affinity with High Church decadence and if ever a piece of theatre is that, surely it's the *Tosca* "Te Deum". To this day it remains the only piece of theatre I secretly would love to direct.'[45]

The 'High Church decadence' that Lloyd Webber so admires and identifies with is very different from the simple sincerity and liberal idealism of Oscar Hammerstein's Unitarian Universalism. It is less innocent and straightforward, more knowing, and also darker and more shadowy. Lloyd Webber is less the true heir to Sullivan, the lover of life and light, whom he resembles in several ways, than to Lehár, with whom he shares that darker, lonelier sense of spiritual yearning. Relatively few critics have recognized this—one who did was the English jazz musician and broadcaster Steve Race in a letter to *The Times* in May 1997 after it had accused Lloyd Webber of 'reinventing some of the under-appreciated melodies of Haydn, Handel, Purcell, Faure and Puccini' in *Sunset Boulevard*. He wrote: 'He is neither Sondheim nor Gershwin, but he is a fine stage composer in the tradition of Lehár, Romberg, Friml and—yes—Ivor Novello.'[46]

As well as standing essentially in that operetta tradition which has been so under-valued for its serious and spiritual qualities, Lloyd Webber also belongs to that increasingly rare breed of composers in musical theatre whose tunes precede rather than follow the lyrics. This has given his music the chance to soar spiritually, emotionally, and in other respects. They have indeed been songs without words and in that lies their particular power and impact. In his own words, 'Melody fascinates, even obsesses me. There isn't a moment when it isn't somewhere at the back of my mind.'[47] It is this

SPIRITUAL YEARNING AND HIGH CHURCH AESTHETICS   155

obsession with melody that makes Lloyd Webber's music so memorable and accessible. It also makes for an underlying and unceasing restlessness as he constantly strives for something more and something better. Is this, too, in some sense a spiritual yearning? That is certainly the impression given in Gale Edwards' account of her experience while staying at Sydmonton Court in the run-up to the preview of *Whistle Down the Wind* in summer 1995. One night she was awoken in the early hours by the sound of a piano:

> I crept from the guest room down the great oak staircase in a dressing gown. The door was ajar and there was Andrew in his dressing gown and pyjamas and without batting an eyelid he said, 'Come in Gale, what do you think of this?' and I sat with him until dawn while he tried things out. He was excited, lost, frightened, in need of opinions. It was one of the most wonderful hours of my life.
>
> And I felt I could die happy because I'd been at the work face and seen how it works. I felt privileged to stand there and see it, and be a part of it. I felt I saw through some kind of window into Andrew's soul. He was not a celebrity or a world-famous composer. Just a man at a piano searching for the right tune.[48]

Is it too fanciful to suggest that, like the organist in Adelaide Procter's poem so memorably set by Sullivan, what Andrew Lloyd Webber was, and is, indeed, ever searching for is that elusive 'Lost Chord' which will 'flood the crimson twilight', 'calm the fevered spirit', and 'link all perplexed meanings into one perfect peace'? His obsession with melody is at root a spiritual search. Perhaps it will find its fulfilment in a return to the *Requiem* and in further sacred works.

Notes

1. Michael Coveney, *Cats on a Chandelier* (London: Hutchison, 1999), 261.
2. Ibid , 274
3. Ellis Nassour, *Rock Opera: The Creation of Jesus Christ Superstar* (New York: Hawthorn Books, 1973), 81.
4. Megan Rosenfeld, 'For The Love of Lloyd Webber', *The Washington Post*, 23 August 1992.
5. Coveney, *Cats on a Chandelier*, 206.
6. Keith Richmond, *The Musicals of Andrew Lloyd Webber* (London: Virgin, 1995), 96.
7. Coveney, *Cats on a Chandelier*, 12.
8. *Daily Telegraph*, 8 April 1988.
9. Manuscript copy of sermon given to the author by Don Lewis' widow, Ann, and quoted with her permission.
10. Michael Walsh, *Andrew Lloyd Webber: His Life and Works* (New York: Harry Abrams, 1997), 12.
11. Andrew Lloyd Webber, *Unmasked: A Memoir* (London: HarperCollins, 2019), 10.

12. Ibid., 17.
13. Ibid., 21–2.
14. *Ibid.,* 18–19.
15. Tim Rice, *Oh, What A Circus* (London: Hodder & Stoughton, 1999), 41.
16. Ibid., 59.
17. Ibid., 134.
18. Terence Copley, 'Children "Theologising" in Religious Education', *Education Today* 51 (April 2001). For a detailed analysis of the theological resonances and weaknesses of *Joseph* and the extent to which it distorts the Biblical story and is actually closer to the Islamic Yusuf of the Qur'an than the Judaeo-Christian figure in Genesis, see my book, *You've Got to Have a Dream* (London: SCM Press, 2004), 113–21.
19. Walsh, *Andrew Lloyd Webber*, 58.
20. Ibid., 123.
21. Ibid., 168.
22. Richmond, *The Musicals*, 98.
23. Lloyd Webber, *Unmasked*, 409.
24. Ibid., 410.
25. Ibid., 418.
26. Ibid., 423.
27. Ibid., 431. Lloyd Webber writes erroneously of the *Offertorium* that 'it is not theologically part of the Requiem Mass' and there is a typographical error *monte* for *morte*.
28. Ibid., 432.
29. Stephen Citron, *The New Musical: Sondheim and Lloyd Webber* (London: Chatto & Windus, 2001), 327.
30. Walsh, *Andrew Lloyd Webber*, 170.
31. Ibid., 172.
32. Citron, *The New Musical*, 326.
33. Ibid., 172.
34. Laurie Winer, 'Stage Wizard', *The Connoisseur* (September 1988), 149.
35. Richmond, *The Musicals*, 108.
36. Lloyd Webber, *Unmasked*, 479.
37. *Daily Telegraph*, 3 July 1998; Coveney, *Cats on a Chandelier*, 273. There is a much more detailed analysis of the theological message in the songs in *Whistle Down the Wind* in Ian Bradley, *You've Got to Have a Dream: The Message of the Musical* (London: SCM Press, 2004), 180–87.
38. Theatregoers' programme, *The Beautiful Game* (2000). The songs in *The Beautiful Game* are analysed in detail in Bradley, *You've Got to Have a Dream*, 192–4.
39. Serena Davies, 'Andrew Lloyd Webber's populist anthem hit the mark', *Daily Telegraph*, 8 May 2023.
40. Lloyd Webber, *Unmasked*, 193.
41. Interview with Dominic Cavendish, *Daily Telegraph*, 5 May 2023.
42. Coveney, *Cats on a Chandelier*, 218.
43. Leah Broad, *Quartet: How Four Women Changed the Musical World* (London: Faber & Faber, 2023), 370.
44. Coveney, *Cats on a Chandelier*, 218, 219.
45. Lloyd Webber, *Unmasked*, 32–3.
46. Coveney, *Cats on a Chandelier*, 203.
47. Lloyd Webber, *Unmasked*, 486.
48. Coveney, *Cats on a Chandelier*, 241.

8

The two Jesuses

Godspell and *Jesus Christ Superstar*

Students taking my Theology of the Musical course could be certain of one question appearing on their examination papers as it cropped up every year: a comparison of the portrayals of Jesus in *Godspell* and *Jesus Christ Superstar*.

These two musicals, which opened in New York within five months of one another in 1971, have much in common. Their creators were in their early twenties—indeed, Stephen Schwartz, composer of *Godspell*, and Andrew Lloyd Webber, composer of *Jesus Christ Superstar*, were born in the same month, March 1948. They were imbued with the values of the times—iconoclastic, anti-establishment, pushing the boundaries—and influenced by the rock musicals of the late 1960s, notably *Hair*, the self-styled 'American Tribal Love-Rock Musical' that had opened off-Broadway in 1967 (*Godspell* has been memorably described as '*Hair* with a haircut') and The Who's 1969 rock opera album *Tommy* about a deaf, mute, and blind boy who becomes a pinball champion and religious leader. Both *Godspell* and *Jesus Christ Superstar* were hugely popular, being turned into films in 1973, and remain so today more than half a century after their creation. They also remain the most interesting representations of Jesus on the musical stage.

But there, the similarities end. The portrayal of Jesus could not be more different in these two shows. In *Godspell*, he is a gentle, innocent, clown-like leader of the gang who derives his authority from his charisma and appealing teaching style through stories and parables. The Jesus of *Jesus Christ Superstar*, by contrast, is an angry, petulant adolescent who is aloof from his disciples and almost unremittingly anguished and intense.

Although, technically speaking, *Jesus Christ Superstar* precedes *Godspell*, having started life as a single record released in November 1969 and then as an LP issued in October 1970, in terms of performance, *Godspell* came first, having premiered in its original version at the Studio Theatre of the Carnegie Mellon University in December 1970, with subsequent performances at Café

Music of the Night. Ian Bradley, Oxford University Press. © Ian Bradley 2025.
DOI: 10.1093/9780197699775.003.0009

158   MUSIC OF THE NIGHT

La MaMa, East Manhattan, in March 1971. An extended and revised version, with lyrics and music by Stephen Schwartz, premiered at the Cherry Tree Theatre in Greenwich Village in May 1971, five months before *Jesus Christ Superstar* opened on Broadway at the Mark Hellinger Theater. So it is with *Godspell* that I begin.

John-Michael Tebelak and the genesis of *Godspell*

In its original conception, *Godspell* had a clear Christian orientation. It was the brainchild of John-Michael Tebelak. As a boy, he had been much taken by the chanting, the incense and the rich colours in the Russian Orthodox Church, which his Czech grandparents attended after coming as immigrants to the USA. With his parents, he also attended the Episcopal Cathedral in Cleveland, Ohio. His sister Trudy believes that his passion for theatre and drama may well have been inspired by his early exposure to religious ritual and pageantry. She recalls that 'when we came home from church, John-Michael would redo the church service. It was cute. He would take a cloth to make an altar, and burn candles, and do the communion—all the dramatic parts.'[1]

As a teenager, Tebelak seriously toyed with the idea of becoming an Episcopal priest. However, the lure of the theatre proved stronger and in 1966, he enrolled in the drama programme at Carnegie-Mellon University. In the words of Leon Katz, one of his professors there, 'He was truly religious. But he was also of the 1960s. So the two things were there in an odd combination.'[2] In fact, the two streams would come together in his master's project, which involved directing a stage production of either a classic or modern work. He obtained special permission to write his own play. Fascinated by mythology and its relationship with theatre, Tebelak originally looked at doing something based on Greek myths, but he found them too remote and turned instead to stories from the Christian tradition with which he had grown up and was more familiar. He began by reading miracle and mystery plays but found them heavy-going. Then, one afternoon, he read all four of the New Testament Gospels in a single sitting: 'I became terribly excited because I found what I wanted to portray on stage: Joy! I found a great joy, a simplicity—some rather comforting words in the Gospel itself, in these four books. I began immediately to adapt it.'[3]

Fired with the joy that he had found in the Gospels, Tebelak took himself to the Easter morning sunrise service at the Episcopal Cathedral in Pittsburgh.

THE TWO JESUS 159

The congregation were grumbling about the snow and apparently lacking in any Resurrection spirit. The clergy were no better:

> An old priest came out and mumbled into a microphone, and people mumbled things back, and then everyone got up and left. Instead of healing the burden, or resurrecting the Christ, it seems those people had pushed him back into the tomb. They had refused to let him come out that day.[4]

Tebelak's negative experience was further confirmed when a policeman who had been sitting two pews in front of him approached him as he was coming out of the Cathedral and asked to search him. He clearly thought that the young man in the hippie clothes was a drug addict who had ducked into the service to escape the snowstorm. In Tebelak's words,

> It angered me so much that I went home and realized what I wanted to do with the Gospels: I wanted to make it the simple, joyful message that I felt the first time I read them and recreate the sense of community, which I did not share when I went to that service.[5]

The play on which Tebelak embarked for his master's degree project thus had an evangelistic as much as a theatrical or academic purpose. It was designed to celebrate the joy at the heart of the Gospels, which he felt the church had lost and suppressed. He called it *The Godspell*, taking up an old English word for Gospel with connotations of magic, and expressed the hope that it would 'weave God's spell over the audience'. He told Peggy Gordon, one of the original cast members, that he wanted the audience 'to get so drenched and embraced by love and joy' that they would become 'transformed'.[6] He also had a more specific agenda, expressed later when he noted that he had written *Godspell* as 'a statement against the organised church—as an indictment of it for keeping religion so serious and removed from the people . . . it was designed to be part of the Jesus awareness'.[7]

Tebelak's play was essentially a straight dramatization of the parables from St Matthew's Gospel framed by key incidents at the beginning and end of Jesus' ministry: his identification and baptism by John the Baptist and his betrayal by Judas and crucifixion. Most of the dialogue, and the lyrics of several of the original songs, come straight out of the Bible. The characters are confined to Jesus and his disciples. At the beginning of the second act, three of the disciples dress up as Pharisees and bombard Jesus with questions such as 'By whose authority are you acting like this?' And after the Last Supper,

·160   MUSIC OF THE NIGHT

there is a dream sequence in which the disciples become devils and test Jesus' faith. But other key figures in the Biblical story of Jesus, such as the chief priests, Pilate, and Herod, do not appear at all. Indeed, the whole emphasis is on the self-contained, tightly knit community that Jesus forms with his disciples, who include several women. Neither he nor they have any interaction with anyone else. They almost seem cut off from the rest of the world, an impression reinforced by the fact that the action takes place in an urban playground surrounded by a high wire fence. There are intriguing, if probably unintentional, theological and Biblical resonances here, both of the Marcan secrecy motif and the Johannine emphasis on Jesus and those who follow him standing in opposition to the world.

Tebelak introduced several features which would become key hallmarks of all subsequent productions of *Godspell*. Perhaps the most striking is the portrayal of Jesus with the characteristic face make up of a clown and the fact he paints the faces of his disciples in a similar manner. Tebelak had been deeply influenced by reading *The Feast of Fools,* a seminal work first published in 1969 by Harvey Cox, a radical professor of divinity at Harvard University. As its subtitle, 'A Theological Essay on Festivity and Fantasy', suggests, Cox wanted to emphasize the elements of celebration and fantasy that he felt had been lost in modern Christianity and to champion medieval notions of the feast of fools and of Christ as Harlequin. In taking up this image, Tebelak was drawing not just on 1960s progressive Christian theology but also on Biblical texts such as Paul's description of Christianity in 1 Corinthians 1.23 as 'foolishness to the Greeks' and Jesus' portrayal of himself as the Lord of the Dance in his statement in Matthew 11.17: 'We played for you and you would not dance'. It is sometimes erroneously suggested that Jesus and the disciples are depicted in *Godspell* as hippies. As Stephen Schwartz has pointed out: 'the characters in *Godspell* were never supposed to be hippies. They were supposed to be putting on "clown" garb to follow the example of the Jesus character as conceived by John Michael Tebelak, according to the "Christ as clown" theory propounded by Harvey Cox among others.'[8]

The originality and significance of portraying Jesus as a clown were well summarized by Dean Pitchford, a Yale English major raised as a Catholic who was recruited as a typist for the first production of *Godspell* and went on to play Jesus in several revivals:

The clown concept was pure genius. . . with *Godspell* I thought of Jesus as the greatest prankster of them all, the most infectious fun meister. What a wonderful way to think of Jesus, because religion had always showed him

THE TWO JESUS   161

as a very serious man with a very serious mission. . . *Godspell* opened my eyes. This is funny. All my life I've been worshipping a tragic story. What about giving people another version of that story?[9]

Another significant feature of *Godspell*, which has been maintained from the beginning, is having John the Baptist and Judas played by the same actor. They are, in fact, the only two characters apart from Jesus who retain their Biblical names in the show—the other disciples, who include women as well as men, simply assume the names of the actors who are playing them. Both John the Baptist and Judas stand slightly apart from the other disciples, but in some ways, they are also the closest to Jesus and the ones who most clearly recognize him for what he is—the one baptising him and the other betraying him. In the words of the script notes, the composite figure of John/Judas is 'both Jesus' lieutenant and most ardent disciple and the doubter who begins to question and rebel. He is the most serious and intellectual of the group'.[10]

This characterization raises significant theological questions, especially in the portrayal of Judas. According to Don Scardino, who has played Jesus in more than 1000 performances and also directed one of the New York revivals of *Godspell*, Tebelak's view of Judas was deeply influenced by the Greek writer Nikos Kazantzakis' 1955 novel *The Last Temptation of Christ*, which, along with *The Feast of Fools*, he encouraged cast members to read:

> The book says Judas is his ally, his closest friend. It's almost as if Jesus is saying that the others are my children in a way. 'They are my disciples so they cannot betray me. You are the only one who can do this because you love me the most. And if you love me the most, you will help me complete what I must do'. Judas, being human, is confused and feels betrayed himself, but runs off to do it because he has to do it.[11]

In the betrayal scene in *Godspell*, instead of Judas kissing Jesus to identify him to the Roman soldiers, Jesus kisses him, signifying his love and forgiveness as well as his understanding of what needs to be done. Judas is subsequently reintegrated into the community. Wallace Smith, who played John the Baptist/Judas in the 2011 Broadway Revival, has written that, while it might seem logical for him to be played as a villain,

> In *Godspell* we focus on a community of people that have to learn how to really love one another. Judas happens to be the one that needs the most love and forgiveness. I think one of the most beautiful things in this show

162   MUSIC OF THE NIGHT

is that they bring him back into the community even though he feels he's not worthy to be a part of it anymore. I don't think of him as [the enemy]. I think of him as somebody who really wants to do the right thing, but, in all human nature, we all have things we need to work on.[12]

Although he had initially found them rather heavy-going, Tebelak drew on some of the features found in medieval mystery plays, including exuberant dressing up and singing, performance and enactment of the parables, emphasis on community and celebration, and concern to involve the audience. For Robert Ellis, professor of English at Worcester State University, *Godspell* is in many ways their heir and successor, especially in terms of closing the cultural gap between subject and audience: 'When a modern theatergoer takes in "Godspell," he is seeing the closest approximation our times have made to the medieval religious drama.'[13]

The original opening of the show, sometimes but not always kept in later revivals, features the disembodied voice of God, as spoken by Jesus, making a profound theological utterance which begins, 'My name is known: God and King. I am most in majesty, in whom no beginning may be and no end'. This is immediately followed by a lengthy prologue, 'The Tower of Babble', in which the world's leading philosophers, including Socrates, Aquinas, Luther, Leonardo da Vinci, Gibbon, Nietzsche, Jean-Paul Sartre and Buckminster Fuller, compete to express their own views of God and the meaning of life, ending up in a cacophonous and chaotic war of words which is silenced by the blowing of the shofar, the ancient ram's horn used as a call to prayer on Jewish holy days, by John the Baptist to signal the coming of Christ. The clear implication is that without the integrative presence of Jesus, everyone is simply pursuing their own ideas and agendas, and there is no cooperation and community but just confusion.

The songs which Tebelak introduced and interspersed among the dramatized recitations of the parables and beatitudes came almost entirely from existing traditional Christian texts, originally set to music by Duane Bolick, a fellow student at Carnegie-Mellon. They included four hymns which he had taken from the Episcopal Hymnal: 'O bless the Lord, my soul', an adaptation of Psalm 103 by the early nineteenth-century Scottish-born hymn writer, James Montgomery; the harvest hymn, 'We plough the fields and scatter', based on a late eighteenth-century German poem by Matthias Claudius; 'The Peoples' Anthem' by the Victorian Chartist activist Ebenezer Elliott, 'When wilt thou save the people', with its radical expression of the

Christian social gospel and call for a bias to the poor; and 'Turn back, O man, forswear thy foolish ways', a song of repentance written in the midst of the First World War by the English author Clifford Bax. There was also an adaptation of the lines from Psalm 137, 'We hanged our harps upon the willows'; a setting of John the Baptist's line in Mark 1.3: 'Prepare the way of the Lord'; and an adaptation of the thirteenth-century prayer by Richard of Chichester,

> O most merciful redeemer, friend and brother,
> may I know thee more clearly,
> love thee more dearly,
> and follow thee more nearly, day by day.

Stephen Schwartz's involvement in *Godspell*

While well received at its first performances, *Godspell* would probably have sunk into relative oblivion and languished as just another college show with promise were it not for Stephen Schwartz being brought in to write a new score. He was approached by producers Edgar Lansbury and Joe Beruh, who saw the potential of the show and wanted to bring it to a much wider audience. They gave it a new subtitle, 'A musical based on the Gospel According to St Matthew', emphasizing its Biblical basis. Watching Tebelak's original show on its last night at the Café La Mama, Schwartz found it 'theatrically inventive, original and, above all, hilarious . . . and I don't mean satirical let's-make-fun-of-religion funny, I mean the humor that arises from human beings behaving according to human foibles. And then at the end, it was suddenly and unexpectedly moving and uplifting.'[14]

Schwartz came to *Godspell* with a very different approach from Tebelak. For him, it was not an evangelistic project designed to be part of the Jesus awareness movement and to shame the church for killing the joy of the Gospel. He went so far as to write in an email to one of my students, '*Godspell* was never meant to be a musical version of the story of Jesus. It is rather a story about the formation of a community and what happens to it when its charismatic leader and founder has gone.'[15]

Schwartz produced an infectiously lively score for *Godspell* in a style that he described as 'pop pastiche' and likened to Lloyd Webber's *Joseph and the Amazing Technicolor Dreamcoat*. As well as re-setting the existing hymns and

164   MUSIC OF THE NIGHT

songs, he added several new ones for which he supplied lyrics and music. He also converted several passages of dialogue into song and made significant changes to improve the flow and pace of the show, shortening the prologue while bringing in new philosophers, including Galileo, Hegel, Jonathan Edwards, and Lafayette Ronald Hubbard, the founder of Scientology.

True to his 'Reluctant Pilgrim' persona, as discussed in Chapter 6, when writing about *Godspell*, Schwartz has always emphasized his own non-Christian background and insisted that for him, it was purely and simply about the formation and survival of a community and had no religious dimension. Yet at the same time, he took a good deal of care and trouble with the specifically Christian texts and in several instances significantly enhanced their message. He converted Jesus' long speech taken from Matthew 23, beginning 'Alas for you, lawyers and pharisees', into a song, feeling that this would give his angry outburst against hypocrisy much more impact. After 'sitting with the Bible [he used a King James version which he kept near his piano] and going through that section', he produced lyrics and a tune that he described as the most 'musical theatre' of all the numbers in the show.[16]

Another of the new songs that Schwartz wrote shows the extent of his concern to be faithful to the Bible and the nuances of the Gospels. It was written for one of the disciples to sing during a scene in Act 1, which both he and Tebelak felt was heavy on dialogue and short on music. He took his inspiration from a remark made in the previous scene about the importance of listening to Moses and the prophets. Specifically referencing Elijah and Jezebel, and mentioning the promised Land, 'Learn your lessons well' begins by picturing a swath of sinners 'sitting yonder and letting their minds wander' instead of studying the good Lord's rules. As Carol de Giere has commented, Schwartz's lyrics have something of the old-fashioned Sunday School lesson about them.[17]

Schwartz also put a lot of thought into the vaudeville soft shoe shuffle duet 'All for the best' that he wrote for Jesus and Judas. He suggested it to Tebelak because he felt that it was important that the two characters should connect emotionally: 'I said, if Judas is going to betray Jesus in the second act, you have to see that they're friends and allies in the first act, so they need to do a musical number together'. Jesus' lyrics, about how grim life can be here on earth but how we will be blessed in heaven, are directly inspired by the line in Matthew 5.12: 'Great is your reward in the kingdom of heaven'. Judas' cynical counterpoint revels in the good life that so many enjoy, unjustly, here and now. In Schwartz's words,

THE TWO JESUES   165

What I tried to do was have him say that the rich people and the lucky get all the stuff... and present the image of the self-interested 'best' hanging onto their mountains of money without a care for the rest of humanity ... By having Jesus and Judas be at odds with one another philosophically in the song's lyrics, and yet performing and dancing together as a team, it helps to illustrate the paradox in their relationship in a way dialogue never could.[18]

One of Schwartz's alterations to Tebelak's original libretto actually had the effect of making it more respectful of the Christian narrative. In the original finale, Jesus had the line 'Oh God, I'm busted' as he hung on the wire. Schwartz felt that this trivialized the crucifixion, and he persuaded Tebelak to drop it. Once again, the Reluctant Pilgrim was proving himself to have a high level of religious awareness and sensitivity. Overall, the effect of Schwartz's contribution was to make *Godspell* a far more polished and enjoyable show and considerably enhance its box office appeal and commercial potential without in any way diminishing its religious message or spiritual resonances.

The Jesus of *Godspell*

The question of Jesus' divinity is left deliberately uncertain in *Godspell*. This is why there is no resurrection scene. Jesus' body is taken down from the wire fence on which he has been crucified—significantly, perhaps, there is no cross—and carried shoulder high by the disciples as they sing 'Long live God'. Many see this song, and Jesus' appearance for the curtain call, as implying his resurrection. Tebelak himself is on record as saying to a fan that the resurrection is, in fact, signalled at the end when the chorus 'Long live God' speeds up and segues into 'Prepare ye the way of the Lord', although this could be taken as more suggestive of a second coming. Schwartz predictably takes a rather different line, writing on his website forum in response to a question about why the disciples are rejoicing at the end despite the fact that Jesus has died and there is no resurrection:

The ending is meant to be ambiguous. GODSPELL is about the formation of a community that is going to carry on the teachings of Jesus and spread his messages, and that is what they are rejoicing about. Regardless of whether or not one believes in the divinity of Jesus, the gift of his messages is something everyone has cause to celebrate (one need only glance at the

166 MUSIC OF THE NIGHT

current state of the world to wish more people, including many who pro-
fess to be Christians, actually lived by those messages.) But in any event,
the end of GODSPELL has always left it up to the individual viewer to de-
cide whether or not Jesus rises from the dead—I would argue that it can be
interpreted either way. And I would think you would agree with me that it is
the message and teachings he brought to the world that are most important
in any event.[19]

Not a few liberal Christians would agree with this assessment that Jesus'
actions and teaching and their impact are more important than whether he
himself was actually physically resurrected.

The lack of a definite resurrection is one of the main features of *Godspell*
that has provoked the ire of fundamentalists, many of whom are also uneasy
about the portrayal of Jesus as a Superman-shirted and face-painted clown.
In *You've Got to Have a Dream,* I quote from a website entitled 'Godspell—
The Ultimate Blasphemy'. But there have also been many testimonies to the
musical's spiritual power by Christians who are not over-concerned about its
ambiguity over Jesus' resurrection. For Robert Ellis:

> In *Godspell* Christ is one of us. That playground fence we have all scaled
> becomes His cross. We are invited, in late medieval fashion, to participate
> in the agony . . . We do not know what to do about this death or even what
> to make of it, but we are together in our feeling, and we do not come away
> overwhelmed by the futility of the death. The festal freshness of the first act
> has passed into an extended sobriety. *Godspell,* lacking the Resurrection
> which would soon follow in the medieval cycle, cannot end comically or
> joyously. Within its limits it is too honest . . . But even a Christ who does not
> rise from the dead affirms a religious mystery. *Godspell* may illustrate the
> limits of belief in our society, but it does proclaim anew for our generation
> some measure of the Good News.[20]

The film version of *Godspell* and more recent productions

Several recent stage productions of *Godspell* have changed the original
ending and substituted the song 'Beautiful city', written by Schwartz for the
1973 film version, which is largely shot in an empty New York, and rewritten

following the 1991 Los Angeles riots. Sung in the film by Jesus and John the Baptist as they hold hands and lead the disciples skipping through the city, it looks forward to the building out of ruins and rubble of 'a beautiful city ... not of angels ... but of man'. It leans more towards being an expression of idealist humanist optimism than of specifically Christian hope and faith, but its exuberant anthemic structure gives it a spiritual quality which hovers somewhere between the sacred and the secular.

The film added other details which reinforce the emphasis on Jesus as a charismatic leader whom people want to follow. It opens with a sequence showing those who are later to become his disciples about their normal jobs, among them a waitress in a diner, a parking attendant, a taxi driver, and a ballet dancer. Leaving their places of work in response to the call of John the Baptist, who comes over Brooklyn Bridge pushing a handcart and singing 'Prepare ye the way of the Lord', they congregate by the Bethesda Fountain in Central Park to be baptised in a joyful, exuberant splash-around. Jesus appears, standing slightly apart, and gets himself baptised by John before singing 'God save the people' and joining the disciples in a joyful dance through the park. Another significant change made in the film is in its treatment of the parable of the sheep and the goats where, unlike in the original stage version, Jesus comes back to rescue the goats, who have been left bleating and apparently damned, and tells them to join the saved sheep, effectively proclaiming a theology of universal salvation.

Godspell remains a favourite of high school and college music and drama groups, especially in the US, retaining its original freshness and innocence and continuing to raise significant theological and philosophical questions. Its great strength is that it can function both as a Christian musical pointing up the joy of the good news of the Gospel, as Tebelak originally intended and as a more secular show exploring and celebrating the formation of community, as emphasized by Schwartz. Some productions play up the Christian element by having the cast come out on stage or go down into the auditorium during the interval with trays of wine or grape juice, which they invite the audience to share as though in a celebration of communion. The 2002 touring production by Stephen Schwartz's son, Scott, went further and had John the Baptist apparently baptise the audience by flicking them with a sponge dipped in a bucket of water after baptizing Jesus. Not surprisingly, the many Christians who have been involved in professional productions tend to

168   MUSIC OF THE NIGHT

play up the religious element. For Don Scardino, 'The show is blessed by the spirit of Christ. The spirit descends upon the show, takes over, and leads everybody through it . . .the show is divinely inspired'.[21] He cites testimonies of those who have given up drugs, patched up broken relationships, and gone back to reading the Bible after seeing the show. *Godspell* is much more popular than *Jesus Christ Superstar* for performance by church groups, although this may have as much to do with its greater accessibility and simplicity as with its religiosity.

Thanks partly perhaps to Tebelak's premature death in 1985, his more specifically Christian vision of *Godspell* has diminished over the years, and the more secular, humanist view of Schwartz has come to prevail in many professional productions. There are several clear pointers to this trend, such as the frequent dropping of the song 'Learn your lessons well' with its somewhat preachy tone, and the tendency of stage productions increasingly to follow the film in ending with 'We can build a beautiful city' rather than with 'Long Live God' segueing into 'Prepare Ye the Way of The Lord'. Stephen Schwartz's son, Scott, who directed successful tours of *Godspell* in the USA and UK in 2001 and 2002, shares his father's belief that it is not a religious work, despite his own innovation with John the Baptist 'baptising' the audience, as noted above, which might seem to contradict this:

> The show was ultimately meant for an audience that did not need to be religious or believe in Jesus as the son of God, but would hopefully come to respect him as a very good and wise man... I think that what the show really is about is a group of people who are strangers, and these strangers come together slowly under the leadership of a man who happens to be named Jesus but could just as well be called Daniel or Jonathan. This guy has some messages that he wants to get out there, and they're very good messages, all around the theme of love thy neighbour. What happens is these strangers get to know each other and come together to form a community . . . Once this community is formed, it's about the challenges that communities go through in the real world, specifically the challenge of losing the leader and then seeing what happens.[22]

Some recent productions have sought much more emphatically to downplay the religious elements. One such, directed by Richard Carroll in 2022 in Sydney, Australia, was set in an LGBTQ + community bar festooned with rainbow flags and with the Progress Pride Flag hanging on the wall. It starred

THE TWO JESUS 169

Billie Palin as a female Jesus. For the *Guardian* critic Cassie Tongue, there was one fundamental flaw:

> Carroll can't quite commit to the show's religious core. Every time Jesus delivers a commandment, Palin is directed with a knowing or mocking twist to throw the phrasing away, as though embarrassed by the holiness. That's fair; in a queer-coded space with a diverse cast, it's easy to remember not all people have been included in the church's good word. In the inner workings of a musical about celebrating that word, however, this direction falls flat.
>
> This isn't to say that musical adaptations of religious texts can't interrogate, subvert or challenge. But for a new interpretation to work, there needs to be a level of deep, if not sincere, engagement with the source.
>
> Carroll's *Godspell* spends so much time apologising for or deflecting from the musical's most directly Biblical quotes and aspects that it isn't able to show how a community can come together to care for each other. The members of the ensemble don't have clearly telegraphed individual motivations or relationships, which means that even when they all join in recreating parables, we don't see how or why this is the moment they're able to let go and let God in, as it were.[23]

Tongue's critique argues, quite rightly in my view, that at least some acknowledgement of the religious influences behind *Godspell*, and of the Biblical references and spiritual resonances which suffuse it, is necessary to bring out the theme of community which more modern and more secular directors see as being at its heart. We are brought back to the key importance of the characterization of Jesus who, in Stephen Schwartz's words, 'is the driving force in the show' and 'must be the most charismatic individual in the cast. High energy, charming, funny, gentle but with strength. He is the sort of person others instinctively follow'.[24]

The genesis of *Jesus Christ Superstar*

The casting requirements for *Jesus Christ Superstar* are rather different. Judas is in many ways a more charismatic and certainly a more thoughtful figure than the anguished, angry, and distinctly uncharming Jesus, who is portrayed not as a natural leader of the gang whom others would instinctively follow

170 MUSIC OF THE NIGHT

but rather as a lonely outsider of the kind portrayed in Albert Camus' famous novel. The fact is that *Jesus Christ Superstar* is a wholly different beast from *Godspell*, with a much less overtly Christian genesis and original agenda.

Following the success of *Joseph and the Amazing Technicolor Dreamcoat*, Rice and Lloyd Webber toyed with writing a musical about Richard the Lionheart and the Crusades, provisionally entitled *Come Back Richard, Your Country Needs You*. They also explored the Biblical story of King David as told in the first book of Samuel and got as far as writing a song, 'Samuel, Samuel, this is the first book of Samuel'. But neither theme inspired them, and they responded to a suggestion from Dean Martin Sullivan at St Paul's Cathedral to move from the Old Testament to the New and 'take Christ down from the stained glass window'.[25] Ignoring the advice of their Jewish agent, David Land, that they should do anything other than tackle the life of Jesus, they enthusiastically turned to a story and a character with whom they were already familiar thanks to their many hours of compulsory worship at school. In Lloyd Webber's words, 'If one had religion sort of rammed down one's throat when one was in school, it was inevitable, I should think, that Christ would be one of the first subjects one would choose'.[26] Rice forsook the *Wonder Book of Bible Stories* that he had used for *Joseph* and turned instead to the US Roman Catholic bishop Fulton Sheen's *Life of Christ* for its calibration and comparison of the four Gospel writers' accounts of the last week of Jesus' life.

Although the original suggestion for *Jesus Christ Superstar* had come from the Dean of St Paul's Cathedral, it was in no way conceived as a Christian musical. Neither Lloyd Webber nor Rice were motivated by the religious faith and enthusiasm that had inspired Tebelak to write *Godspell*. Lloyd Webber's religious beliefs were discussed in the previous chapter. Rice's were more straightforward. As he himself put it, 'Technically, I'm Church of England, which is really nothing. But I don't follow it. I wouldn't say I was a Christian. I have nothing against it.'[27] If anything, the prime motivation of the two young collaborators was commercial—here was a good, strong, daring subject for a rock opera that would break boundaries, attract attention, and propel them into a much bigger league. That is not to say that they were wholly cynical about it and did not have a more serious interest in the subject. Rice got the idea of the title from a description of the Welsh singer Tom Jones in *Melody Maker* as 'The world's Number One Superstar'. He had long been fascinated by the character of Judas in the Gospel stories and was very taken by a line in a Bob Dylan song on his 1964 album *The Times They*

Are A-Changin' which asked the question as to 'whether Judas Iscariot had God on his side?'.

These two influences are very evident in the song that formed the A-side of the pop single released in November 1969 to launch the whole 'Superstar' project. Re-using the tune about the first book of Samuel that Lloyd Webber had originally written for the putative musical about King David, it put into Judas' mouth a whole series of questions about exactly who Jesus was and what his sacrifice on the Cross was all about. Interviewed about it, Rice freely admitted,

> Neither of us is religious: we just want to put on a good show. We're not trying to make any particular religious point. If people want to read into it that Christ was God or not, then they can ... We feel that there are certain questions which it is fair to ask about Christ and the basic theme of the record is quite simply, "What's it all about?".[28]

The B-side of the single featured an orchestral piece by Lloyd Webber, later titled *John 19:41* by Rice. Played just after the crucifixion scene at the end of the show, it also formed the basis for Jesus' song 'Gethsemane'. It was, in Lloyd Webber's own words,

> a very Richard Straussian arrangement for heavily divided strings. I already knew what I would compose for the crucifixion and my instinct was that this music would become its coda. I wanted the antithesis to the stark horror of Jesus's death, something overripe and more stained-glass window than wooden nails, that hinted at how Jesus became sentimentalized in paintings like Holman Hunt's *Light of the World* or the Baroque excesses of southern Italy.[29]

The two quotations above suggest a dichotomy between the approaches of librettist and composer, with the former wanting to ask awkward and gritty questions about Jesus' identity and the latter seeking to envelop him in sentimental Pre-Raphaelite and Baroque excesses in keeping with his own High Anglican aesthetic tastes. The overall feel of the single, which made it to number 14 in the US singles chart, and the double long-playing album that followed it in October 1970 and sold two million copies within twelve months, leant very much towards the former rather than the latter approach. The same is true of the stage version for which it provided the taster. Aside

172   MUSIC OF THE NIGHT

from the camp ragtime two-step song for King Herod, which recycled a tune originally written for *Come Back Richard, Your Country Needs You* and was introduced to bring some much-needed light relief, the mood of *Jesus Christ Superstar* is unremittingly serious and intense, far more so than *Godspell*. Its through-sung score, harsh, shrieked vocal lines, extensive use of pulsating bass guitars, and 5/4 and 7/8 time signatures, and its 'in your face', angst-ridden atmosphere make it the first significant rock opera and also the first of the gloomy-doomy mega-musicals that were to dominate the London stage for the next two decades and more.

Reactions to *Jesus Christ Superstar*

Attacked by fundamentalist Christians, Jews, militant secularists, and atheists alike, *Jesus Christ Superstar* was welcomed by liberal clergy and theologians who had achieved a dominant position in many mainstream churches in Britain by the end of the 1960s. This was especially true of the Church of England. For the enthusiasts of what became known as 'South Bank religion', which flourished in London throughout the 1960s and 1970s and was associated particularly with Mervyn Stockwood, Bishop of Southwark from 1959 to 1980, the questions raised about Jesus and brought to a wide audience through the medium of rock music were relevant and welcome. They echoed points that had been made in the best-selling book 'Honest to God' by the Bishop of Woolwich, John Robinson, published in 1963. Robinson's successor, David Sheppard, a former England cricketer who came from the Evangelical wing of the Church of England, announced in 1972 that, despite not being a fan of pop music, he found himself playing the *Superstar* album 'at every opportunity. Why? Because it grips me so much and it seems to me to be an utterly genuine attempt of two young men to enter into the story of the Cross.'[30] From the church's liberal wing, Martin Sullivan enthused over *Superstar*, writing this endorsement for the sleeve of the original single:

> There are people who may be shocked by this record. I asked them to listen to it and think again. It is a desperate cry. 'Who are you, Jesus Christ?' is the urgent enquiry, and a very proper one at that. The onus is on the listener to come up with his replies. If he is a Christian let him answer for Christ. The singer says, 'Don't get me wrong, I only want to know'. He is entitled to some response.[31]

THE TWO JESUS 173

Sullivan expressed his desire to stage the musical in St Paul's Cathedral. This was kiboshed when the *Daily Express* printed a wholly erroneous story that John Lennon, who had recently declared that the Beatles were bigger than Jesus, would play Christ with his wife Yoko Ono as Mary Magdalene. Also aborted was a proposed one-off performance on the stage used for the famous passion play in Oberammergau, Austria.

In the US, first reactions to *Jesus Christ Superstar* were predictably mixed. An irate nun stood outside the Mark Hellinger Theater on its opening night carrying a banner declaring 'I am a Bride of Christ, not Mrs Superstar', while a Catholic priest in New Jersey used the lyrics of the title song as the basis for a sermon in which he said, 'this is exactly what the youth are asking today'. Billy Graham denounced the musical as bordering on 'blasphemy and sacrilege' because of its failure to acknowledge the divine aspect of Jesus and its absence of a Resurrection scene. However, he went on to concede that 'the opera asks questions millions of young people are asking ... and if it causes religious discussion and leads young people to search their bibles, to that extent it may be beneficial'.[32] In reviewing the 1973 film, the liberal Protestant weekly, *The Christian Century*, applauded it as the first Biblical film to portray Jesus 'in a first century setting with twentieth century sensitivity' and described it as 'superb cinema and stimulating theology', while the conservative *Christianity Today* found it 'a theological disaster'.[33]

The characters of Judas and Jesus in *Jesus Christ Superstar*

If one can hear the words through the intense shrieked falsettos and the over-amplification, there are undoubtedly many theological points to ponder in *Jesus Christ Superstar*. Throughout the show, Judas is portrayed as a much stronger and more intelligent character than the angst-ridden Jesus. His opening soliloquy sets him apart from the rest of the disciples, whom he criticizes for having 'too much heaven on their minds' and for their adulation of Jesus, who has become too big for his boots and started believing that the things people say about him are true. More prominent than the Judas of *Godspell*, he shares some of the same characteristics and beliefs, notably that Jesus has abandoned what should be his main role as a political activist and opponent of Roman oppression. Indeed, what Schwartz writes about him in *Godspell* could apply equally to the Judas of *Superstar*: 'Judas wants Jesus to be more of a revolutionary—to sweep out the old order and the fat cats, by

174 MUSIC OF THE NIGHT

violent means if necessary. When he begins to see that Jesus' philosophy is to "turn the other cheek", he grows disillusioned, and this is what leads to the betrayal.'[34] For Rice, 'Judas did not think of himself as a traitor. He did what he did, not because he was basically evil, but because he was intelligent.'[35] He felt Jesus was getting out of control as people began worshipping him as a god.

Judas' dominant role in *Superstar* is reinforced by the fact that it is he rather than Jesus who undergoes a resurrection, re-appearing after his suicide to ask the stream of questions in the title song. Asking why and when Jesus appeared when he did, and probing the nature and meaning of his sacrifice, could well form the starting point for a Christological dissertation or church discussion group.

Jesus, by contrast, acts more like a petulant adolescent, telling the crowds of cripples and beggars who gather round him to go away, losing his temper with his disciples, and haranguing God in the anguished and almost unbearably intense 'Gethsemane' soliloquy. In that song, he describes himself as 'sad and tired' and begs that the cup of poison may be taken away from him but ultimately accepts that, if it is what God wants, he will face death by crucifixion. He is perhaps seen at his most angst-ridden and self-pitying during the Last Supper when he passes around the wine and bread to his self-satisfied disciples, who are congratulating themselves that they will be remembered long after their deaths. 'For all you care, this wine could be my blood', he tells them, 'for all you care, this bread could be my body'. This remarkable statement, which turns the conventional Christian understanding of the Eucharist on its head, conveys a real sense of Jesus as the man of sorrows, despised and rejected, the one who, in the words of John's Gospel, 'came to his own, and his own received him not'.

In an early radio interview, Tim Rice spelt out clearly the approach that he and Andrew Lloyd Webber took to Jesus in their musical:

We approached the opera from the point of view of Christ the man, rather than Christ the god. We had been well coached in the mechanics of Christianity and its legends and beliefs. That was drummed into us at school. They treated the legends so we decided to treat the bloke as a man. We read the gospels very carefully and that was it. What we did not read was eighty-three other people's interpretations of Christ because we didn't want to be affected by their views.[36]

THE TWO JESUS 175

Several points emerge from this statement, not least the fact that, despite his insistence that the focus is on the human Jesus, Rice calls him 'Christ', perhaps unconsciously testifying to the lasting influence of the High Anglican Lancing College where he had been at school. There is also his insistence that he and Lloyd Webber took their cue straight from their reading of the Gospels and without reference to any secondary sources. In fact, their portrayal of Jesus as a fallible human being, never sure of himself or of whether or not he is God, tied in with the way he had been depicted in Kazantzakis' *The Last Temptation of Christ*, although this novel was not as direct an influence as it was for Tebelak. It had also been suggested in Pasolini's 1964 film, *The Gospel According to St Matthew*. There were cultural currents anticipating and encouraging this kind of interpretation, just as there were theological movements supporting Tebelak's very different depiction of Jesus as a clown.

The Jesus of *Superstar* is both a less attractive and in some ways a more human figure than the Jesus of *Godspell*, although both maintain a certain distance from others. Rice has written that 'We tried to humanize Christ because, for me, I find Jesus as portrayed in the Gospels as a God a very unrealistic figure'.[37] In Mary Magdalene's words in her ballad, 'I don't know how to love him', 'he's a man, he's just a man' and yet one who both scares and attracts her. For some, this humanizing of Jesus has proved very appealing. I have met and interviewed two fans who came back to church and regained their faith as a direct result of seeing the show. In both cases, they told me that what attracted them was the 'humanness of Jesus ... so different from the anaemic Jesus portrayed in Sunday School'.

Unlike *Godspell*, *Superstar* focuses on Jesus' passion and trial rather than on his teaching, and it features the other characters portrayed in the Gospel. Pontius Pilate is given a wistful, haunting solo, 'I dreamed I met a Galilean', set in the dark key of B flat minor. Herod is caricatured as a cruel and camp villain, and Caiaphas, Annas, and the other Jewish priests are depicted as grotesque figures with outrageous costumes and distorted voices. There are no hymns or settings of traditional psalms and prayers, as in *Godspell*, although the exuberant chorus, 'Hosanna, Heysanna', sung by the crowd as Jesus enters Jerusalem could come straight out of a Palm Sunday liturgy and I have indeed used it in church worship in that way. Like *Godspell*, *Superstar* has no resurrection scene. The audience is left with the crucifixion in keeping with the emphasis throughout on the human rather than the divine side of Jesus. This is not to say that Jesus is portrayed as being without

176 MUSIC OF THE NIGHT

any aura or charisma. Mary Magdalene has quite clearly been changed and moved through her interaction with him. So, in his own way, has Pilate, who describes him as 'a most amazing man'.

More recent productions of *Jesus Christ Superstar*

If productions of *Godspell* over the last fifty years have moved in the direction of downplaying the specifically religious dimension that was there at the beginning, the opposite has tended to happen with *Jesus Christ Superstar*. The original 1971 Broadway production was full of garish spectacle and over-the-top visual effects, with huge angels swinging about on psychedelic wings, dancing dwarfs and lepers, and a crucifixion scene set on a dazzling golden triangle. The London production, which opened in August 1972, was simpler and starker, as was the 1973 film version made on location in Israel and directed by Norman Jewison. A new, less glitzy production by Gale Edwards, which focused more intensely on the relationship between Jesus and Judas, began a two-year run in London in 1996, was the basis for a video version released in 2000, and came to New York the same year. Some recent productions have emphasized the theme of social justice and portrayed Jesus and his disciples primarily as political and economic agitators. In the 2012 UK Arena tour, Ben Forster as Jesus raised a huge red flag like the one waved by the student revolutionaries in the ABC café in *Les Misérables*. A production which I saw at the Baden Stadttheater in Austria in 2014 was much more upbeat and positive as well as more overtly Christian, ending with (the presumably resurrected) Jesus walking through the audience, saying 'And remember, I am with you till the end of time', and engaging in a lively rock and roll routine with Judas. The 2020 open air production in London's Regent's Park, directed by Timothy Sheader and toured throughout Britain in 2023 and 2024, returned to emphasizing Jesus's spiritual intensity and anguish and enhanced the theme of sacrifice by the use of a huge illuminated red cross lying on the ground throughout the performance. As in the film version of *Les Misérables*, to be considered in the next chapter, the presence of this uncompromisingly Christian image drew attention to the religious aspect of the story. *Superstar* has become more spiritual as *Godspell* has become more secular.

Notes

1. Carol de Giere, *The Godspell Experience: Inside a Transformative Musical* (Bethel, CT: Scene 1 Publishing, 2014), 36.
2. Ibid., 36.
3. Interview with Thomas Barker, originally published in *Dramatics Magazine*, January 1975, reprinted in de Giere, *The Godspell Experience*, 325.
4. Ibid., 326.
5. Ibid., 326.
6. Ibid., 313.
7. Joseph Barton, 'The *Godspell* Story', *America*, 12 December 1971.
8. Carol de Giere, *Defying Gravity: The Creative Career of Stephen Schwartz* (New York: Applause, 2008), 475.
9. De Giere, *The Godspell Experience*, 128.
10. Stephen Schwartz, '*Godspell* script notes and revisions', 1999, quoted in Ian Bradley, *You've Got to Have a Dream: The Message of the Musical* (London: SCM Press, 2004), 135.
11. De Giere, *The Godspell Experience*, 142.
12. Michael Gioia, 'The leading men: The men of *Godspell*—Two sides of Wallace Smith: John and Judas', *Playbill*, 14 December, 2011.
13. Robert Ellis, '*Godspell* as Medieval drama', *America*, 23 December 1972, https://www.americam agazine.org/issue/100/godspell-medieval-drama.
14. De Giere, *The Godspell Experience*, x.
15. Bradley, *You've Got to Have a Dream*, 142.
16. De Giere, *The Godspell Experience*, 229–30.
17. Ibid., 193.
18. Ibid., 207–9.
19. Stephen Schwartz, *Stephen Schwartz Answers Questions about the Godspell Movie*, from the archive of the StephenSchwartz.com Forum, 4, https://stephenschwartz.com/wp-content/uplo ads/2017/04/Godspell_movie.pdf.
20. Ellis, '*Godspell* as Medieval drama'.
21. De Giere, *The Godspell Experience*, 315.
22. Programme for 2002 UK tour of *Godspell* (John Good Holbrook, 2002).
23. Cassie Tongue, 'Godspell review: Good tunes can't save a deeply uncool musical', *Guardian*, 30 October 2022.
24. Schwartz, '*Godspell* script notes and revisions', in Bradley, *You've Got to Have a Dream*, 134.
25. Keith Richmond, *The Musicals of Andrew Lloyd Webber* (London: Virgin, 1995), 26.
26. Ellis Nassour, *Rock Opera: The Creation of Jesus Christ Superstar* (New York: Hawthorn Books, 1973), 28.
27. Interview in *Spartanburg Herald-Journal*, 27 November 1982.
28. Michael Walsh, *Andrew Lloyd Webber: His Life and Works* (New York: Harry Abrams. 1997), 63.
29. Andrew Lloyd Webber, *Unmasked: A Memoir* (London: HarperCollins, 2019), 116.
30. Richmond, *The Musicals of Lloyd Webber*, 28.
31. Tim Rice, *Oh, What A Circus* (London: Hodder & Stoughton, 1999), 177.
32. Nassour, *Rock Opera*, 190.
33. *Christian Century*, 27 June 1973; *Christianity Today*, 12 October 1973.
34. De Giere, *The Godspell Experience*, 143.
35. Nassour, *Rock Opera*, 39–40.
36. Ibid., 37.
37. Ibid., 38.

9

The road to Calvary and the circle of life

Les Misérables and *The Lion King*

Three musicals dominated Broadway and London's West End in the last two decades of the twentieth century. One of them, *The Phantom of the Opera*, has already been discussed. This chapter looks at the other two, *Les Misérables* and *The Lion King*, contrasting in many respects but, like *Phantom*, sharing strong religious influences and spiritual resonances.

Les Misérables

Les Misérables is not just one of the most successful and popular musicals of the last fifty years; it is also without doubt the most explicitly religious and spiritually loaded. In his Easter Day sermon in Canterbury Cathedral in 1999, George Carey, the Archbishop of Canterbury, said that the encounter between Jean Valjean and the Bishop of Digne 'offers us the finest description of grace outside the New Testament. That moment of "grace" set Valjean on his way to redemption and wholeness.'[1] I agree with him. Indeed, I took this encounter and its consequences as the starting point for a sermon on forgiveness that I preached before the late Queen Elizabeth II in Crathie Kirk, the parish church of Balmoral Castle, in 2002. In a subsequent conversation over lunch, the Queen told me she had never seen *Les Misérables*. I urged her to do so and was amused to read some time later that she had held a special command performance at Windsor Castle to celebrate the centenary of the *Entente Cordiale* between the United Kingdom and France in the presence of the French president, Jacques Chirac.

As I have recounted in *You've Got to Have a Dream*, it was the experience of attending a matinée performance of *Les Misérables*, where the audience was made up largely of high school students, that awakened me to the spiritual power of musicals. Their awed silence throughout the performance and their utter absorption in the great drama of redemption were palpable.

Music of the Night. Ian Bradley, Oxford University Press. © Ian Bradley 2025.
DOI: 10.1093/9780197699775.003.0010

Overheard conversations in the interval and at the end of the performance confirmed that these young people had been genuinely moved and uplifted by what they had seen and heard on stage. That afternoon in the theatre had exposed them to the deep theological themes of grace, redemption, sacrificial love, and the power of forgiveness.

There are many other testimonies to the spiritual power of this particular musical. I know personally of three people who have undergone 'conversions' to Christianity as a result of watching a performance and being blown away by the saintliness of the Bishop of Digne and the Christ-like character of Jean Valjean. Many of its songs have been taken up for pastoral, liturgical, and communal use. Fantine's 'I dreamed a dream', with its poignant depiction of a girl being abandoned by the man who spent a summer by her side, has been used in counselling abused women and helping them to express their feelings. 'Empty chairs at empty tables' became a popular anthem of lament for those who died of HIV Aids from the mid-1980s onwards. Valjean's song, 'Bring him home', praying for the safe return of Marius when he has gone to fight with the revolutionary students, has been much used in the context of remembering those caught up in wars and conflicts. It was regularly played on US TV networks and sung in churches during the 2003–2011 Iraq War. I recall American students in my Theology of the Musicals Class during this period playing it most movingly over images of fighting. It continues to be sung regularly at veterans' parades. In the November 2023 British Legion Festival of Remembrance at the Royal Albert Hall, London, in the presence of the King and other members of the royal family, it was memorably sung by the tenor Alfie Boe following a presentation on the training of Ukrainian military chaplains in the UK and at the start of the most solemn part of the evening, when an altar is assembled from drums for the religious service remembering those killed in conflict. I know that I am not the only minister of religion to have led a church congregation in singing the great student anthem, 'Do you hear the people sing', with its Biblically inspired lines about beating swords into ploughshares and living again in freedom in the garden of the Lord.

Several of those who have written about *Les Misérables* see religious themes as being at its heart. Edward Behr notes in his book about the making of the show:

The universal aspect of *Les Misérables* has less to do with political upheavals and revolution than with the eternal truths about human nature—and

180   MUSIC OF THE NIGHT

belief in God. In essence, the story of John Valjean is that of a sudden, Pauline conversion, and a determination to retain the almost impossible ethical standards he has set himself. The quest for saintliness is the one thing that all religions have in common.[2]

For Scott Miller, writing in his director's guide to musical theatre, 'It is a show about the nobility of the human spirit, faith, redemption, and other spiritual concepts. Religion and spirituality—as well as the distortion of it and the lack of it—informs most of the action of the show.'[3]

The 'Christianization' of *Les Misérables* in its successive versions

What is particularly striking is how *Les Misérables* has become significantly more explicitly religious, and specifically Christian, in each of its successive incarnations. The original French concept album, which was released shortly before the show's Paris opening in 1980, has relatively little spiritual content. The Bishop of Digne, who is so central to Victor Hugo's novel on which the musical is based, and to the theme of forgiveness, makes no appearance at all. The action in the original French show begins in the factory in Montreuil-sur-Mer run by the mayor, Monsieur Madeleine, the name assumed by Jean Valjean after he has settled down to respectability. There are few mentions of God—Fantine's song, 'J'avais rêvé d'une autre vie', has none, unlike its later English version, 'I dreamed a dream', with its reference to her early dream 'that God would be forgiving'. There is a reference to the road to Calvary (*le chemin de Calvaire*) in the original Act 2 (later Act 1) finale, but no mention of discovering what 'our God in heaven has in store'. The musical ends with Valjean dying in his bed in the presence of Marius and Cossette but with no appearance by the deceased Fantine or the bishop.

There is one interesting theological note in the original French version that comes right at the end, with a hymn sung by Valjean to *la lumière* (the light):

> *La lumière, au matin de justice,*
> *Puisse enfin décapiter nos vices*
> *Dans un monde où Dieu pourrait se plaire*
> *S'il décidait un jour de redescendre sur la terre*

THE ROAD TO CALVARY AND THE CIRCLE OF LIFE   181

This translates as:

> The light, on the morning of justice,
> Can finally put to death our vices
> In a world where God could please himself
> If he decided one day to redescend to earth.

This is an unexpected and isolated theological reference in what is otherwise a distinctly secular treatment of Hugo's story, in keeping with the prevailing French principle of *laicité*. Hugo's own religious position was somewhat ambiguous. He largely gave up on traditional Christianity to espouse a kind of humane, enlightened, mildly deist rationalism in the tradition of Voltaire while also espousing a Manichean/Gnostic sense of life as a war between darkness and light. Yet he retained a strong interest in and a certain sympathy for Christianity and an admiration for those who practised its principles as well as preaching them. Although he was fiercely anti-clerical in the spirit of many French intellectuals, his description of the Bishop of Digne, which occupies the first sixty-five pages of the novel, is deeply sympathetic. He is portrayed as a friend of the poor, an 'upright man' with 'an excess of love', who 'prefers deeds to creeds' and gives up his palace to provide twenty-six impoverished invalids with a home while himself living simply in a modest house. Indeed, he comes across as a progenitor of Pope Francis. There are occasions in the novel where Valjean is explicitly portrayed in Christ-like terms.

All of this is largely ignored in the original French version of the musical, which is focused much more on the love interest between Marius and Cosette, the political and social aspects of the story, and the character of Gavroche, who is given a song, 'La faute à Voltaire', which references both Voltaire and Rousseau and could be taken as a kind of hymn to French enlightenment values.

This is not to say that Alain Boublil and his collaborator Claude-Michel Schönberg, the two original French creators of *Les Misérables*, were devoid of religious influences. Both came from practising Jewish backgrounds. Boublil's family were Sephardic Jews in Tunisia, and Schönberg's parents were Hungarian Jews. Schönberg has said: 'We both feel special about Jewish people and when I'm writing a show there is always a part that is typically Jewish. Just listen to the introduction of "Master of the House". It is completely Jewish.'[4] More broadly, there are undoubted echoes of golden age

182   MUSIC OF THE NIGHT

central European operetta in the soaring melodies of the *Les Misérables* score. Cameron Mackintosh has observed of Schönberg: 'his music is squarely in the tradition of Romberg and Friml, those central European composers who founded the American musical'.[5] I would myself say that, like Lloyd Webber in *Phantom* mode, he is rather an heir to the late Léhar, and perhaps even more to the Jewish-born Emmerich Kálmán.

Boublil and Schönberg's next collaboration after *Les Misérables, Martin Guerre*, a fascinating and under-rated musical which deserves to be better known, is set in the middle of the sixteenth-century French wars of religion and points up, not least musically, the contrast between Catholicism and Protestantism.[6] In their original working of *Les Misérables*, by contrast, they showed little interest in the religious dimension. It is rather a tribute to the secular, rational values of the French revolutionary spirit. Although God and his coming again are mentioned in the final number, what Valjean seems to be hymning as *la lumière* is, rather, enlightenment with its associations with justice and the abstract, essentially secular, French values of *liberté, égalité*, and *fraternité*, rather than anything specifically Christian or spiritual.

In marked contrast, the English language version of the show, radically reworked for stage presentation in 1985 by a creative team assembled by Cameron Mackintosh, puts far more emphasis on the religious aspects of the story. It starts where Hugo does, with Valjean as a convict, his escape from parole, and his encounter with the Bishop of Digne, and not halfway through the story in Monsieur Madeleine's factory as the French concept album and original production had done. This makes the crucial moment in the story the bishop's forgiveness of Valjean for repaying his hospitality by stealing his silver, directly leading to Valjean's decisive change from hating everyone to self-sacrificial love and dramatically illustrating the power of forgiveness to beget forgiveness.

According to a footnote in Ethan Mordden's 2021 history of British musical theatre, *Pick a Pocket Or Two*, it was James Fenton, the poet who was brought in to write the English lyrics, who first suggested the earlier start to the musical.[7] His father, John Fenton, was an Anglican priest and leading Biblical scholar who taught New Testament studies at Durham and Oxford University. Also involved in the decision to make this major change from the French original version was John Caird, co-director with Trevor Nunn of the new English version. Like Fenton, Caird, whom we have already encountered for his key role in the creation of *Children of Eden*, was also the son of a prominent New Testament scholar, G.B. Caird. It is tempting to suggest that

THE ROAD TO CALVARY AND THE CIRCLE OF LIFE   183

it is thanks to these two men, with their strong Biblical backgrounds, that the 1985 English language version was much more explicitly Christian than the French original. In fact, as Caird has told me, it was not quite as simple as that:

> The decision to include the opening of the story with Valjean as a convict and his encounter with the Bishop of Digne was taken after a great deal of discussion between James Fenton, Trevor Nunn and myself, in consultation with Alain Boublil and Claude-Michel Schonberg.
>
> Our first instinct was to remove all mention of God from the story throughout, but we became more and more fascinated by Hugo's own personal struggle to equate his passion for social change with his reluctantly entrenched faith in a Christian God.
>
> We realised after a series of meetings that telling the story of *Les Misérables* without God being a central character would be a fruitless task and would only represent half of Hugo's philosophical world.
>
> Having agreed with Trevor on the need for a prologue, James and I mapped it out together.[8]

The introduction of the Bishop of Digne and his encounter with Valjean makes the musical much more explicitly Christian. There is far more focus on Valjean's change of character, brought about by the bishop's act of kindness. The English version picks up Hugo's line that in pardoning Valjean for abusing his hospitality through stealing from him, and indeed, in insisting that he take even more silverware, the bishop is 'buying his soul for God'. There is subsequently much more focus than in the original French version on Valjean's Christ-like character, as he carries others on his shoulders, literally in the case of Marius through the sewers. The ending also becomes more explicitly Christian, with Valjean being led to heaven by the spirit of the departed Fantine, who invites him to come with her 'where chains are no longer binding'. He quotes directly from the Lord's Prayer and ends by saying that, 'To love another person is to see the face of God', making 'God' the last word in the libretto before the reprise of the student anthem in the finale.

Another of the effects of the substantial re-working of the libretto by the British team was to make much more of the contrast in character and outlook between Valjean and Javert. It is their starkly different theological views and conception of God which are particularly highlighted. This was something

184 MUSIC OF THE NIGHT

that both Trevor Nunn and John Caird felt that the original French version had underplayed. Nunn has said that, for him, *Les Misérables* is primarily a show about God, and more specifically about the very different ways in which God is perceived by the three central male characters:

> Javert is someone who believes in a vengeful, Old Testament God who will bring down plague and pestilence on all those who disobey the law; Valjean, in the light of his own experience, has come to believe in redemption and that justice can exist in our world; Thénardier not only believes that God is dead but that he died a long time ago and that we are all fair game for him.[9]

In fact, these are not the only perspectives on God represented by characters in the show. There is also the Bishop of Digne's saintly embodiment of and witness to a divine being of infinite mercy, compassion, and forgiveness, and there is Fantine's loss of faith in the whole idea of a loving and forgiving God, as her dreams are shattered by the reality of life. In the English version, God becomes a dominant and ubiquitous, if unseen, presence throughout the musical. In Cameron Mackintosh's words, 'It is the voice of God through this story which changes and guides the life of Jean Valjean'.[10] God is first mentioned very near the beginning when the bishop blesses Valjean and tells him that he has bought his soul for God. The closing lines of Act 1 include the statement, 'tomorrow we'll discover/what our God in heaven has in store', and the Act 2 showstopper, 'Bring him home', begins with the words 'God on high, hear my prayer'. As we have already noted, 'God' is also the last word in the last song of the show before the reprise of the student anthem in the finale.

The 1985 English version became the template for all subsequent international productions, including the French one premiered in 1991. Its much more explicitly religious emphasis compared to Boublil's 1980 book and libretto is evident even in a number as simple and incidental as the chorus sung at the wedding of Marius and Cosette. In the original French concept album, this is a straightforward celebration of human happiness and love. The English translation invokes the angels of the Lord singing their songs of praise, introducing a metaphysical note into the celebration.

Overall, the English libretto for *Les Misérables* reads almost like a liturgical text, with thirty-one references to God, many of which are in the context of prayers, six references to Jesus (there are none in the original French version), eight mentions each of heaven and of prayer, and four of the soul.

There are also explicit allusions to Calvary, the passion and the blood of Christ, the blood of the martyrs, the way of the Lord, communion, sacrifice, salvation, and sainthood.

The main librettist for the English version of *Les Misérables* was Herbert Kretzmer, the television critic of the *Daily Mail*. He was brought in by Cameron Mackintosh to replace James Fenton, whose lyrics were proving too poetic and who was taking too long to deliver. Kretzmer, one of four sons of Lithuanian Jewish immigrants to South Africa, took six months to bash out the libretto, going back to Hugo's novel and sustaining himself with copious amounts of smoked salmon. Around a third of his new lyrics represented a loose translation of the original French, another third involved a much broader adaptation with little attempt at translation, and the rest were entirely new songs. A self-proclaimed atheist, he seems at first sight an unlikely person to have produced a much more Christian version of the musical. But in his words, 'You don't have to believe in what you're writing, so long as you believe with every sinew that your characters believe it: the theology in the lyrics was written with the utmost sincerity'.[11]

John Caird, who worked very closely with Kretzmer on the lyrics, has a similar perspective, saying, 'I'm not religious myself, my religion is Shakespeare', although he does see close parallels between religion and musical theatre: 'Religion and theatre are almost the same thing with the music, liturgy and deeply emotional literature. I think people go to church and theatre for the same reasons—to have their faith in humanity restored. I go to church as I am fascinated by religion.'[12]

In fact, in their frequent sessions working together on the libretto and lyrics, Caird and Kretzmer found themselves, in Caird's words, 'talking a great deal about God and theology and the nature of belief. I remember Herbie saying to me one day, "I don't believe in God but I'm a profound believer in belief."[13]

Kretzmer added several new songs to the show, including Javert's soliloquy, 'Stars'. Yet there was one that he found particularly difficult to write, a solo for Valjean after he has joined the students at the barricades at night, with Marius sleeping beside him and the treacherous Javert bound as a captive and cowering in the corner. In Kretzmer's words:

We code-named this 'Night Thoughts' to reflect the resentment, anger and jealousy that Valjean would feel as he contemplated this usurper. Yet the music I was given was ridiculously at odds – a stately, hymn-like

186 MUSIC OF THE NIGHT

progression of three ascending notes. The directors came round to discuss it and, as they left at 2 am, Caird said: 'Sounds like a prayer to me.'

The minute he said that, every door seemed to fly open. I was freed from delving into the murkier corners of Valjean's mind and could instead give his blessing to a young couple in love. I stood for the rest of that night in my study and by 5 am, 'Bring Him Home' was written—17 days before the show opened.[14]

Caird also has vivid memories of this occasion:

> I was standing on the doorstep outside Herbie's apartment block, saying my goodbyes, enjoying the fresh air and the night sky after the fug of Herbie's flat. We had rehearsed 'Stars' earlier that day with Roger Allam as Javert, so the idea of prayer and belief and faith in God were strongly in mind. I thought if Javert can address the stars as his personal guides, then Valjean has certainly earned the right to talk direct to the God who has guided his life since his meeting with the Bishop of Digne.[15]

It is somehow appropriate that it was the son of the Congregational minister and professor of the interpretation of holy scripture at Oxford University who pointed out the prayer-like quality of the music that Schönberg had provided for Valjean's soliloquy on the barricades, giving his atheistically in-clined fellow-lyricist the inspiration for one of the most deeply religious and spiritually charged ballads in musical theatre.

The influence of John Caird's theological genes was even more marked in the drafting of the show's final line, 'To love another person is to see the face of God'. Caird has told me that it was inspired by a passage in his father's book, *Language and Imagery of the Bible*.

> The book was published in 1980, and when my Dad died in 1984, I re-read all of his books in succession as a sort of extended wake, I suppose. Herbie and I worked on the lyrics of *Les Mis* all through the spring and early summer of 1985, so a lot of my Dad's brilliant exegesis was fresh in my mind at the time.
>
> In Chapter 4, he refers to 1 John 4:12: 'God himself dwells in us if we love one another; his love is brought to perfection within us.' He goes on to com-ment on 1 John 4:7–9, thus: 'John's argument is that love for God entails love for our fellows, so that one cannot exist without the other; and when

THE ROAD TO CALVARY AND THE CIRCLE OF LIFE   187

we love our fellows it is not merely we who love, but God who loves through us; so that all human love that is genuine is the indwelling of God. God is love, and only by the experience of loving can one have experience of God.'

I remember being very struck by this passage at the time and, looking back now, I have no doubt it was this passage that inspired the final line, 'To love another person is to see the face of God' when Herbie and I were wrestling with the final lyrics of the show.[16]

Caird initially thought that the line 'might be too simplistic, not to say too heretical, a thought as Valjean's last utterance'. However, the rest of the team liked it. The idea of the return of Fantine and Éponine as 'ghostly visitants' to Valjean's deathbed came from Trevor Nunn, and, in Caird's words, 'the line became a shared lyric for the three "loveless" characters in the story, or rather the characters who sacrifice themselves for someone they love'.[17]

Although it represented a considerable 'Christianization' of the French original, the 1985 English stage version did not bring out all the religious references and nuances in Hugo's novel. For example, at the end of the novel, Valjean takes down a copper crucifix from the wall of the room in which he is dying and lays it on the table, saying, 'Behold the great martyr'. Asked if he wants a priest, he replies, 'I have one', and with his finger 'seemed to designate a point above his head where, you would have said, he saw one'. Hugo adds: 'It is probable that the Bishop was indeed a witness of this death-agony.' At the moment of Valjean's death, he sees a light. Hugo writes: 'The night was starless and very dark. Without doubt, in the gloom some almighty angel was standing, with outstretched wings, awaiting his soul.'[18]

These references were picked up in the 2012 film of *Les Misérables* directed by Tom Hooper, which goes even further than the 1985 stage show in reflecting and, indeed, enhancing the religious references and Christian imagery present in Hugo's novel and largely absent from the original French version of the musical. The film's opening sequence, showing Valjean and his fellow members of the chain gang up to their waists in water and hauling ropes in a vast dock, has an almost Old Testament quality to it. Camilla Stephens, Supervising Location Manager, has said that 'the brief was to have a Biblical start to the film'.[19]

What is particularly striking in the film is the prominent role it gives to visual images of the Christian cross. Hugo makes several references to this symbol in his novel, but the film introduces more. The image first appears when Valjean, released on parole, wanders up a bare hillside. Silhouetted

188 MUSIC OF THE NIGHT

against the sky is a prominent cross planted on a cairn on the edge of the hill. As he passes it with his staff, Valjean pauses and sings about being free at last. He looks for all the world like a pilgrim rather than a prisoner on parole. The scene was shot in the foothills of the French Alps with the mountaintop village of Gourdon standing in for Digne—in the words of Debra Hayward, the producer, 'high on a mountain nearer to God'.[20]

The cross appears again in the scene where Valjean is taken in by the Bishop of Digne and steals his silver. There is a brief shot of the crucifix on the wall above the bed where the bishop is sleeping when Valjean commits his theft. As he runs out with his ill-gotten gains, he is surrounded by wooden crosses in the churchyard outside. Later, after he has been caught and pardoned by the bishop, who tells him that he has saved his soul for God, Valjean kneels in front of an altar in the bishop's chapel. Directly looking at the cross on the altar, he asks, 'What have I done, Sweet Jesus?' and embarks on the soliloquy that marks the start of the change of direction in his life and reflects on the bishop's words, 'He told me that I have a soul.' As the soliloquy ends, with Valjean screaming out that 'another story must begin', he is outside in the graveyard that surrounds the church, standing next to another prominent wooden cross. The camera pulls back to reveal a sea of crosses in the walled graveyard on top of the mountain and then pans up to the sky as the great descending chords sound out. The suggestion of heaven is unmistakable. The image of the cross appears prominently again in the scene where Fantine is dying. She sees Cosette through a curtain on which is woven a very prominent cross.

The ending of the film, played out in front of an altar, is also more explicitly Christian than the finale of the stage show. As well as Fantine inviting the dying Valjean to come with her where chains will never bind him, and asking the Lord in heaven to look down on him in mercy, the Bishop of Digne appears standing in front of a church blazing with candlesticks and welcoming him into heaven. So, at last, this third take on the *Les Misérables* musical gets back to the strong Christian themes which are there in Victor Hugo's novel but are missing from both the original French version and the 1985 London production. The significance of this has been noted by the Catholic author, Kenneth Pierce:

> The Christian perspective throughout the entire film is unusually clear for a production of this type and is perhaps even more striking than it is in Victor Hugo's work. Crosses and crucifixes are presented multiple times,

not only as decoration but as a key reading of a film that seems to have borrowed the script from the Beatitudes of the Gospel. The cross, then, does not appear as a masochistic and oppressive aspect of Christianity that Hollywood seems to love to portray, but as an ultimate way of freedom and redemption, a necessary step for the encounter with God's love and light that allows a deeper understanding of our daily lives.[21]

It is not only those coming from a Christian faith perspective who have recognized the strong religious influences and resonances in the film version of *Les Misérables*. The great majority of the comments on YouTube about the closing scene, which has been watched there by some 2.3 million people, point to its religious significance, with the appearance of the bishop and the intimation of heaven being especially singled out. Even many of those who say that they are not themselves religious comment that it makes them believe in heaven.[22] This is undoubtedly a musical that has become increasingly religious and, more explicitly, Christian in its successive incarnations.

The Lion King as a post-Christian musical

The Lion King, the last of the major mega-hit musicals of the twentieth century, has also gone through several different incarnations. Starting life as an animated cartoon film in 1994 with songs by Tim Rice and Elton John, it opened as a stage show on Broadway in 1997 and in the West End in 1999, with a new photorealistic computer-animated film version coming out in 2019. The stage version is the highest-grossing Broadway musical of all time.

It is tempting to identify *The Lion King* as the first distinctively post-Christian musical, rooted as it is in the primal religions of animism and ancestor worship. There is no denying its strong spiritual resonances, apparent from the electrifying opening chorus, 'The circle of life', with its thrilling Zulu chant that celebrates regeneration and rebirth and the evolutionary cycle moving us all through despair and hope, faith, and love.

In his book, *The Gospel According to Disney*, Mark Pinsky observes that *The Lion King* marked a significant departure for the Disney studios, 'cautiously edging away from the Judeo-Christian universe that characterized the company's full-length features since *Snow White*'.[23] At the same time, it also indicated an embrace of spirituality that was not found in earlier films. In a paper entitled 'Disney gets religion', given at the 1998 meeting of

190   MUSIC OF THE NIGHT

the American Academy of Religion, Donald Fadner sees *The Lion King* as marking the beginning of a shift in Disney musicals 'in a much more explicitly religious direction'. He points out that greater-than-human powers had hitherto been represented in Disney musicals as 'magical', involving instantaneous transformations of the conditions of the characters in the story by those possessed of a supernatural power to do such things.

> Starting with *The Lion King*, however, the greater-than-human dimension of the stories has been much more explicitly 'religious' or, perhaps better-put, 'spiritual', i.e. focused on objects of reverence that, while inspiring and supporting the development of the characters, do not intervene directly with magical solutions to their dilemmas. This forces the characters to find within themselves the necessary resources to solve their problems.[24]

It is significant that Rob Minkoff, the director of the original *Lion King* film, described it as attempting 'a level of spirituality, something slightly metaphysical'.[25]

Themes in *The Lion King*—the circle of life and sacred kingship

The underlying theme of the circle of life and regeneration is reinforced by Mufasa's statement to Simba as he shows him the lands which he will one day inherit: 'Life rises from death. Everything is connected in the great circle of life. As a king, you will have to understand it.' Mufasa points out that lions eat other animals, then eventually die, and their biomass nurtures the vegetation, ultimately providing food for other animals. Pinsky comments that 'without question, this is not Christianity's tradition and promise of resurrection'.[26] Yet it echoes the thinking of Victorian Christian poets and divines who believed that the motif of life rising out of death in the natural world is both analogous to and illustrative of the Christian doctrine of resurrection to eternal life. This idea was clearly stated by James Buchanan, a minister in the Free Church of Scotland and Professor of Systematic Theology at New College, Edinburgh, in a treatise published in 1864 where he wrote, 'the future resurrection of the body has its natural analogue in the annual resurrection of nature from the death-like torpor of winter'.[27] It was a theme particularly taken up by John Clare, the farm labourer's son and devout Anglican known as the Northamptonshire peasant poet, for whom the circle of life in the natural world is divinely ordained, with its birth in heaven, and speaks clearly of resurrection and eternal life. Other nineteenth-century poets equally fascinated by the process of recycling in nature took a less explicitly Christian and theological approach while still marvelling at the way life comes out of death. Perhaps the most famous and powerful poetic expression of this theme is 'This Compost', written in 1856 by the American poet Walt Whitman.[28]

I have argued elsewhere that *The Lion King* is both a celebration and affirmation of the doctrine of sacred kingship.[29] Its three leading characters are the good, wise king Mufasa, the evil usurper Scar, and the reluctant heir to the throne, Simba, who eventually comes to realize that he must follow his hereditary duty and destiny and assume the crown in order to rescue the land from famine and anarchy. The musical underlines the themes of cosmic order and sacrifice that are central to primal religious notions of sacred kingship and emphasizes the intimate relationship between the character of the sovereign and the well-being of the land. It also underlines the hereditary aspect of monarchy and explores the theme of ancestor worship. It is only when Simba sees his own reflection in a pool and then sees in the sky the face of his dead father, who tells him that he has forgotten who he is, that he realizes his royal destiny and responsibility. The song 'He lives in you', sung by the baboon shaman Rafiki, conveys the sense of the departed spirits of the ancestors living on in their descendants and the especially strong continuing presence of the departed king.

Christian echoes in *The Lion King*

There are scenes in *The Lion King* which might be interpreted as echoing Christian themes and imagery. One occurs early on when Rafiki anoints the baby Simba, first with juice from the baobab fruit and then with dust, moving his finger across his forehead, in much the same way as a Christian pastor or priest does when baptizing an infant. As Rifiki holds Simba up to the massed animals on the plain beneath Pride Rock, a shaft of light shines down on him, suggesting a heavenly blessing, and all the animals bow down before him. Later, when Simba has his vision of his father in the sky, Mufasa tells

192   MUSIC OF THE NIGHT

him: 'Remember who you are. You are my son, the one true king'. There seem to be echoes here of God's words to Jesus at the time of his baptism, 'You are my beloved son'. Is Mufasa a God-like figure and Simba Christ-like? In this reading, Simba's exile to the wasteland, where he wanders around among the vultures, could be compared to Jesus being tempted in the wilderness among the wild beasts.

Conservative evangelical Christians have been keen to detect Christian influences and parallels in *The Lion King*. They see hints in it of C.S. Lewis' *Chronicles of Narnia*, with its depiction of Aslan the lion as a God- or Christ-like figure. Scar's jealousy of Mufasa is compared to Lucifer's envy towards God in Milton's *Paradise Lost*. The scene where Simba runs through thorn bushes during his exile from the Pride Lands has been seen as evoking Jesus' crown of thorns. Simba has also been likened to Moses. Both start as princes and find their comfortable situations interrupted when the injustices oppressing their peoples are revealed through super-natural means: God speaks to Moses through a burning bush on Mount Horeb, while Mufasa speaks to Simba through the night stars overlooking the African outback. Both fulfil their pre-ordained destinies by rescuing their peoples from oppressive rule. Comparisons have also been made be-tween Simba and Joseph. Both start out as their respective fathers' pride and joy and attract the envy of family members—in Simba's case, his uncle, and in Joseph's, his brothers. Both go into exile from their homelands and ultimately return to positions of power, restoring order and prosperity to the land.[30]

These interpretations are intriguing, but it is important to re-state that *The Lion King* is not a Christian musical but rather locates itself firmly in primal religious traditions. If Simba can be seen in some way as having expelled himself from Paradise and from his heritage, it is not Christian grace that rescues him but rather the meerkat Timon and the warthog Pumbaa with their philosophy of 'Hakuna Matata'—forget your worries and accept life as it is with the bad things that will happen as well as the good. This is not a million miles from the philosophy of life preached by Jesus in Matthew 6:26–34 when he asks, 'Can any one of you by worrying add a single hour to your life?' and commends the birds of the air and the lilies of the field for their more laid-back approach. But it is not a uniquely Christian idea, and it is not presented as such in *The Lion King*.

There is another important message in this musical, again expressed in pagan, animist terms, which is about the sacredness of the land. It is particularly emphasized in the song 'Shadowland', written for the 1997 stage musical by Mark Mancina, Lebohang Morake, and Hans Zimmer. It begins with an African chorus proclaiming that the land of the ancestors is holy and continues with the soloist Nala singing that it is broken and asking that her prayers be the guide to restoration. Based on the song 'Lea Halalela' (The Holy Land) in Lebo M's 1995 album, *Rhythm of the Pride Lands*, itself written as a sequel to the soundtrack of the original *Lion King* animated film, it is a soul power ballad with more than a hint of gospel. The emphasis on prayer is clear, but so is the animist message.

Some critics have been scathing about what they see as the spiritual shallowness of *The Lion King*. For the British journalist Matthew Parris, writing in 1999:

> What did *The Lion King* mean philosophically? The musical was not without a moral, but the moral was, to our rich hinterland of western philosophy, what Grandma Moses is to the heritage of European art. The moral was that good will triumph over evil in the end, the souls of the dead live on in the living, we must respect the natural world and there's a place for every creature under the sun. Absurd, I realise, to expect Hegel or St Augustine in a family show, and the trite can move to tears. It moved me to tears. But trite is trite.
>
> A century which has lost its Christian confidence has found no new moral confidence beyond a sort of Hollywood-sanitised primitivism. Natural law, by Walt Disney, out of Rousseau. If the cast did not quite break into 'Search for the Hero Inside Yourself' to the backing of skin drums, that's probably because it is copyrighted. Halfway through the century now complete, Rogers and Hammerstein, in *Carousel*, were still capable of drawing upon moral ambiguity in a family show. We seem to have lost even that degree of philosophical literacy.[31]

This is unfair. I am not sure that there is that much moral ambiguity in *Carousel*, and it seems too much to be looking for it in *The Lion King*. It does have its cute and cheesy side, but its moral messages about the circle of life, the sacredness of the land, and the need to face your responsibilities rather than avoid them are far from trite. It stands in the tradition of those great twentieth century musicals with clear religious influences and spiritual resonances, while breaking significant new ground in not taking them from either the Jewish or Christian traditions.

194 MUSIC OF THE NIGHT

Notes

1. Ian Bradley, *You've Got to Have a Dream: The Message of the Musical* (London: SCM Press, 2004), 149.
2. Edward Behr, *Les Misérables: History in the Making* (London: Pavilion, 1996), 160.
3. Scott Miller, *From Assassins to West Side Story* (London: Heinemann, 1996), 167.
4. Interview with Brigit Grant, *Jewish News*, 20 April 2020.
5. Mark Steyn, *Broadway Babies Say Goodnight: Musicals Then and Now* (Hoboken, NJ: Taylor and Francis, 2014), 87.
6. For an analysis of this musical, see Bradley, *You've Got to Have a Dream*, 165–8.
7. Ethan Mordden, *Pick A Pocket or Two* (New York, Oxford University Press, 2021), 176.
8. Email from John Caird to the author, 16 February 2024.
9. Behr, *Les Misérables*, 78.
10. '"Les Misérables" Behind the Scenes', YouTube video, 19 February 2020, https://www.youtube.com/watch?v=m-m0WZNofZE3.
11. Interview with Anna Tims, *The Guardian*, 19 February 2013.
12. Alison Dayani, 'Religion and theatre are almost the same thing', *Business Live*, 11 November 2011 https://www.business-live.co.uk/retail-consumer/religion-theatre-same-thing-3916469
13. Email to the author, 16 February 2024.
14. Interview with Anna Tims.
15. Email to the author, 16 February 2024.
16. Email to the author, 4 April 2024.
17. Email to the author, 16 February 2024.
18. Victor Hugo, *Les Misérables* (London: Everyman's Library, 1998), 1428–9.
19. '"Les Misérables" Behind the Scenes'.
20. Ibid.
21. Kenneth Pierce, '*Les Misérables*: The Cross as a way of salvation', *Catholic Link*, 16 May 2013: https://catholic-link.org/recommended-movie-the-les-miserables-2012-the-cross-as-a-way-of-salvation/.
22. https://www.youtube.com/watch?v=88T3elu2wfE.
23. Mark Pinsky, *The Gospel According to Disney* (Louisville, KY: Westminster John Knox Press, 2004), 154.
24. Donald Fadner, 'Disney Gets Religion', conference paper, June 2020, 3–4, https://www.research gate.net/publication/342182716_DISNEY_GETS_RELIGION
25. *New York Daily News*, 12 June 1994.
26. Pinsky, *The Gospel According to Disney*, 154.
27. James Buchanan, *Analogy* (Edinburgh: Johnstone, Hunter, 1864), 368.
28. On this, see Ian Bradley, *Breathers of an Ampler Day: Victorian Views of Heaven* (Durham: Sacristy Press, 2023), Chapter 9.
29. Ian Bradley, *God Save the King: The Sacred Nature of the Monarchy* (London: Darton, Longman & Todd, 2023), 32.
30. For examples of these readings, see Matty S, 'Theology in "The Lion King": A religious analysis of the classic Disney animated film', posted 16 September 2019, https://gothgordongekko.med ium.com/theology-in-the-lion-king-aaaa098b7772#:~:text=Mufasa%20and%20Simba%20re present%20both,crown%20of%20thorns%20Jesus%20donned; 'The Lion King as a Christian story', https://religiousthemesinthelionking.yolasite.com/information.php; and Anthony Perrotta, 'How does "The Lion King" show similarities to the stories of Joseph and Moses in the Bible?', *The Take*, https://the-take.com/read/how-does-the-lion-king-show-similarities-to-the-stories-of-joseph-and-moses-in-the-bible.
31. Matthew Parris, 'Nature in the roar', *The Times*, 18 December 1999.

10

The spiritual show goes on

Mamma Mia! and *The Book of Mormon*

The Lion King was the last big hit musical of the twentieth century. Was it also the last musical to display significant religious influences? Do the hit shows of the twenty-first century display evidence of the steady secularization that has been one of the hallmarks of our age? In fact, there are clear signs of religious influences and spiritual resonances in several more recent shows. This concluding chapter will briefly explore them.

Rent

Before moving into the present century, it is worth giving a shout-out to a musical from the 1990s that has only had the briefest of mentions so far in this book. Jonathan Larson's *Rent* (1996) tackles the scourge of HIV/Aids with a mixture of gritty realism and hope. There is interesting and surely not accidental use of religious language in the repetition of the word 'Glory' in the song that the central character, Roger, sings about the one great song that he dreams of writing before he is carried off by the virus, and in the figure of 'Angel', the transvestite street drummer who radiates love and compassion. There is even a reference to the divine in the lyric 'To sodomy, It's between God and me'. Without any explicitly Christian or other theological underpinning, *Rent* identifies the truth that the deepest human fellowship is to be found in human suffering—in Christian terms, at the foot of the cross. It is a moving and exhilarating testimony to human warmth and connectedness and to both the earthiness and vitality of human existence. In some ways uncompromisingly secular, with its focus on the here and now and living for today, it is also profoundly spiritual in its rootedness and testimony to the fellowship of suffering.

Music of the Night. Ian Bradley, Oxford University Press. © Ian Bradley 2025.
DOI: 10.1093/9780197699775.003.0011

196 MUSIC OF THE NIGHT

Mamma Mia!

Another musical which, strictly speaking, just belongs to the twentieth century is *Mamma Mia!*, which opened in the West End in 1999 and on Broadway in 2001, with the hugely popular movie versions coming out in 2008 and 2018. It is the most successful of a whole string of jukebox musicals, which are essentially compilations of hit songs—in this case, by the Swedish group ABBA—padded out with usually rather inane plots. The story of the deserted Donna Sheridan, her dream of building a hotel on a Greek island, and her relationship with her daughter and best friends is rather more substantial and touching than most jukebox musicals and has an added feminist twist. For English theatre producer Kate Pakenham, it is a very smart, almost Shakespearean story of lost souls washed up onto a magical island, and proves the point that I have been trying to make in this book that musicals, while 'apparently light and flippant and frivolous . . . actually have more depth than you might expect.'[1]

Mamma Mia! certainly has the feel-good factor and uplifting, life-enhancing effect that I identified at the very beginning of this book as an essentially spiritual quality shared by the related genres of operetta and musical theatre. Its pastoral and therapeutic properties were well illustrated when it opened on Broadway within a month of the 9/11 attack on the World Trade Center. Already dubbed 'the Lourdes of musicals' for its curative effect on audiences who cast aside walking sticks, crutches, and inhibitions to dance along to its catchy tunes, it was hailed by the *New York Times* critic as 'just what the city needed and the unlikeliest hit ever to win over cynical sentiment-shy New Yorkers.'[2] I have spoken to several people who watched the second film, *Mamma Mia! Here We Go Again*, to raise their spirits just before going into hospital for a major operation, and I know that I am not the only person to be moved to tears by the scene where Donna, played by Meryl Streep, returns from death to sing 'With all my heart, God bless you' during the baptism of her grandchild.

There are no conscious religious influences behind ABBA's songs. Indeed, the band's most prominent member, Björn Ulvaeus, has made no secret of his atheism and general dislike of religion. But this does not stop some of the songs in the musical from having considerable spiritual depth. For me, the most theologically charged is the simple and soulful ballad 'I have a dream', reminiscent in its opening line of Martin Luther King's famous 1963 speech and of the prophecy made in the Old Testament book of Joel, repeated in the New Testament Book of Acts, that God will pour out his spirit so that the old will dream dreams and the young see visions. It contains the lines, 'I believe in angels, something good in everything I see', and 'When I know the time is right for me, I'll cross the stream'. The many moving comments on YouTube, where the song has been viewed more than thirty million times, indicate that it has often accompanied people's dying moments and brought enormous consolation to the bereaved and those suffering from depression.

Some years ago, grieving parents in England wanted to put the line 'I believe in angels, something good in everything I see' on the gravestone of their teenage daughter who had died in particularly tragic circumstances. The Church of England refused them permission on the grounds that this was not suitable language for a churchyard. This decision showed not just pastoral insensitivity but theological cloth-headedness. As well as speaking words of hope to the grieving parents, it proclaims two central tenets of the Christian faith: a belief in angels and a conviction that the world that God created is basically good and everyone and everything has something of the divine within them and is not beyond redemption.

Jane Eyre

There is much more conscious Christian theology in one of the first musicals of the twenty-first century, *Jane Eyre*, an adaptation of Charlotte Bronte's classic nineteenth-century novel, with music by Paul Gordon and lyrics by John Caird, which premiered on Broadway in 2000. In Caird's words, 'The whole story is driven by the theme of forgiveness. Christianity and Christian values run through the work as they did throughout the life of their author, another daughter of the cloth.'[3]

A review of a production at the Royal Academy of Music in 2023 by Chris Omaweng noted:

Victorian Protestant Christianity is very much embraced—there was so much religious content in places that I started to wonder if someone was going to sing a ridiculously high-pitched prayer a la *Les Misérables*. I suppose there's something to be said for the power of forgiveness, and how

198   MUSIC OF THE NIGHT

(without necessarily converting to any given religion) it can help a person heal emotional and psychological wounds of the past.[4]

Andrew Lippa and *The Addams Family*

Andrew Lippa, responsible, among other works, for the music and lyrics of *The Addams Family* (2009), is almost certainly the most religiously engaged and committed of those currently working in musical theatre. Born and raised Jewish, he sang as a lay cantor in a synagogue for many years and was commissioned in 1998 by the Jewish Federation of Greater Vancouver to write an anthem for a concert celebrating Israel's fiftieth birthday. However, finding that Judaism did not fulfil his need to 'get closer to God and closer to himself', he joined the One Spirit Learning Alliance, an interfaith seminary and community based in New York, of which he is a prominent and active member. He has said that he is particularly led to 'writing about religion. Religion from the point of view of people believing in something bigger than yourself'.[5]

There are certainly distinct religious and spiritual resonances in several songs from *The Addams Family*, notably 'Death is just around the corner', 'Move towards the darkness', Gomez's 'Happy-sad', and Fester's 'The moon and me'. Even more overtly religious is Lippa's 2016 double bill musical, *I Am Anne Hutchinson/I Am Harvey Milk*, which links the stories of the seventeenth-century Puritan activist, Anne Hutchinson, and the twentieth-century Jewish gay rights campaigner, Harvey Milk. God is directly referenced and appealed to in several songs, especially although not exclusively by Hutchinson. Reviewing the first night, the critic David Friscic wrote: 'Throughout the evening a linkage was developed between the more overtly religious Hutchinson and the morality of Milk in honoring the authenticity of each human being God has made'.[6]

The Book of Mormon

Even more than *The Sound of Music* and *Fiddler on the Roof*, *The Book of Mormon* (2011) has a religious and faith-based community as its subject matter. The stage set resembles the entrance to a Mormon temple, with the Angel Moroni on the top, and the story revolves around the exploits of

Mormon missionaries in Uganda. There are songs about heaven and the Bible, and one about Jesus 'manning up', which could serve as an anthem for muscular Christianity. The power ballad, 'I believe', sung by Elder Price with its line, 'I believe that God has a plan for all of us', could be construed as a testament to the power of religious faith. Jesus makes several appearances, dressed in white robes with lit-up stripes.

Yet there is also a lot of blasphemy, sexual innuendo, and crudity. While some of the native Africans' chants resemble Gospel songs and are highly derivative of the chants in *The Lion King*, their basic message is 'F**k you, God'. There is a strange scene set in Hell with a variation on the well-known Sunday School hymn, which transforms into 'Jesus hates you, this you know'. Most shockingly, a Mormon missionary 'baptizes' a local girl whom he finds hot. It is the first time for both of them, and little is left to the imagination in what is essentially a sexual coupling dressed up as a religious sacrament.

Matt Stone, who conceived and wrote *The Book of Mormon* in collaboration with Trey Parker and Robert Lopez, has described himself as ethnically Jewish due to his mother being Jewish but in religious terms as an atheist. He characterizes the musical as 'an atheist's love letter to religion'.[7] Central to its story is the redemption of the over-confident and ultra-smooth Elder Price, who learns humility when the geeky and tubby Elder Cunningham proves a far more successful missionary than he is. There is a subsidiary message about not taking religious texts too seriously. Elder Cunningham converts an entire Ugandan village to Mormonism on the basis of stories that he makes up himself. He has never actually read the Book of Mormon. The moral seems to be that if you make people happy, it doesn't really matter too much what your particular creed is.

Although distinctly ambivalent in its approach to religious faith and presenting a satirical and caricatured take on Mormonism, *The Book of Mormon* has been widely taken up as a recruiting tool by the Church of Jesus Christ of Latter-day Saints, which regularly advertises in playbills and programmes to encourage theatre-goers to learn more about the Book of Mormon, with phrases like 'you've seen the play, now read the book', and 'the book is always better'. When asked in January 2015 if he had met any Mormons who disliked the musical, Josh Gad, who created the role of Elder Cunningham in the original Broadway run, stated 'In the 1.5 years I did that show, I never got a single complaint from a practising Mormon ... To the contrary, I probably had a few people—a dozen—tell me they were so *moved* by the show that they took up the Mormon faith.'[8]

200 MUSIC OF THE NIGHT

Come From Away and *Hamilton*

Come From Away (2013), which tells the story of passengers in the thirty-eight planes which were ordered to land at Gander International Airport, Newfoundland, following the 9/11 terrorist attacks, has a particularly affecting number entitled 'Prayer' in which the hymn 'Make me a channel of your peace' is sung by Christians, with Jews, Muslims, and Hindus joining in and contributing their own prayers in Hebrew, Arabic, and Hindi, blending to make a moving interfaith act of worship.

Hamilton (2015), which has almost certainly been the most popular musical of the twenty-first century, does not have anything like the spiritual and religious resonances of *Les Misérables*, which it closely resembles in its structure and staging. It is true that there are religious references scattered throughout the libretto. Moses' claiming of the Promised Land gets an early mention in the song 'My shot'. The appearance of the importuning temptress, Maria Reynolds, leads Hamilton to pray, 'Lord, show me how to say no to this. I don't know how to say no to this, but my God, she looks so helpless, and her body's saying, "Hell yes."'. Reflecting on his descent from Jonathan Edwards, the eighteenth-century revivalist preacher who played a key role in the first Great Awakening of evangelical Christianity, Aaron Burr sings that 'my grandfather was a fire and brimstone preacher, but there are things that homilies and hymns won't teach you'. But none of these amount to a significant theological statement or spiritual prompt.

The nearest that *Hamilton* comes to expressing deep religious themes is in the song 'It's quiet uptown', which is sung by Alexander Hamilton and his wife, Eliza, following the death of their son, Philip, in a duel. Hamilton sings, 'I take the children to church on Sunday. A sign of the cross at the door and I pray. That never used to happen before.' This signal of his change of heart and contrition over his infidelity to Eliza is matched by her statement that 'There's a grace too powerful to name' and her forgiveness of her erring husband, which is reinforced by the chorus' repeated line 'Forgiveness. Can you imagine?'

Although this song does speak of redemption and salvation through forgiveness, this is not the ultimate message of the musical. Rather, as underlined in its closing number, Eliza's 'Who lives? Who dies? Who tells your story?', it is about how you are remembered in history. I found watching and listening to *Hamilton* overall a secular rather than a spiritual experience, although others clearly disagree, among them Kevin Cloud, pastor of

Midwest Fellowship in Overland Park, Kansas, who has written *God and Hamilton: Spiritual Themes from the Life of Alexander Hamilton and the Broadway Musical He Inspired* (2018).

Conclusion

I have been conscious throughout writing this book of the danger of imposing my own liberal Christian views on others and finding religious influences and spiritual resonances where they were never intended or consciously present among librettists and composers of musical theatre. I hope I have been true to the intentions of the creators, although inevitably, what I have written is my interpretation, coloured by my own theological interests and beliefs.

What I hope that I have shown in this book is that there are religious influences and spiritual resonances, sometimes unexpected and surprising, in an art form that is often dismissed as shallow, sentimental, and secular. Of course, operettas and musicals exist primarily to entertain, and it is on their ability to do that they should ultimately be judged. In the words of Jeremy Sams, responsible for the book of *Chitty Chitty Bang Bang* (is that one I should have included? I don't think so, and it's too late now), writing musicals is 'basically trying to put magic in a bottle and it's really hard. Audiences are unanimous in recognizing that this is something they want and need. That's because most people at some point in their lives have been made happy by a musical'.[9]

I do believe that the key feel-good factor found in those operettas and musicals that lift our spirits and get us tapping our toes and humming or whistling the tunes as we come out of the theatre and for weeks afterwards can be regarded as spiritual. They spread joy and administer balm in our troubled, disordered world. But operettas and musicals aren't just about escapism—there is, too, that music of the night which takes us into deeper, more ambiguous, and more unsettling realms. In the words of composer Tim Sutton:

In a great musical, you're hoping to see many different elements, from comedy and drama to introspection. You have a chance to experience a whole range of emotions. A well-crafted score should be able to display all those factors and it's the mark of a really well-rounded theatre composer

202 MUSIC OF THE NIGHT

and lyricist to be able to flex in all these directions. As audience members, we're looking to see how flawed but sympathetic heroes fail, learn and grow through the course of the show. The richer the nature of the score, the better the experience for an audience.[10]

There are close analogies between musical theatre and religious worship and ritual. I have already quoted John Caird on this theme, and I explored it in more detail in *You've Got to Have a Dream*, where I wrote:

> People approach a musical much as they approach a service of worship in a church. They dress up, they come from a variety of places and backgrounds to congregate together in rows of seats that are not unlike church pews in their fixed settings and close proximity. There is a sense of awe and expectancy as they wait for the orchestra to strike up and the curtain to rise. The level of audience participation is generally much greater in musicals than it is in so-called straight plays. There is often an element of singing or clapping along with the performers on stage. Musicals also provide their audiences with a spiritual experience of some depth, which can move people to tears and engage their emotions in a way that is more than mere entertainment or escapism.[11]

This is something that is recognized more by practitioners than by critics. It is well described by Aisha Wheatley, president of the Cambridge University Musical Theatre Society, who notes in respect of the audience reaction to musicals: 'that cheering and screaming and whooping offers a different feeling than you get from a moving piece of straight theatre, where the audience are quite subdued'.[12]

This may seem to point to excess and ramped-up emotion (precisely, of course, what atheists and other detractors say is happening in much religious worship), but it also suggests connection, empathy, and engagement. For me, these are spiritual values. In all sorts of ways, operettas and musicals feed our souls—they are life-enhancing, offering joy and uplift, and they are also pastoral and therapeutic, representing our fears, hurts, and doubts, and providing hope and inspiration. We climb every mountain till we find our dream (or, as in Maria's case, God's dream for us). We hear the people sing and we join in the crusade. We recognize our place in the circle of life. All this is simultaneously reassuring and challenging. And constantly, there are new interpretations, new productions, new songs, and new scores. The spiritual show goes on.

Notes

1. *Cambridge University Alumni Magazine*, no. 96, Easter term 2022, 36.
2. 'Mom Had a Trio (And a band Too), *New York Times*, 19 October 2001.
3. Email to the author, 21 February 2024.
4. https://www.crazychris.net/post/jane-eyre-musical-royal-academy-of-music.
5. Mark Horowitz, 'Andrew Lippa on God, bigotry and writing and playing Harvey Milk', *DC Theater Scene*, 15 April 2016, https://dctheatrescene.com/2016/04/15/andrew-lippa-god-bigotry-writing-playing-harvey-milk/.
6. *DC Theater Arts*, 25 April 2016. https://dctheaterarts.org/2016/04/25/review-2-anne-hutchinsoni-harvey-milk-strathmore/.
7. Xeni Jardin, 'The Book of Mormon, Matt Stone and Trey Parker's Broadway Musical', *Boing Boing*, 9 March 2011. https://boingboing.net/2011/03/09/the-book-of-mormon-m.html.
8. Comments by Josh Gad in response to questions posed on reddit.com, 2015. https://www.reddit.com/r/IAmA/comments/2rkb6g/comment/cngn9js/.
9. *Cambridge University Alumni Magazine*, no. 96, Easter term 2022, 37.
10. Ibid., 38.
11. Ian Bradley, *You've Got to Have a Dream: The Message of the Musical* (London: SCM Press, 2004), 14–15.
12. *Cambridge University Alumni Magazine*, no. 96, Easter term 2022, 38.

Recommended further reading

Richard Traubner's *Operetta* (Gollancz, 1984) remains a standard work on the subject, supplemented by Micaela Baranello, *The Operetta Empire* (Berkeley and Los Angeles: University of California Press, 2021) and *The Cambridge Companion to Operetta* (Cambridge: Cambridge University Press, 2019). The most recent study of Offenbach is Laurence Selenick, *Jacques Offenbach and the Making of Modern Culture* (Cambridge: Cambridge University Press, 2017) and the best and most recent biography of Lehár is Stefan Frey, *Franz Lehar: Der Letzte Operettenkonig. Eine Biographie* (Vienna: Böhlau, 2020), so far only available in German.

Michael Ainger's *Gilbert and Sullivan: A Dual Biography* (Oxford: Oxford University Press, 2002) provides a lively survey of the Savoy operas. For individual biographies of the two collaborators, see Andrew Crowther, *Gilbert of Gilbert & Sullivan* (Gloucestershire: The History Press, 2011) and Ian Bradley, *Arthur Sullivan: A Life of Divine Emollient* (Oxford: Oxford University Press, 2021).

In my view, the two most readable overviews of twentieth-century musical theatre remain John Bush Jones' *Our Musicals, Ourselves* (Hanover, NH: Brandeis University Press, 2003) and Mark Steyn's *Broadway Babies Say Goodnight* (London: Faber and Faber, 1997). A more academic approach is provided by Raymond Knapp, *The American Musical and the Performance of Personal Identity* (Princeton, NJ: Princeton University Press, 2006) and the Jewish contribution to the genre is well covered in Andrea Most, *Making Americans: Jews and the Broadway Musical* (Cambridge, MA: Harvard, 2004).

Hugh Fordin's *Getting to Know Him* (London: Random House, 1977) is a solid biography of Oscar Hammerstein. Also worth reading is Laurie Winer, *Oscar Hammerstein II and the Invention of the Musical* (New Haven, CT: Yale University Press, 2023). *The Letters of Oscar Hammerstein II*, edited by Mark Horowitz (New York: Oxford University Press, 2022) are a superb resource, soon to be supplemented by another collection of his hitherto unpublished papers.

Alisa Solomon's *Wonder of Wonders* (New York: Metropolitan Books, 2013) is the only book you need to read on *Fiddler on the Roof*—it says it all.

The literature on Sondheim is vast and somewhat intimidating. Meryle Secrest, *Stephen Sondheim: A Life* (London: Bloomsbury, 1999) provides a clear, straightforward biography. Carol de Giere does a similarly good job on Stephen Schwartz's life and work in *Defying Gravity* (New York: Applause, 2008). The same author's *The Godspell Experience* (Bethel, CT: Scene 1 Publishing, 2014) is splendidly comprehensive and revelatory.

The most insightful biography of Andrew Lloyd Webber remains Michael Coveney's *Cats on a Chandelier* (London: Hutchison, 1999). The composer's autobiography, *Unmasked: A Memoir* (New York: HarperCollins, 2019) is also well worth reading and more up-to-date.

Index

For the benefit of digital users, indexed terms that span two pages (e.g., 52–53) may, on occasion, appear on only one of those pages.

Addams Family, The, 198
Aleicheim, Sholem (Solomon Rabinivitz),
  83–84, 85
Audran, Edmond, 16–17

Baranello, Micaela, 7, 25–26
Beautiful Game, The, 130–32, 143, 149–51
Behr, Edward, 179
Belle Hélène, La, 13
Berlin, Irving, 52, 72
Bernstein, Leonard, 94–95, 151–52
  Mass, 110, 111–13, 120
Bjornson, Maria, 146
Blood Brothers, 150
Bock, Jerry, 84–85, 86–87
Bolick, Duane, 162–63
Bonhoeffer, Dietrich, 98–99
Book of Mormon, The, 75, 198–99
Boublil, Alain, 181–82, 183, 184
Bradley, Kathryn, 55, 69
Brightman, Sarah, 141–42, 143–44, 148
Bush Jones, John, 50, 55, 89

Caird, George, 115–16, 182–83
Caird, John
  and *Children of Eden*, 115–20
  and *Les Misérables*, 182–84, 185–87, 197, 202
Carousel, 52–53, 54–55, 61, 62–66, 68–69, 72–
  73, 80, 85, 106, 140–41, 193
Carroll, Richard, 168–69
Cats, 130–33, 139–41, 147
Children of Eden, 110, 114–20, 122, 126,
  128, 182–83
Citron, Stephen, 70, 144–45
'Climb every mountain', 80–81
Climb High, 95, 96
Come From Away, 200
Company, 4–5, 97–98, 99–100, 106
Contes d'Hoffman, Les, 13
Conway, David, 14–15
Copenhaver, Martin, 107–8

Coveney, Michael, 131–32, 139, 147,
  149, 153–54
Cox, Harvey, 160
Crowther, Andrew, 35–36, 47–48

Dahlhaus, Carl, 7
Darwin, Charles, 35–36
De Giere, Carol, 112, 115, 126, 164
Delibes, Léo, 16–17
Desert Song, The, 8, 50
Dies Irae theme, 13, 17, 103
Doggett, Alan, 136–37
Drei Engel Auf Erden, 3
Duffy, Sister Gregory, 76–78, 80–81
Dybbuk, The, 83–84

Eden, David, 35, 38–39, 48
Edwards, Gale, 154–55, 176
Eliot, T.S., 139, 140
Ellis, Robert, 162, 166
Elton, Ben, 150–51
Emerald Isle, The, 40–41, 42
Endlich Allein, 22–23
Erlanger, Jules, 15
Evita, 130–31, 132–33
Eysler, Edmund, 25

Fadner, Donald, 121, 189–90
Fall, Leo, 3, 25–26
Fenton, James, 182–83, 185
Fenton, John, 182–83
Fiddler on the Roof, 83–91
Findon, Benjamin, 37, 38–39
Fledermaus, Die, 19
Flower Drum Song, 69
Fogelman, Lauren, 99–100
Follies, 98, 107
Fordin, Hugh, 55, 70
Francis, Ben, 99
Frey, Stefan, 4–5
Friml, Rudolf, 8, 50, 154, 181–82

208 INDEX

Gad, Josh, 199
Ganzl, Kurt, 73
Gilbert and Sullivan, 28–48
   collaboration, 42–44
   serious side, 29
   See also individual comic operas
Gilbert and Sullivan Yiddish Light Opera
   Company, 3–4
Gilbert, W. S., 1, 28–29, 94, 96
   death fixation, 33–37, 45, 46
   pessimism and cynicism, 29–30, 38
   partnership with Sullivan, 42–44, 47–48
Godspell, 110, 111, 112–13, 114, 115,
   122, 157–69
   film, 166–67
   genesis, 158–63
   portrayal of Jesus, 165–66
   recent versions, 167–69
   Stephen Schwartz's involvement, 163–65
Goggin, Dan, 82–83
Gondoliers, The, 35, 36, 43–44
Gottin der Vernauft, Die, 19–20, 23
Grande Duchesse de Gerolstein, La, 13
Grove, George, 38–39, 47
Guys and Dolls, 75
Gypsy, 98–99

H.M.S. Pinafore, 28–29, 33, 35–36
Hair, 157
Halévy, Jacques Fromenthal, 14–15
Hall, Dr Francis, 58–60, 71, 73, 80
Hamilton, 9, 200–1
Hammerstein, Alice, 56–57
Hammerstein, Oscar II, 5, 50–73, 75–78, 80, 81,
   110, 120, 150–51
   characterisation as Jewish, 51–53, 83–84
   belief in brotherhood of man, 67–69
   faith and religious belief, 61–62, 70–71
   influence on Richard Rodgers, 71–72
   influence on Stephen Sondheim, 71, 95–96,
   106, 107
   Unitarian Universalism, 53–58, 59–60, 64–
   66, 69, 118, 143, 154
Hare, David, 5–6
Harnick, Sheldon, 51, 84–85, 86–87, 88
Hart, Lorenz, 52–53, 72
Hobson, Harold, 4–5
Hooper, Tom, 140, 187
Horowitz, Mark, 52, 53
Hugo, Victor, 121, 180, 181, 182, 183,
   185, 187–89
Hunchback of Notre Dame, The, 110, 121–22

Into the Woods, 98, 100, 105–6, 119–20, 121
Iolanthe, 33, 45, 46

Jane Eyre, 197–98
Jesus Christ Superstar, 113, 114, 131–32, 138–39,
   151–52, 157–58, 167–68
   characterisation of Jesus & Judas, 173–76
   genesis, 169–72
   recent productions, 176
   reception, 172–73
Joseph and His Amazing Technicolor Dreamcoat,
   114, 133, 136–39, 163–64, 170
Jullien, Louis Antoine, 17

Kálmán, Emmerich, 4–5, 9, 25, 181–82
Keck, Jean-Christophe, 12–13
Kenrick, John, 7, 9
King and I, The, 3, 69, 78–79, 143
Knapp, Raymond, 2–3, 101–2, 106
Knight, Beverley, 3
Knoppert, Emily, 90
Kracauer, Siegfried, 10–12
Kretzmer, Herbert, 185

Land des Lächelns, Das, 25–26
Larson, Jonathan, 150, 195
Lehár, Franz, 5, 8, 9, 20–26, 40–41, 102, 148,
   154, 181–82
   Catholicism, 20–21, 22
   loneliness, 22–23
   religious beliefs, 21–22
   view of operetta, 24–25
   See also individual operettas
Léon, Viktor, 23, 25–26
Lerner, Alan Jay, 67–68, 148
Lewis, C.S., 116, 192
Lewis, Canon Don, 133
Lion King, The, 3, 178, 189–93, 195, 199
Lippa, Andrew, 198
Lisanby, Charles, 114–16
Liszt, Franz, 21–22, 40–41, 154
Little Night Music, A, 93, 100, 101–2, 107
Lloyd Webber, Andrew, 5, 22, 130–55, 160–61,
   170–72, 174–75
   church music, 151–53
   faith, 132–33, 134–35
   High Church aesthetic, 153–54
   Requiem, 141–44
   similarity to Lehár, 8, 148, 154, 181–82
   spiritual yearning, 131–32, 139, 147, 155
   See also individual musicals
Lloyd Webber, William (Bill), 130–31, 134

INDEX 209

Look to the Lilies, 82–83
Lost Chord, The, 39–40, 44–45, 155
Lustige Witwe, Die, 20, 21, 24–26

Mackintosh, Cameron, 115–16, 181–82, 184, 185
Mamma Mia!, 196
Mam'zelle Nitouche, 16
Mariage aux Lanternes, Le, 13
Martin Guerre, 182
Mary Poppins, 2–3
McDermott, Fr Jim, 100–1
McLaughlin, Robert, 97–99, 102
Menken, Alan, 121
Merrily We Roll Along, 96, 98–99, 107
Messager, André, 16–17
Mikado, The, 30–32, 34–35, 36, 42, 44, 46
Minkoff, Rob, 190
Misérables, Les, 104, 105, 115–16, 122, 123, 140–41, 176, 178–89
  Christianization of successive versions, 5, 180–89
Mordden, Ethan, 73, 95, 105, 182–83
Morgan, Mother Josephine, 79
Most, Andrea, 2, 52
Mostel, Zero, 87

Niedermeyer, Louis, 16–17
Novello, Ivor, 4–5
Nunn, Trevor, 140, 148, 182–84, 187
Nunsense, 82–83

Offenbach, Isaac, 9–11, 42
Offenbach, Jacques, 9–14, 17
  Catholic music, 12–13
  Jewish music of, 10–11
  religious beliefs, 12, 13–14
Oklahoma!, 9, 50, 52–53, 68–69, 70, 78–79, 95
Orphée aux Enfers, 13–14

Pacific Overtures, 103
Patience, 28–29, 42, 44–45
Phantom of the Opera, The, 5, 8, 21, 130–32, 143, 144–48, 153–54, 178
Pinsky, Mark, 121, 189–91
Pipe Dream, 69
Pippin, 114
Pirates of Penzance, The, 34, 43–44
Porter, Cole, 72, 82
Pourvoyeur, Robert, 10
Prince, Hal, 98, 101

Prince of Egypt, The, 110, 122–26, 128
Princess Ida, 28–29, 37
Puccini, Giacomo, 148, 154

Rent, 150, 195
Rice, Tim, 136–38, 149, 170–75, 189
Richter, Caspar, 8
Robbins, Jerry, 86–88
Rodgers and Hammerstein, 8, 26, 28, 71, 72, 75, 76, 80, 82, 84, 98, 135–36, 150–51, 186
  See also individual musicals
Rodgers, Richard, 71, 82, 83–84, 135–36
  atheism, 63, 71–72, 73
  collaboration with Hammerstein, 50, 51, 68–69
  identification as Jewish, 52–53
  research for *Sound of Music,* 78–79
Roger, Victor, 16–17
Romberg, Sigmund, 8, 50
Ronger, Louis-Auguste, 15–16
Rose Marie, 8, 50
Rose von Stambul, Die, 3, 25–26
Ruddigore, 34

Scardino, Dan, 161, 167–68
Schirmer, Ulf, 20, 22, 24
Schön Ist Die Welt, 23
Schönberg, Claude-Michel, 181–83, 186
Schwartz, Stephen, 110–28
  and *Godspell,* 160, 163–68, 173–74
  involvement in Bernstein *Mass,* 111–13
  religious views, 127–28
  upbringing, 110
  See also individual musicals
Secrest, Meryle, 93, 94–95, 97
Selenick, Laurence, 9, 11
Show Boat, 69
Sister Act, 82–83
Smith, Wallace, 161–62
Solomon, Alisa, 85, 89–90
Sondheim, Stephen, 4–5, 93–108
  cynicism, 97–99
  influence of Hammerstein on, 50, 71, 95–96
  secularism and spirituality, 5, 93–94, 106–8
  upbringing, 94–95, 97
  See also individual musicals
Sorcerer, The, 33
Sound of Music, The, 5, 8, 50, 75–83, 86–87, 91, 95, 135–36, 198–99
South Pacific, 26, 52, 68, 69, 95, 135, 143
Stein, Joseph, 84–85, 86–87, 88
Steinman, Jim, 149

210 INDEX

Steyn, Mark, 8, 68–69, 72, 96
Stone, Matt, 199
Strauss, Johann, 8, 17–18, 19–20, 23
Strauss, Oscar, 24–25
Stravinsky, Igor, 29
Sullivan, Arthur, 8, 22, 35, 37, 94, 102, 151–52, 154, 155
  as church musician, 40–42, 133–34, 144
  Christian faith, 1, 5, 29–30, 38–42
  collaboration and relationship with W.S.Gilbert, 28, 29–30, 42–48, 71, 96
  love of life, 2, 37–38
Sullivan, Martin, 137, 170, 172–73
Sunday in the Park With George, 97, 100, 107
Suppé, Franz von, 17–18
Sweeney Todd, 97, 101, 102–5, 121, 148
Sweet Charity, 75

Taymor, Julie, 3
Tebelak, John-Michael, 111, 158–65, 167–68, 170–71, 175
Tommy, 157
Tongue, Cassie, 168–69

Traubner, Richard, 7–8

Vasseur, Léon, 16–17
Vogelhändler, Der, 18–19

Walsh, Michael, 133–34, 138–39, 144–45
War Requiem (Britten), 134–35, 141
West Side Story, 94–95, 98–99, 107, 111, 135
Wheeler, Hugh, 93, 103–4
Whistle Down the Wind, 130–33, 143, 149, 151–52, 154–55
Wicked, 126–27
Williamson, Malcolm, 131
Willner, Alfred, 23
Winer, Laurie, 51–52, 61, 106

Yeomen of the Guard, The, 33, 34–35, 45–46, 47–48
'You'll never walk alone', 72–73, 85, 106

Zarewitsch, Der, 5, 24–25
Zeller, Carl, 18–19
Zigeunerbaron, Der, 19